A

SYSTEM OF INSTRUCTION

IN

THE PRACTICAL USE

OF

THE BLOWPIPE.

BEING A

GRADUATED COURSE OF ANALYSIS FOR THE USE OF STUDENTS

AND ALL THOSE ENGAGED IN THE EXAMINATION OF METALLIC COMBINATIONS.

NEW YORK:
H. BAILLIÈRE, 290 BROADWAY,
AND 219 REGENT STREET, LONDON.
PARIS: J. B. BAILLIÈRE ET FILS, RUE HAUTEFEUILLE.
MADRID: C. BAILLY-BAILLIÈRE, CALLE DEL PRINCIPE.
1858.

W. H. Tinson, Printer and Stereotyper, 43 Centre Street.

TABLE OF CONTENTS.

PART I.

PART II.

PART III.

PREFACE.

It is believed the arrangement of the present work is superior to that of many of its predecessors, as a vehicle for the facilitation of the student's progress. While it does not pretend to any other rank than as an introduction to the larger works, it is hoped that the arrangement of its matter is such that the beginner may more readily comprehend the entire subject of Blowpipe Analysis than if he were to begin his studies by the perusal of the more copious works of Berzelius and Plattner.

When the student shall have gone through these pages, and repeated the various reactions described, then he will be fully prepared to enter upon the study of the larger works. To progress through them will then be but a comparatively easy task.

The arrangement of this little work has been such as the author and his friends have considered the best that could be devised for the purpose of facilitating the progress of the student. Whether we have succeeded is left for the public to decide. The author is indebted to several of his friends for valuable contributions and suggestions.

S.

CINCINNATI, *June*, 1857.

THE BLOWPIPE.

Part First.

THE USE OF THE BLOWPIPE.

Perhaps during the last fifty years, no department of chemistry has been so enriched as that relating to analysis by means of the Blowpipe.

Through the unwearied exertions of men of science, the use of this instrument has arrived to such a degree of perfection, that we have a right to term its use, "Analysis in the *dry* way," in contradistinction to analysis "in the *wet* way." The manipulations are so simple and expeditious, and the results so clear and characteristic, that the Blowpipe analysis not only verifies and completes the results of analysis in the wet way, but it gives in many cases direct evidences of the presence or absence of many substances, which would not be otherwise detected, but through a troublesome and tedious process, involving both prolixity and time; for instance, the detection of manganese in minerals.

Many substances have to go through Blowpipe manipulations before they can be submitted to an analysis in the wet way.

The apparatus and reagents employed are compendious and small in number, so that they can be carried easily while on scientific excursions, a considerable advantage for mineralogists and metallurgists.

The principal operations with the Blowpipe may be explained briefly as follows :

(*a.*) By *Ignition* is meant the exposure of a substance to such a degree of heat, that it glows or emits light, or becomes red-hot. Its greatest value is in the separation of a volatile substance from one less volatile, or one which is entirely fixed at the temperature of the flame. In this case we only take cognizance of the latter or fixed substance, although in many instances we make use of ignition for the purpose of changing the conditions of a substance, for example, the sesqui-oxide of chromium (Cr^2O^3) in its insoluble modification ; and as a preliminary examination for the purpose of ascertaining whether the subject of inquiry be a combination of an organic or inorganic nature.

The apparatus used for this purpose are crucibles of platinum or silver, platinum foil, a platinum spoon, platinum wire or tongs, charcoal, glass tubes, and iron spoons.

(*b.*) *Sublimation* is that process by which we convert a solid substance into vapor by means of a strong heat. These vapors are condensed by refrigeration into the solid form. It may be termed a distillation of a solid substance. Sublimation is of great consequence in the detection of many substances ; for nstance, arsenic, antimony, mercury, etc.

The apparatus used for the purposes of sublimation consist of glass tubes closed at one end.

(*c.*) *Fusion.*—Many substances when exposed to a certain degree of heat lose their solid form, and are converted into a liquid. Those substances which do not become converted into the liquid state by heat, are said to be infusible. It is a convenient classification to arrange substances into those which are fusible with difficulty, and those which are easily fusible. Very often we resort to fusion for the purpose of decomposing a substance, or to cause it to enter into other combinations, by which means it is the more readily detected. If insoluble substances are fused with others more fusible (reagents) for the purpose of causing a combination which is soluble in water and acids, the operation is termed *unclosing*. These substances are particularly the silicates and the sulphates of the alkaline earths. The usual reagents resorted to for this purpose are carbonate of soda (NaO, CO^2), carbonate of potash (KO, CO^2), or still better, a mixture of the two in equal parts. In some cases we use the hydrate of barytes (BaO, HO) and the bisulphate of potash ($KO, 2SO^3$). The platinum spoon is generally used for this manipulation.

Substances are exposed to fusion for the purpose of getting a new combination which has such distinctive characteristics that we can class it under a certain group; or for the purpose of ascertaining at once what the substance may be. The reagents used for this purpose are borax ($NaO, 2BrO^3$) and the microcosmic salt (NaO, NH^4O, PO^5, HO). Charcoal and the platinum wire are used as supports for this kind of operation.

(*d.*) *Oxidation.*—The chemical combination of any substance with oxygen is termed *oxidation*, and the products are termed *oxides*. As these oxides have qualities differing from those which are non-oxidized, it therefore frequently becomes necessary to convert substances into oxides; or, if they are such, of a lower degree, to convert them into a higher degree of oxidation. These different states of oxidation frequently present characteristic marks of identity sufficient to enable us to draw conclusions in relation to the substance under examination. For instance, the oxidation of manganese, of arsenic, etc. The conditions necessary for oxidation, are high temperature and the free admission of air to the substance.

If the oxidation is effected through the addition of a substance containing oxygen (for instance, the nitrate or chlorate of potash) and the heating is accompanied by a lively deflagration and crackling noise, it is termed *detonation*. By this process we frequently effect the oxidation of a substance, and thus we prove the presence or the absence of a certain class of substances. For instance, if we detonate (as it is termed by the German chemists) the sulphide of antimony, or the sulphide of arsenic with nitrate of potash, we get the nitrate of antimony, or the nitrate of arsenic. The salts of nitric or chloric acid are determined by fusing them with the cyanide of potassium, because the salts of these acids detonate.

(*e.*) *Reduction.*—If we deprive an oxidized substance of its oxygen, we term the process *reduction.* This is effected by fusing the substance under examination with another which possesses a greater affinity for oxygen. The agents used for reduction are hydrogen, charcoal, soda, cyanide of potassium, etc. Substances generally, when in the unoxidized state, have such characteristic qualities, that they cannot very readily be mistaken for others. For this reason, reduction is a very excellent expedient for the purpose of discerning and classifying many substances.

B. UTENSILS.

We shall give here a brief description of the most necessary apparatus used for analysis in the dry way, and of their use.

The Blowpipe is a small instrument, made generally out of brass, silver, or German silver, and was principally used in earlier times for the purpose of soldering small pieces of metals together. It is generally made in the form of a tube, bent at a right angle, but without a sharp corner. The largest one is about seven inches long, and the smallest about two inches. The latter one terminates with a small point, with a small orifice. The first use of the blowpipe that we have recorded is that of a Swedish mining officer, who used it in the year 1738 for chemical purposes, but we have the most meagre accounts of his operations. In 1758 another Swedish mining officer, by the name of Cronstedt, published his "Use of the Blowpipe in

Chemistry and Mineralogy," translated into English, in 1770, by Van Engestroem. Bergman extended its use, and after him Ghan and the venerable Berzelius (1821). The blowpipe most generally used in chemical examinations is composed of the following parts: (*Fig.* 1.) A is a little reservoir made air-tight by grinding the part B into it. This reservoir serves the purpose of retaining the moisture with which the air from the mouth is charged. A small conical tube is fitted to this reservoir. This tube terminates in a fine orifice. As this small point is liable to get clogged up with soot, etc., it is better that it should be made of platinum, so that it may be ignited. Two of these platinum tubes should be supplied, differing in the size of the orifice, by which a stronger or lighter current of flame may be projected from it. Metals, such as brass or German silver, are very liable to become dirty through oxidation, and when placed between the lips are liable to impart a disagreeable taste. To avoid this, the top of the tube must be supplied with a mouthpiece of ivory or horn C. The blowpipe here represented is the one used by Ghan, and approved by Berzelius. The trumpet mouthpiece was adopted by Plattner; it is pressed upon the lips while blowing, which is less tiresome than holding the mouthpiece between the lips, although many prefer the latter mode.

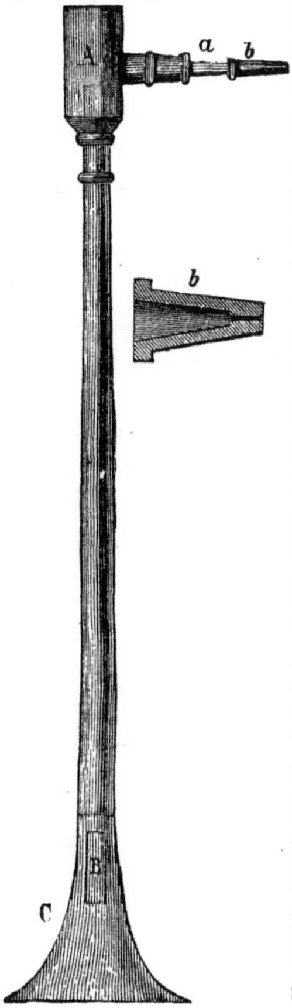

Dr. Black's blowpipe is as good an instrument and cheaper.

It consists of two tubes, soldered at a right angle; the larger one, into which the air is blown, is of sufficient capacity to serve as a reservoir.

A chemist can, with a blowpipe and a piece of charcoal, determine many substances without any reagents, thus enabling him, even when travelling, to make useful investigations with means which are always at his disposal. There are pocket blowpipes as portable as a pencil case, such as Wollaston's and Mitscherlich's; these are objectionable for continued use as their construction requires the use of a metallic mouthpiece. Mr. Casamajor, of New York, has made one lately which has an ivory mouthpiece, and which, when in use, is like Dr. Black's.

The length of the blowpipe is generally seven or eight inches, but this depends very much upon the visual angle of

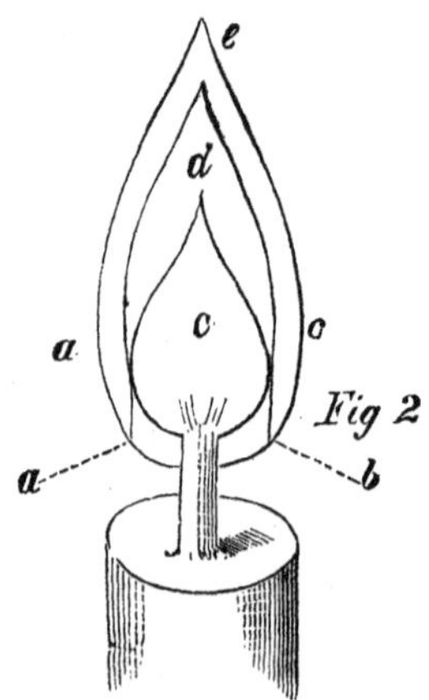

Fig 2

the operators. A short-sighted person, of course, would

require an instrument of less length than would suit a far-sighted person.

The purpose required of the blowpipe is to introduce a fine current of air into the flame of a candle or lamp, by which a higher degree of heat is induced, and consequently combustion is more rapidly accomplished.

By inspecting the flame of a candle burning under usual circumstances, we perceive at the bottom of the flame a portion which is of a light blue color (*a b*), *Fig.* 2, which gradually diminishes in size as it recedes from the wick, and disappears when it reaches the perpendicular side of the flame. In the midst of the flame there is a dark nucleus with a conical form (*c*). This is enveloped by the illuminating portion of the flame (*d*). At the exterior edge of the part *d* we perceive a thin, scarcely visible veil, *a, e, c,* which is broader near the apex of the flame. The action of the burning candle may be thus explained. The radiant heat from the flame melts the tallow or wax, which then passes up into the texture of the wick by capillary attraction until it reaches the glowing wick, where the heat decomposes the combustible matter into carbonated hydrogen (C^4H^4), and into carbonic oxide (CO).

While these gases are rising in hot condition, the air comes in contact with them and effects their combustion. The dark portion, *c*, of the flame is where the carbon and gases have not a sufficiency of air for their thorough combustion; but gradually they become mixed with air, although not then sufficient for complete combustion. The hydrogen is first oxidized or burnt, and then the carbon is attacked by the air, although particles of carbon are separated, and it is these, in a state of intense ignition, which produce the illumination. By bringing any oxidizable substance into this portion of the flame, it oxidizes very quickly in consequence of the high temperature and the free access of air. For that reason this part of the flame is termed the oxidizing flame, while the illuminating portion, by its tendency to abstract oxygen for the purpose of complete combustion, easily reduces oxidated substances brought into it, and it is, therefore, called the flame of reduction. In the oxidizing flame, on the contrary, all the carbon which exists in the interior of the flame is oxidized into carbonic acid (CO^2) and carbonic oxide (CO), while the blue color of the cone of the flame is caused by the complete combustion of the carbonic oxide. These two portions of the flame—the oxidizing and the reducing—are the principal agents of blowpipe analysis.

If we introduce a fine current of air into a flame, we notice the following: The air strikes first the dark nucleus, and forcing the gases beyond it, mixes with them, by which oxygen is mingled freely with them. This effects the complete combustion of the gases at a certain distance from the point of the blowpipe. At this place the flame has the highest temperature, forming there the point of a blue cone. The illuminated or reducing portion of the flame is enveloped outside and inside by a very hot flame, whereby its own temperature is so much increased that in this reduction-flame many substances will undergo fusion which would prove perfectly refractory in a common flame. The exterior scarcely visible part loses its form, is diminished, and pressed more to a point, by which its heating power is greatly increased.

The Blast of Air.—By using the blowpipe for chemical purposes, the effect intended to be produced is an uninterrupted steady stream of air for many minutes together, if necessary, without an instant's cessation. Therefore, the blowing can only be effected with the muscles of the cheeks, and not by the exertion of the lungs. It is only by this means that a steady constant stream of air can be kept up, while the lungs will not be injured by the deprival of air. The details of the proper manner of using the blowpipe are really more difficult to describe than to acquire by practice; therefore the pupil is requested to apply himself at once to its practice, by which he will soon learn to produce a steady current of air, and to distinguish the different flames from each other. We would simply say that the tongue must be applied to the roof of the mouth, so as to interrupt the communication between the passage of the nostrils and the mouth. The operator now fills his mouth with air, which is to be passed through the pipe by compressing the muscles of the cheeks, while he breathes through the nostrils, and uses the palate as a valve. When the mouth becomes nearly empty, it is replenished by the lungs in an instant, while the tongue is momentarily withdrawn from the roof of the mouth. The stream of air can be continued for a long time, without the least fatigue or injury to the lungs. The easiest way for the student to accustom himself to the use of the blowpipe, is first to learn to fill the mouth with air, and while the lips are kept firmly closed to breathe freely through the nostrils. Having effected this much, he may introduce the mouthpiece of the blowpipe between his lips. By inflating the cheeks, and breathing through the nostrils, he will soon learn to use the instrument without the least fatigue. The air is forced through the tube against the flame by the action of the muscles of the cheeks, while he continues to breathe without interruption through the nostrils. Having become acquainted with this process, it only requires some practice to produce a steady jet of flame. A defect in the nature of the combustible used, as bad oil, such as fish oil, or oil thickened by long standing or by dirt, dirty cotton wick, or an untrimmed one, or a dirty wickholder, or a want of steadiness of the hand that holds the blowpipe, will prevent a steady jet of flame. But frequently the fault lies in the orifice of the jet, or too small a hole, or its partial stoppage by dirt, which will prevent a steady jet of air, and lead to difficulty. With a good blowpipe the air projects the entire flame, forming a horizontal, blue cone of flame, which converges to a point at about an inch from the wick, with a larger, longer, and more luminous flame enveloping it, and terminating to a point beyond that of the blue flame.

To produce an efficient flame of oxidation, put the point of the blowpipe into the flame about one third the diameter of the wick, and about one twelfth of an inch above it. This, however, depends upon the size of the flame used. Blow strong enough to keep the flame straight and horizontal, using the largest orifice for the purpose. Upon examining the flame thus produced, we will observe a long, blue flame, *a b*, Fig. 3, which letters correspond with the same letters in Fig. 2. But this flame has changed its form, and contains all the combustible gases. It forms now a thin, blue cone, which converges to a point about an inch from the wick. This point of the

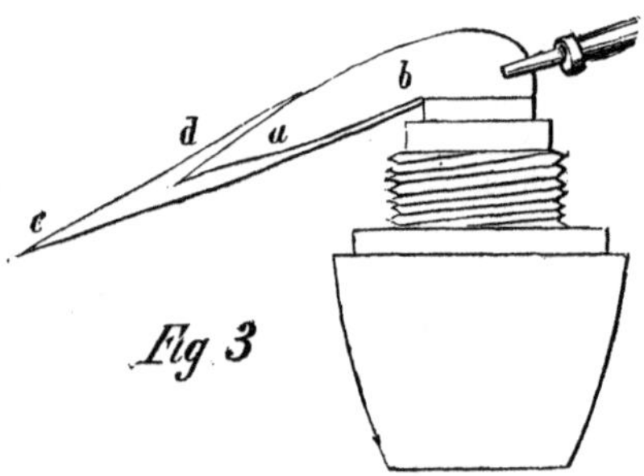

Fig 3

flame possesses the highest intensity of temperature, for there the combustion of the gases is the most complete. In the original flame, the hottest part forms the external envelope, but here it is compressed more into a point, forming the cone of the blue flame, and likewise an envelope of flame surrounding the blue one, extending beyond it from *a* to *c*, and presenting a light bluish or brownish color. The external flame has the highest temperature at *d*, but this decreases from *d* to *c*.

If there is a very high temperature, the oxidation is not effected so readily in many cases, unless the substance is removed a little from the flame; but if the heat be not too high, it is readily oxidized in the flame, or near its cone. If the current of air is blown too freely or violently into the flame, more air is forced there than is sufficient to consume the gases. This superfluous air only acts detrimentally, by cooling the flame.

In general the operation proceeds best when the substance is kept at a dull red heat. The blue cone must be kept free from straggling rays of the yellow or reduction flame. If the analysis be effected on charcoal, the blast should not be too strong, as a part of the coal would be converted into carbonic oxide, which would act antagonistically to the oxidation. The oxidation flame requires a steady current of air, for the purpose of keeping the blue cone constantly of the same length. For the purpose of acquiring practice, the following may be done: Melt a little molybdenic acid with some borax, upon a platinum wire, about the sixteenth of an inch from the point of the blue cone. In the pure oxidation flame, a clear yellowish glass is formed; but as soon as the reduction flame reaches it, or the point of the blue cone touches it, the color of the bead changes to a brown, which, finally, after a little longer blowing, becomes quite dark, and loses its transparency. The cause of this is, that the molybdenic acid is very easily reduced to a lower degree of oxidation, or to the oxide of molybdenum. The flame of oxidation will again convert this oxide into the acid, and this conversion is a good test of the progress of the student in the use of the blowpipe. In cases where we have to separate a more oxidizable substance from a less one, we use with success the blue cone, particularly if we wish to determine whether a substance has the quality, when submitted to heat in the blue cone, of coloring the external flame.

A good *reduction* flame can be obtained by the use of a small orifice at the point of the blowpipe. In order to produce such a flame, hold the point of the blowpipe higher above the wick, while the nozzle must not enter the flame so far as in the production of the oxidation flame. The point of the blowpipe should only touch the flame, while the current of air blown into it must be stronger than into the oxidation flame. If we project a stream, in the manner mentioned, into the flame, from the smaller side of the wick to the middle, we shall perceive the flame changed to a long, narrow, luminous cone, *a b*, Fig. 4,

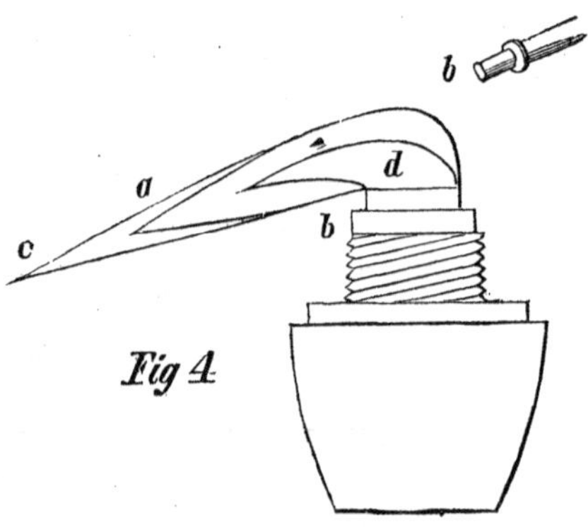

Fig 4.

the end *a* of which is enveloped by the same dimly visible blueish colored portion of the flame *a, c,* which we perceive in the original flame, with its point at *c.* The portion close above the wick, presenting the dull appearance, is occasioned by the rising gases which have not supplied to them enough oxygen to consume them entirely. The hydrogen is consumed, while the carbon is separated in a state of bright ignition, and forms the internal flame.

Directly above the wick, the combustion of the gases is least complete, and forms there likewise, as is the case in the free flame, a dark blue nucleus *d.*

If the oxide of a metal is brought into the luminous portion of the flame produced as above, so that the flame envelopes the substance perfectly, the access of air is prevented. The partially consumed gases have now a strong affinity for oxygen, under the influence of the intense heat of that part of the flame. The substance is thus deprived of a part, or the whole, of its oxygen, and becomes *reduced* according to the strength of the affinity which the substance itself has for oxygen. If the reduction of a substance is undertaken on platinum, by fusion with a flux, and if the oxide is difficult to reduce, the reduction will be completely effected only in the luminous part of the flame. But if a substance be reduced on charcoal, the reduction will take place in the blue part of the flame, as long as the access of air is cut off; but it is the luminous part of the flame which really possesses the greatest reducing power.

The following should be observed in order to procure a good reduction flame:

The wick should not be too long, that it may make a smoke, nor too short, otherwise the flame will be too small to produce a heat strong enough for reduction.

The wick must be free from all loose threads, and from charcoal.

The blast should be continued for a considerable time without intermission, otherwise reduction cannot be effected.

For the purpose of acquiring practice, the student may fuse the oxide of manganese with borax, upon a platinum wire, in the oxidation flame, when a violet-red glass will be obtained; or if too much of the oxide be used, a glass of a dark color and opaque will be obtained. By submitting this glass to the reduction flame, it will become colorless in correspondence to the perfection with which the flame is produced. Or a piece of tin may be fused upon charcoal, and kept in that state for a considerable time, while it presents the appearance of a bright metal on the surface. This will require dexterity in the operator; for, if the oxidation flame should chance to touch the bright metal only for a moment, it is coated with an infusible oxide.

COMBUSTION.—Any flame of sufficient size can be used for blowpipe operations. It may be either the flame of a candle of tallow or wax, or the flame of a lamp. The flame of a wax candle, or of an oil lamp is most generally used. Sometimes a lamp is used filled with a solution of spirits of turpentine in strong alcohol. If a candle is used, it is well to cut the wick off short, and to bend the wick a little toward the substance experimented upon. But candles are not the best for blowpipe operations, as the radiant heat, reflecting from the substance upon the wax or tallow, will cause it to melt and run down the side of the candle; while again, candles do not give heat enough. The lamp is much the most desirable. The subjoined figure, from Berzelius, is perhaps the best form of lamp. It is

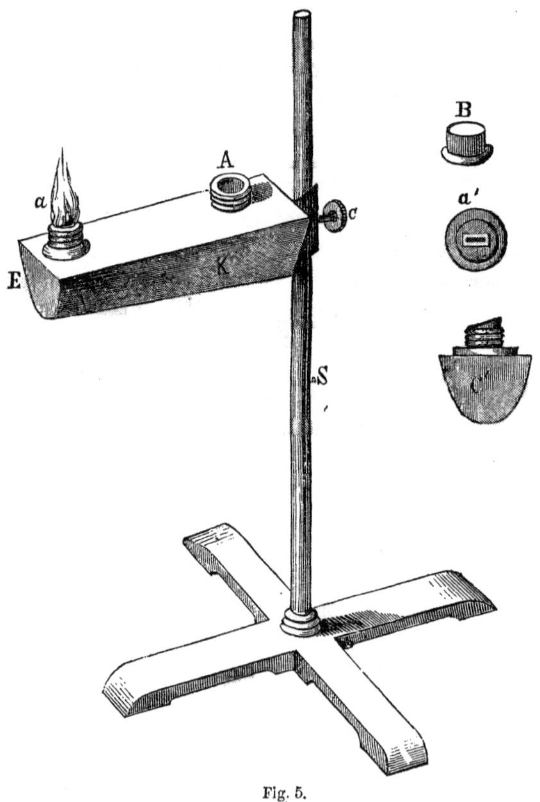

Fig. 5.

made of japanned tin-plate, about four inches in length, and has the form and arrangement represented in Fig. 5. K is the lamp, fastened on the stand, S, by a screw, C, and is movable upwards or downwards, as represented in the figure. The posterior end of the lamp may be about one inch square, and at its anterior end, E, about three-quarters of an inch square. The under side of this box may be round, as seen in the figure. The oil is poured into the orifice, A, which has a cap screwed over it. C′ is a wick-holder for a flat lamp-wick. *a* is a socket containing the wick, which, when not in use, is secured from dirt by the cap. The figures B and *a′* give the forms of the cap and socket. The best combustible for this lamp is the refined rape-seed oil, or pure sweet oil. When this lamp is in use, there must be no loose threads, or no charcoal on the wick, or these will produce a smoky flame. The wick, likewise, should not be pulled up too high, as the same smoky flame would be produced.

THE SPIRIT-LAMP.—This is a short, strong glass lamp, with a cap, B, Fig. 6, fitted to it by grinding, to prevent the evaporation of the alcohol. The neck *a* contains a tube C, made of silver, or of tin plate, and which contains the wick. Brass

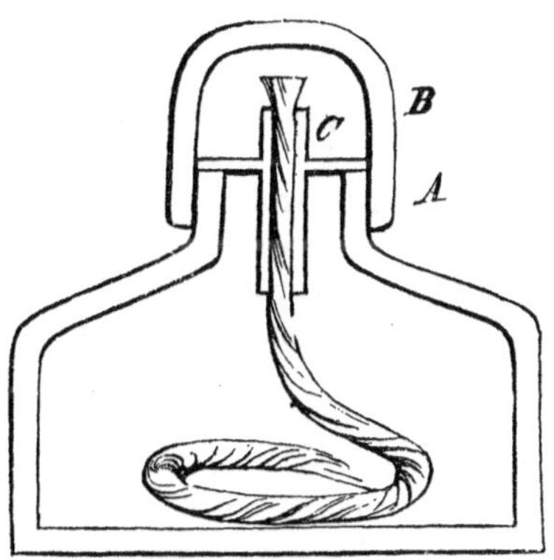

Fig. 6.

would not answer so well for this tube, as the spirits would oxidize it, and thus impart color to the flame. The wickholder must cover the edge of the neck, but not fit tight within the tube, otherwise, by its expansion, it will break the glass. It is not necessary that alcohol, very highly rectified, should be burnt in this lamp, although if too much diluted with water, enough heat will not be given out. Alcohol of specific gravity 0.84 to 0.86 is the best.

This lamp is generally resorted to by blowpipe analysts, for the purpose of experiments in glass apparatus, as the oily combustibles will coat the glass with soot. Some substances, when exposed to the dark part of the flame, become reduced and, *in statu nascendi*, evaporated ; but by passing through the external part of the flame, they become oxidized again, and impart a color to the flame. The spirit flame is the most efficient one for the examination of substances the nature of which we wish to ascertain through color imparted to the flame, as that of the spirit-lamp being colorless, is, consequently, most easily and thoroughly recognized by the slightest tinge imparted to it.

It is necessary that in operating with such minute quantities of substances as are used in blowpipe analysis, that they should have some appropriate support. In order that no false results may ensue, it is necessary that the supports should be of such a nature that they will not form a chemical combination with the substance while it is exposed to fusion or ignition. Appropriate supports for the different blowpipe experiments are charcoal, platinum instruments, and glass tubes.

(*a.*) *Charcoal.*—The value of charcoal as a support may be stated as follows :

1. The charcoal is infusible, and being a poor conductor of heat, a substance can be exposed to a higher degree of heat upon it than upon any other substance.

2. It is very porous, and therefore allows easily fusible substances (such as alkalies and fluxes) to pass into it, while other substances less fusible, such as metals, to remain unabsorbed.

3. It has likewise a great reducing power.

The best kind of charcoal is that of pinewood, linden, willow, or alderwood, or any other soft wood. Coal from the firwood sparkles too freely, while that of the hard woods contains too much iron in its ashes. Smooth pieces, free from bark and knots, should be selected. It should be thoroughly burnt, and the annual rings or growths should be as close together as possible.

If the charcoal is in masses, it should be sawed into pieces about six inches in length by about two inches broad, but so that the year-growths run perpendicular to the broadest side, as the other sides, by their unequal structure, burn unevenly.

That the substance under examination may not be carried off by the blast, small conical concavities should be cut in the broad side of the charcoal, between the year-growths, with a conical tube of tin plate about two or three inches long, and one quarter of an inch at one end, and half an inch at the other. These edges are made sharp with a file. The widest end of this charcoal borer is used for the purpose of making cavities for cupellation.

In places where the proper kind of charcoal is difficult to procure, it is economical to cut common charcoal into pieces about an inch broad, and the third of an inch thick. In each of these little pieces small cavities should be cut with the small end of the borer. When these pieces of charcoal are required for use, they must be fastened to a narrow slip of tin plate, one end of which is bent into the form of a hook, under which the plate of charcoal is pushed.

In general, we use the charcoal support where we wish to reduce metallic oxides, to prevent oxidation, or to test the fusibility of a substance. There is another point to which we would direct the student. Those metals which are volatile in the reduction flame, appear as oxides in the oxidation flame. These oxides make sublimates upon the charcoal close in the vicinity of the substance, or where it rested, and by their peculiar color indicate pretty correctly the species of minerals experimented upon.

(*b.*) *Platinum Supports.*—The metal platinum is infusible in the blowpipe flame, and is such a poor conductor of heat that a strip of it may be held close to that portion of it which is red hot without the least inconvenience to the fingers. It is necessary that the student should be cognizant of those substances which would not be appropriate to experiment upon if placed on platinum. Metals should not be treated upon platinum apparatus, nor should the easily reducible oxides, sulphides, nor chlorides, as these substances will combine with the platinum, and thus render it unfit for further use in analysis.

(*c.*) *Platinum Wire.*—As the color of the flame cannot be well discerned when the substance is supported upon charcoal, in consequence of the latter furnishing false colors, by its own reflection, to the substances under examination, we use platinum wire for that purpose, when we wish to examine those substances which give indications by the peculiar color which they impart to fluxes. The wire should be about as thick as No. 16 or 18 wire, or about 0.4 millimetre, and cut into pieces about from two and a half to three inches in length. The end of each piece is crooked. In order that these pieces should remain clear of dirt, and ready for use, they should be kept in a glass of water. To use them, we dip the wetted hooked end into the powdered flux (borax or microcosmic salt) some of which will adhere, when we fuse it in the flame of the blowpipe to a bead. This bead hanging in the hook, must be clear and colorless. Should there not adhere a sufficient quantity of the flux in the first trial to form a bead sufficiently large, the hook must be dipped a second time in the flux and again submitted to the blowpipe flame. To fix the substance to be examined to the bead, it is necessary, while the latter is hot, to dip it in the powdered substance. If the hook is cold, we moisten the powder a little, and then dip the hook into it, and then expose it to the oxidation flame, by keeping it exposed to a regular blast until the substance and the flux are fused together, and no further alteration is produced by the flame.

The platinum wire can be used except where reduction to the metallic state is required. Every reduction and oxidation experiment, if the results are to be known by the color of the fluxes, should be effected upon platinum wire. At the termination of the experiment or investigation, if it be one, to clean the wire, place it in water, which will dissolve the bead.

(*d.*) *Platinum Foil.*—For the heating or fusing of a substance, whereby its reduction would be avoided, we use platinum foil as a support. This foil should be of the thickness of good writing paper, and from two and a half to three inches long, by about half an inch broad, and as even and smooth as possible. If it should become injured by long use, cut the injured end off, and if it should prove too short to be held with the fingers, a pair of forceps may be used to grasp it, or it may be placed on a piece of charcoal

(*e.*) *Platinum Spoon.*—When we require to fuse substances with the acid sulphate of potash, or to oxidize them by detonation with nitrate of potash, whereby we wish to preserve the oxide produced, we generally use a little spoon of platinum, about from nine to fifteen millimetres * in diameter, and shaped as represented in Fig. 7. The handle of this spoon is

Fig. 7.

likewise of platinum, and should fit into a piece of cork, or be held with the forceps.

(*f.*) *Platinum Forceps or Tongs.*—We frequently are necessitated to examine small splinters of metals or minerals directly in the blowpipe flame. These pieces of metallic substances are held with the forceps or tongs represented as in

* The French millimetre is about the twenty-fifth part of an English inch.

Fig. 8, where *a c* is formed of steel, and *a a* are platinum

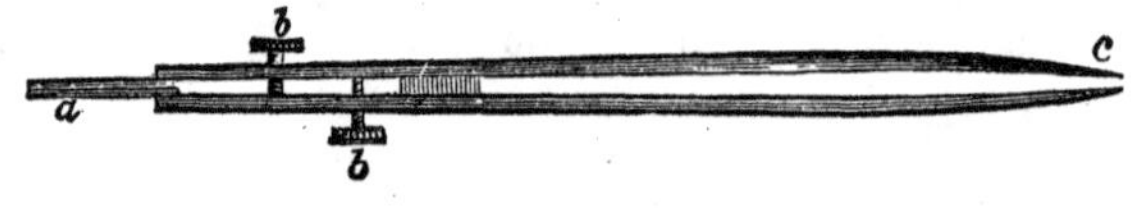

Fig. 8.

bars inserted between the steel plates. At *b b* are knobs which by pressure so separate the platinum bars *a a*, that any small substance can be inserted between them.

(*g.*) *Iron Spoons.*—For a preliminary examination iron spoons are desirable. They may be made of sheet iron, about one-third of an inch in diameter, and are very useful in many examinations where the use of platinum would not be desirable.

(*h.*) *Glass Tubes.*—For the separation and recognition of volatile substances before the blowpipe flame, we use glass tubes. These should be about one-eighth of an inch in diameter, and cut into pieces about five or six inches in length. These tubes should have both ends open.

Tubes are of great value in the examination of volatile substances which require oxidizing or roasting, and heating with free access of air. Also to ascertain whether a substance under examination will sublimate volatile matter of a certain appearance. Such substances are selenium, sulphur, arsenic, antimony, and tellurium. These substances condense on a cool part of the tube, and they present characteristic appearances, or they may be recognized by their peculiar smell. These tubes must be made of the best kind of glass, white and difficult of fusion, and entirely free from lead. The substance to be examined must be put in the tube near one end, and exposed to the flame of the blowpipe. The end containing the substance must be held lower than the other end, and must be moved a little over the spirit-lamp before a draught of air is produced through the tube. It is a good plan to have a number of these tubes on hand. After having used a tube we cut off that end of it which contained the substance, with a file, and clean it from the sublimate, either by heating it over the spirit-lamp, or with a piece of paper wound around a wire. It sometimes happens that the substance falls out of the tube

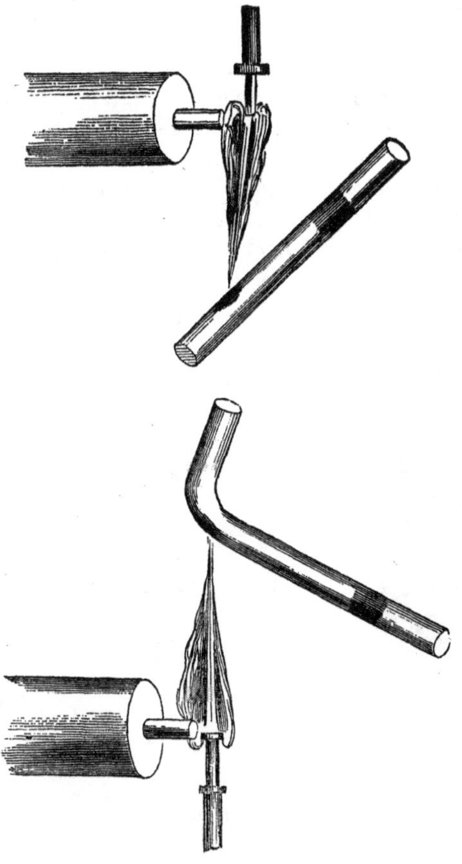

Fig. 9.

before it becomes sufficiently melted to adhere to the glass. To obviate this, we bend the tube not far from the end, at an obtuse angle, and place the substance in the angle, whereby the tube may be lowered as much as necessary. Fig. 9 will give the student a comprehension of the processes described, and of the manner of bending the tubes.

(*i.*) *Glass Tubes closed at one End.*—If we wish to expose volatile substances to heat, with the exclusion of air as much as possible, or to ascertain the contents of water, or other volatile fluids, or for the purpose of heating substances which will decrepitate, we use glass tubes closed at one end. These tubes must be about one-eighth of an inch wide, and from two to three inches in length. They should be made of white glass, difficult of fusion, and free from lead. They should be closed at one end, as figured in the margin, Fig. 10.

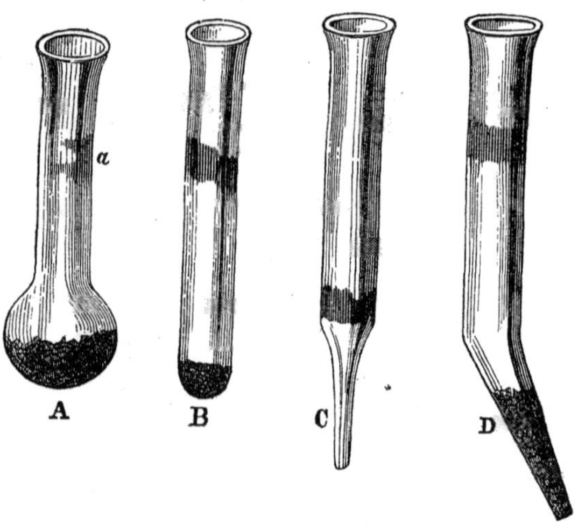

Fig. 10.

When a substance is to be examined for the purpose of

ascertaining whether it contains combustible matter, as sulphur or arsenic, and where we wish to avoid oxidation, we use these tubes without extending the closed end, in order that there may be as little air admitted as possible, as is represented in tube B. But when a substance to be examined is to be tested for water, or other incombustible volatile matters, we employ tubes with little bulbs blown at one end, such as represented at tube A. Here there is room for a circulation of air at the bottom of the tube, by which the volatile matter rises more easily. In some cases, it is necessary to draw the closed end out to a fine point, as in the tubes C and D. Either one or the other of these tubes is employed, depending upon the nature of the substance used. The sublimates condense at the upper part of the tube *a*, and can be there examined and recognized. These tubes, before being used, must be thoroughly dried and cleaned. In experimenting with them, they should not be exposed at once to the hottest part of the flame, but should be submitted to the heat gradually. If the substance is of such a nature that it will sublime at a low heat, the tube should be held more horizontal, while a higher heat is attained by bringing the tube to a more vertical position.

VARIOUS APPARATUS NECESSARY.

Edulcorator or Washing Bottle.—Take a glass bottle of the capacity of about twelve ounces, and close the mouth of it very tight with a cork, through which a short glass tube is fitted airtight. The external end of this tube is drawn out to a point, with a very fine orifice. The bottle should be filled about half full of water. By blowing air into the bottle through the tube, and then turning it downwards, the compressed air will expel a fine stream of water through the fine orifice with considerable force. We use this washing bottle, Fig. 11, for the purpose of rinsing the small particles of coal from the reduced metals.

Fig. 11.

Agate Mortar and Pestle.—This mortar is used for the purpose of pulverizing hard substances, and for mixing fluxes. As this mortar will not yield to abrasion, there is no danger of any foreign matter becoming mixed with the substance pulverized in it. It should be cleaned after use with pumice stone. Steel mortars are very useful for the pulverization of hard bodies; but for all those substances which require great care in their analysis, and which can be obtained in very minute quantity, the agate mortar alone should be used.

A *hammer* made of steel is necessary. This should have the edge square.

A small *anvil*, polished on the surface, is also required. It is frequently used to test the malleability of metals.

A *knife*, for the purpose of ascertaining the hardness of minerals.

The student should also be provided with several three-edged files, and likewise with some flat ones.

A *microscope*, an instrument with two lenses, or with such a combination of lenses, that they may be used double or single, is frequently necessary for the examination of blowpipe experiments, or the reaction of the fluxes. Common lenses, howsoever cheap they may be, are certainly not recommended. A microscope with achromatic lenses can now be purchased so cheap that there is no longer any necessity of procuring one with the common lens. Besides, there is no reliability whatever to be placed in the revelations of the common lens ; while on the contrary, the deceptive appearances which minute objects assume beneath such lenses are more injurious than otherwise. A small cheap set of magnifying glasses are all that is required for the purpose of blowpipe analysis, Fig. 12.

Fig. 12.

A small *magnet* should be kept on hand, for the purpose of testing reduced metals.

Nippers, for the purpose of breaking off pieces of minerals for analysis, without injuring the entire piece, are indispensable, Fig 13.

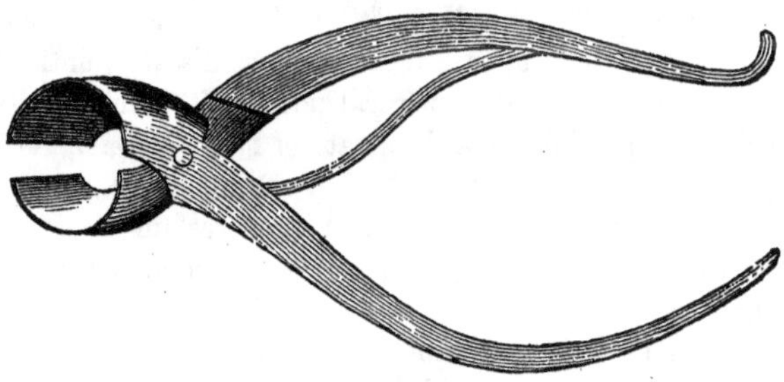

Fig. 13.

A pair of *scissors* is required to trim the wick of the lamp, and for the trimming of the edge of platinum foil.

A small *spatula* should be kept for the purpose of mixing substances with fluxes.

THE REAGENTS.

Those substances which possess the property of acting upon other substances, in such a characteristic manner that they can be recognized, either by their color, or by their effervescence, or by the peculiar precipitation produced, are termed *reagents.* The phenomena thus produced is termed *reaction.* We use those reagents, or *tests,* for the purpose of ascertaining the presence or the absence of certain substances, through the peculiar phenomena produced when brought in contact with them.

The number of reagents employed in blowpipe analysis is not great, and therefore we shall here give a brief description of their preparation and use. It is indispensably necessary that they should be chemically pure, as every admixture of a foreign substance would only produce a false result. Some of them have a strong affinity for water, or are deliquescent, and consequently absorb it greedily from the air. These must be kept in glass bottles, with glass stoppers, fitted air-tight by grinding.

A. REAGENTS OF GENERAL USE.

1. *Carbonate of Soda.*—(NaO, CO^2) Wash the bicarbonate of soda ($NaO, 2CO^2$) upon a filter, with cold water, until the filtrate ceases to give, after neutralization with diluted nitric acid (NO^5), a precipitate with nitrate of baryta, (BaO, NO^5), or nitrate of silver, (AgO, NO^5). That left upon the filter we make red hot in a platinum, silver, or porcelain dish. One atom of carbonic acid is expelled, and the residue is carbonate of soda.

A solution of soda must not be changed by the addition of sulphide of ammonium. And when neutralized with hydrochloric acid, and evaporated to dryness, and again dissolved in water, there must be no residue left.

Carbonate of soda is an excellent agent in reduction, in consequence of its easy fusibility, whereby it causes the close contact of the oxides with the charcoal support, so that the blowpipe flame can reach every part of the substance under examination.

For the decomposition and determination of insoluble substances, particularly the silicates, carbonate of soda is indispensable. But for the latter purpose, we use with advantage a mixture of ten parts of soda and thirteen parts of dry carbonate of potash, which mixture fuses more easily than the carbonate of soda alone.

2. *Hydrate of Baryta* (BaO, HO).—This salt is used sometimes for the detection of alkalies in silicates. Mix one part of the substance with about four parts of the hydrate of baryta, and expose it to the blowpipe flame. The hydrate of baryta combines with the silicic acid, and forms the super-basic silicate of baryta, while the oxides become free. The fused mass must be dissolved in hydrochloric acid, which converts the oxides into chlorides. Evaporate to dryness, and dissolve the residue in water. The silicic acid remains insoluble.

The hydrate of baryta is prepared by mixing six parts of finely powdered heavy-spar (BaO, SO_3) with one part of charcoal and one and a half parts of wheat flour, and exposing this mixture in a Hessian crucible with a cover to a strong and continuous red heat. The cooled chocolate-brown mass must be boiled with twenty parts of water, and, while boiling, there must be added the oxide of copper in sufficient quantity, or until the liquid will not impart a black color to a solution of acetate of lead (PbO, $\bar{A}$). The liquid must be filtered while hot, and as it cools the hydrate of baryta appears in crystals. These crystals must be washed with a little cold water, and then heated at a low temperature in a porcelain dish until the crystal water is expelled. The hydrate of baryta melts by a low red heat without losing its water of hydration.

3. *Bisulphate of Potassa* (KO, $2SO^3$).—At a red heat the half of the sulphuric acid of this salt becomes free, and thus

separates and expels volatile substances, by which we can recognize lithium, boracic acid, nitric acid, fluoric acid, bromine, iodine, chlorine; or it decomposes and reveals some other compounds, as, for instance, the salts of the titanic, tantalic and tungstic acids. The bisulphate of potash is also used for the purpose of converting a substance into sulphate, or to free it at once from certain constituents. These sulphates are dissolved in water, by which we are enabled to effect the separation of its various constituents.

PREPARATION.—Two parts of coarsely powdered sulphate of potash are placed in a porcelain crucible, and one part of pure sulphuric acid is poured over it. Expose this to heat over the spirit-lamp, until the whole becomes a clear liquid. The cooled mass must be of a pure white color, and may be got out of the crucible by inverting it. It must be kept in a fine powder.

4. *Oxalate of Potassa* ($KO, \bar{O}$).—Dissolve bioxalate of potash in water, and neutralize with carbonate of potash. Evaporate the solution at a low heat to dryness, stirring constantly towards the close of the operation. The dry residue is to be kept in the form of a powder.

The oxalate of potash, at a low red heat, eliminates a considerable quantity of carbonic oxide, which, having a strong affinity for oxygen, with which it forms carbonic acid, it is therefore a powerful agent of reduction. It is in many cases preferable to carbonate of soda.

5. *Cyanide of Potassium* (Cy, K).—In the dry method of analysis, this salt is one of the most efficient agents for the reduction of metallic oxides. It separates not only the metals from their oxygen compounds, but likewise from their sulphur compounds, while it is converted through the action of the oxygen into carbonate of potash, or, in the latter case, combines with the sulphur and forms the sulphureted cyanide of potassium. This separation is facilitated by its easy fusibility. But in many cases it melts too freely, and therefore it is better to mix it, for blowpipe analysis, with an equal quantity of soda. This mixture has great powers of reduction, and it is easily ab-

sorbed by the charcoal, while the globules of reduced metal are visible in the greatest purity.

PREPARATION.—Deprive the ferrocyanide of potassium (2KCy +FeCy) of its water by heating it over the spirit-lamp in a porcelain dish. Mix eight parts of this anhydrous salt with three parts of dry carbonate of potash, and fuse the mixture by a low red heat in a Hessian, or still better, in an iron crucible with a cover, until the mass flows quiet and clear, and a sample taken up with an iron spatula appears perfectly white. Pour the clear mass out into a china or porcelain dish or an iron plate, but with caution that the fine iron particles which have settled to the bottom, do not mix with it. The white fused mass must be powdered, and kept from the air. The cyanide of potassium thus prepared, contains some of the cyanate of potassa, but the admixture does not deteriorate it for blowpipe use. It must be perfectly white, free from iron, charcoal, and sulphide of potassium. The solution of it in water must give a white precipitate with a solution of lead, and when neutralized with hydrochloric acid, and evaporated to dryness, it must not give an insoluble residue by dissolving it again in water.

6. *Nitrate of Potassa, Saltpetre* (KO, NO^5).—Saturate boiling water with commercial saltpetre, filter while hot in a beaker glass, which is to be placed in cold water, and stir while the solution is cooling. The greater part of the saltpetre will crystallize in very fine crystals. Place these crystals upon a filter, and wash them with a little cold water, until a solution of nitrate of silver ceases to exhibit any reaction upon the filtrate. These crystals must be dried and powdered.

Saltpetre, when heated with substances easy of oxidation, yields its oxygen quite readily, and is, therefore, a powerful means of oxidation. In blowpipe analysis, we use it particularly to convert sulphides (as those of arsenic, antimony, &c.) into oxides and acids. We furthermore use saltpetre for the purpose of producing a complete oxidation of small quantities of metallic oxides, which oxidize with difficulty in the oxidation flame, so that the color of the bead, in its highest state of oxidation, shall be visible, as for instance, manganese dissolved in the microcosmic salt.

7. *Biborate of soda, borax*—($NaO + 2BO^3$).—Commercial borax is seldom pure enough for a reagent. A solution of borax must not give a precipitate with carbonate of potassa; or, after the addition of dilute nitric acid, it must remain clear upon the addition of nitrate of silver, or nitrate of baryta. Or a small piece of the dry salt, fused upon a platinum wire, must give a clear and uncolored glass, as well in the oxidation flame as in the reduction flame. If these tests indicate a foreign admixture, the borax must be purified by re-crystallization. These crystals are washed upon a filter, dried, and heated, to expel the crystal water, or until the mass ceases to swell up, and it is reduced to powder.

Boracic acid is incombustible, and has a strong affinity for oxides when fused with them; therefore, it not only directly combines with oxides, but it expels, by fusion, all other volatile acids from their salts. Furthermore, boracic acid promotes the oxidation of metals and sulphur, and induces haloid compounds, in the oxidation flame, to combine with the rising oxides. Borates thus made, melt generally by themselves; but admixed with borate of soda, they fuse much more readily, give a clear bead. Borax acts either as a flux, or through the formation of double salts.

In borax, we have the action of free boracic acid, as well as borate of soda, and for that reason it is an excellent reagent for blowpipe analysis.

All experiments in which borax is employed should be effected upon platinum wire. The hook of the wire should be heated red hot, and then dipped into the powdered borax. This should be exposed to the oxidation flame, when it will be fused to a bead, which adheres to the hook. This should be then dipped into the powdered substance, which will adhere to it if it is hot; but if the bead is cool, it must be previously moistened. Expose this bead to the oxidation flame until it ceases to change, then allow it to cool, when it should be exposed to the reduction flame. Look for the following in the oxidation flame :

(1.) Whether the heated substance is fused to a clear bead or not, and whether the bead remains transparent after cooling. The beads of some substances, for instance those of the alkaline earths, are clear while hot ; but upon cooling, are milk-white and enamelled. Some substances give a clear bead when heated and when cold, but appear enamelled when heated intermittingly or with a flame which changes often from oxidation to reduction, or with an unsteady flame produced by too strong a blast. The reason is an incomplete fusion, while from the basic borate compound a part of the base is separated. As the boracic acid is capable of dissolving more in the heat, a bead will be clear while hot, enamelled when cold, as a part in the latter instance will become separated.

(2.) Whether the substance dissolves easily or not, and whether it intumesces from arising gases.

(3.) Whether the bead, when exposed to the oxidation flame, exhibits any color, and whether the color remains after the bead shall have cooled, or whether the color fades.

(4.) Whether the bead exhibits any other reaction in the reduction flame.

The bead should not be overcharged with the substance under examination, or it will become colored so deeply as not to present any transparency, or the color light enough to discern its hue.

8. *Microcosmic Salt—Phosphate of Soda and Ammonia*—(NaO, $NH^4O + PO^5$).—Dissolve six parts of phosphate of soda ($2NaO$, HO, PO^5), and one part of pure chloride of Ammonium (NH^4Cl.), in two parts of boiling water, and allow it to cool. The greatest part of the formed double salt crystallizes, while the mother-liquid contains chloride of sodium, and some of the double salt. The crystals must be dissolved in as little boiling water as possible, and re-crystallized. These crystals must be dried and powdered.

When this double salt is heated, the water and the ammonia

escape, while the incombustible residue has a composition similar to borax, viz., a free acid and an easily fusible salt. The effect of it is, therefore, similar to the borax. The free phosphoric acid expels, likewise, most other acids from their combinations, and combines with metallic oxides.

For supports, the platinum wire may be used, but the hook must be smaller than when borax is used, or the bead will not adhere. As for all the other experiments with this salt, the microscosmic salt is used the same as borax.

9. *Nitrate of Cobalt.*—(CoO, NO^5).—This salt can be prepared by dissolving pure oxide of cobalt in diluted nitric acid, and evaporating to dryness with a low heat. The dry residue should be dissolved in ten parts of water, and filtered. The filtrate is now ready for use, and should be kept in a bottle with a glass stopper. If the pure oxide of cobalt cannot be procured, then it may be prepared by mixing two parts of finely powdered *glance of cobalt* with four parts of saltpetre, and one part of dry carbonate of potassa with one part of water free from carbonate of soda. This mixture should be added in successive portions into a red-hot Hessian crucible, and the heat continued until the mass is fused, or at least greatly diminished in volume. The cooled mass must be triturated with hot water, and then heated with hydrochloric acid until it is dissolved and forms a dark green solution, which generally presents a gelatinous appearance, occasioned by separated silica. The solution is to be evaporated to dryness, the dry residue moistened with hydrochloric acid, boiled with water, filtered and neutralized while hot with carbonate of ammonia, until it ceases to give an acid reaction with test-paper. This must now be filtered again, and carbonate of potassa added to the filtrate as long as a precipitate is produced. This precipitate is brought upon a filter and washed thoroughly, and then dissolved in diluted nitric acid. This is evaporated to dryness, and one part of it is dissolved in ten parts of water for use.

The oxide of cobalt combines, with strong heat in the oxidation flame, with various earths and infusible metallic oxides, and thus produces peculiarly colored compounds, and is therefore used for their detection; (alumina, magnesia, oxide of zinc, oxide of tin, etc.) Some of the powdered substance is heated upon charcoal in the flame of oxidation, and moistened with a drop of the solution of the nitrate of cobalt, when the oxidation flame is thrown upon it. Alumina gives a pure blue color, the oxide of zinc a bright green, magnesia a light red, and the oxide of tin a bluish-green color; but the latter is only distinctly visible after cooling.

The dropping bottle, is the most useful apparatus for the purpose of getting small quantities of fluid. It is composed of a glass tube, drawn out to a point, with a small orifice. This tube passes through the cork of the bottle. By pressing in the cork into the neck of the bottle, the air within will be compressed, and the liquid will rise in the tube. If now we draw the cork out, with the tube filled with the fluid, and pressing the finger upon the upper orifice, the fluid can be forced out in the smallest quantity, even to a fraction of a drop.

10. *Tin.*—This metal is used in the form of foil, cut into strips about half an inch wide. Tin is very susceptible of oxidation, and therefore deprives oxidized substances of their oxygen very quickly, when heated in contact with them. It is employed in blowpipe analysis, for the purpose of producing in glass beads a lower degree of oxidation, particularly if the substance under examination contains only a small portion of such oxide. These oxides give a characteristic color to the bead, and thus are detected. The bead is heated upon charcoal in the reduction flame, with a small portion of the tin, whereby some of the tin is melted and mixes with the bead. The bead should be reduced quickly in the reduction flame, for by continuing the blast too great a while, the oxide of tin separates the other oxides in the reduced or metallic state, while we only require that they shall only be converted into a sub-oxide, in order that its peculiar color may be recognized in the bead. The addition of too much tin causes the bead

to present an unclean appearance, and prevents the required reaction.

11. *Silica* (SiO^3).—This acid does not even expel carbonic acid in the wet way, but in a glowing heat it expels the strongest volatile acids. In blowpipe analysis, we use it fused with carbonate of soda to a bead, as a test for sulphuric acid, and in some cases for phosphoric acid. Also with carbonate of soda and borax, for the purpose of separating tin from copper.

Finely powdered quartz will answer these purposes. If it cannot be procured, take well washed white sand and mix it with two parts of carbonate of soda and two parts of carbonate of potassa. Melt the materials together, pound up the cooled mass, dissolve in hot water, filter, add to the filtrate hydrochloric acid, and evaporate to dryness. Moisten the dry residue with hydrochloric acid, and boil in water. The silica remains insoluble. It should be washed well, dried, and heated, and then reduced to powder.

12. TEST-PAPERS.—(*a.*) *Blue Litmus Paper.*—Dissolve one part of litmus in six or eight parts of water, and filter. Divide the filtrate into two parts. In one of the parts neutralize the free alkali by stirring it with a glass rod dipped in diluted sulphuric acid, until the fluid appears slightly red. Then mix the two parts together, and draw slips of unsized paper, free from alkali, such as fine filtering paper. Hang these strips on a line to dry, in the shade and free from floating dust. If the litmus solution is too light, it will not give sufficient characteristic indications, and if too dark it is not sensitive enough. The blue color of the paper should be changed to red, when brought in contact with a solution containing the minutest trace of free acid ; but it should be recollected that the neutral salts of the heavy metals produce the same change.

(*b.*) *Red Litmus Paper.*—The preparation of the red litmus paper is similar to the above, the acid being added until a red color is obtained. Reddened litmus paper is a very sensitive reagent for free alkalies, the carbonates of the alkalies, alkaline earths, sulphides of the alkalies and of the alkaline earths, and alkaline salts with weak acids, such as boracic acid. These substances restore the original blue color of the litmus.

(*c.*) *Logwood Paper.*—Take bruised logwood, boil it in water, filter, and proceed as above. Logwood paper is a very delicate test for free alkalies, which impart a violet tint to it. It is sometimes used to detect hydrofluoric acid, which changes its color to yellow.

All the test-papers are to be cut into narrow strips, and preserved in closely stopped vials. The especial employment of the test-papers we shall allude to in another place.

B. ESPECIAL REAGENTS.

13. *Fused Boracic Acid* (BO^3).—The commercial article is sufficiently pure for blowpipe analysis. It is employed in some cases to detect phosphoric acid, and also minute traces of copper in lead compounds.

14. *Fluorspar* ($CaFl^2$).—This substance should be pounded fine and strongly heated. Fluorspar is often mixed with boracic acid, which renders it unfit for analytical purposes. Such an admixture can be detected if it be mixed with bisulphate of potassa, and exposed upon platinum wire to the interior or blue flame. It is soon fused, the boracic acid is reduced and evaporated, and by passing through the external flame it is reoxidized, and colors the flame green. We use fluorspar mixed with bisulphate of potassa as a test for lithia and boracic acid in complicated compounds.

15. *Oxalate of Nickel* ($NiO, \bar{O}$).—It is prepared by dissolving the pure oxide of nickel in diluted hydrochloric acid. Evaporate to dryness, dissolve in water, and precipitate with oxalate of ammonia. The precipitate must be washed with caution upon a filter, and then dried. It is employed in blowpipe analysis to detect salts of potassa in the presence of sodium and lithium.

16. *Oxide of Copper* (CuO).—Pure metallic copper is dis-

solved in nitric acid. The solution is evaporated in a porcelain dish to dryness, and gradually heated over a spirit-lamp, until the blue color of the salt has disappeared and the mass presents a uniform black color. The oxide of copper so prepared must be powdered, and preserved in a vial. It serves to detect, in complicated compounds, minute traces of chlorine.

17. *Antimoniate of Potassa* (KO, SbO^5).—Mix four parts of the bruised metal of antimony, with nine parts of saltpetre. Throw this mixture, in small portions, into a red-hot Hessian crucible, and keep it at a glowing heat for awhile after all the mixture is added. Boil the cooled mass with water, and dry the residue. Take two parts of this, and mix it with one part of dry carbonate of potassa, and expose this to a red heat for about half an hour. Then wash the mass in cold water, and boil the residue in water ; filter, evaporate the filtrate to dryness, and then, with a strong heat, render it free of water. Powder it while it is warm, and preserve it in closed vials. It is used for the detection of small quantities of charcoal in compound substances, as it shares its oxygen with the carbonaceous matter, the antimony becomes separated, and carbonate of potassa is produced, which restores red litmus paper to blue, and effervesces with acids.

18. *Silver Foil.*—A small piece of silver foil is used for the purpose of detecting sulphur and the sulphides of the metals, which impart a dark stain to it. If no silver foil is at hand, strips of filtering paper, impregnated with acetate of lead, will answer in many cases.

19. *Nitroprusside of Sodium* ($Fe^2Cy^5, NO^2, 2Na$).—This is a very delicate test for sulphur, and was discovered by Dr. Playfair. This test has lately been examined with considerable ability by Prof. J. W. Bailey, of West Point. If any sulphate or sulphide is heated by the blowpipe upon charcoal with the carbonate of soda, and the fused mass is placed on a watch-glass, with a little water, and a small piece of the nitroprusside of sodium is added, there will be produced a splendid purple color. This color, or reaction, will be produced from any substance contain-

ing sulphur, such as the parings of the nails, hair, albumen, etc. In regard to these latter substances, the carbonate of soda should be mixed with a little starch, which will prevent the loss of any of the sulphur by oxidation. Coil a piece of hair around a platinum wire, moisten it, and dip it into a mixture of carbonate of soda, to which a little starch has been added, and then heat it with the blowpipe, when the fused mass will give with the nitroprusside of sodium the characteristic purple reaction, indicative of the presence of sulphur. With the proper delicacy of manipulation, a piece of hair, half an inch in length, will give distinct indications of sulphur.

Preparation.—The nitroprussides of sodium and potassium (for either salt will give the above reactions), are prepared as follows: One atom (422 grains) of pulverized ferrocyanide of potassium is mixed with five atoms of commercial nitric acid, diluted with an equal quantity of water. One-fifth of this quantity (one atom) of the acid is sufficient to transfer the ferrocyanide into nitroprusside; but the use of a larger quantity is found to give the best results. The acid is poured all at once upon the ferrocyanide, the cold produced by the mixing being sufficient to moderate the action. The mixture first assumes a milky appearance, but after a little while, the salt dissolves, forming a coffee-colored solution, and gases are disengaged in abundance. When the salt is completely dissolved, the solution is found to contain ferrocyanide (red prussiate) of potassium, mixed with nitroprusside and nitrate of the same base. It is then immediately decanted into a large flask, and heated over the water-bath. It continues to evolve gas, and after awhile, no longer yields a dark blue precipitate with ferrous salts, but a dark green or slate-colored precipitate. It is then removed from the fire, and left to crystallize, whereupon it yields a large quantity of crystals of nitre, and more or less oxamide. The strongly-colored mother liquid is then neutralized with carbonate of potash or soda, according to the salt to be prepared, and the solution is boiled, whereupon it generally deposits a green or brown precipitate, which must be separated by filtration. The liquid then contains nothing but nitroprusside and nitrate of potash or soda. The nitrates being the least soluble, are first crystallized, and the remaining liquid, on farther evaporation, yields crystals of the nitroprusside. The sodium salt crystallizes most easily.—(PLAYFAIR.)

As some substances, particularly in complicated compounds, are not detected with sufficient nicety in the dry way of analysis, it will often be necessary to resort to the wet way. It is therefore necessary to have prepared the reagents required for such testing, as every person, before he can become an expert blowpipe analyst, must be acquainted with the characteristic tests as applied in the wet way.

Part II.

INITIATORY ANALYSIS.

Qualitative analysis refers to those examinations which relate simply to the presence or the absence of certain substances, irrespective of their quantities. But before we take cognizance of special examinations, it would facilitate the progress of the student to pass through a course of Initiatory Exercises. These at once lead into the special analysis of all those substances susceptible of examination by the blowpipe. The Initiatory Analysis is best studied by adopting the following arrangement:

1. Examinations with the glass bulb.
2. " with the open tube.
3. " upon charcoal.
4. " in the platinum forceps.
5. " in the borax bead.
6. " in microcosmic salt.
7. " in the carbonate of soda bead.
8. Confirmatory examinations.

1. EXAMINATIONS WITH THE GLASS BULB.

The glass of which the bulb is made should be entirely free from lead, otherwise fictitious results will ensue. If the bulb be of flint glass, then by heating it, there is a slightly iridescent film caused upon the surface of the glass, which may easily be mistaken for arsenic. Besides, this kind of glass is easily fusible in the oxidating flame of the blowpipe, while, in the reducing flame, its ready decomposition would preclude its use entirely. The tube should be composed of the potash or hard Bohemian glass, should be perfectly white, and very thin, or the heat will crack it.

The tube should be perfectly clean, which can be easily attained by wrapping a clean cotton rag around a small stick, and inserting it in the tube. Before using the tube, see also that it is perfectly dry.

The quantity of the substance put into the tube for examination should be small. From one to three grains is quite sufficient, as a general rule, but circumstances vary the quantity. The sides of the tube should not catch any of the substance as it is being placed at the bottom of the tube, or into the bulb. If any of the powder, however, should adhere, it should be pushed down with a roll of clean paper, or the clean cotton rag referred to above.

In submitting the tube to the flame, it should be heated at first very gently, the heat being increased until the glass begins to soften, when the observations of what is ensuing within it may be made.

If the substance be of an organic nature, a peculiar empyreumatic odor will be given off. If the substance chars, then it may be inferred that it is of an organic nature. The matters which are given off and cause the empyreumatic odor, are a peculiar oil, ammonia, carbonic acid, acetic acid, water, cyanogen, and frequently other compounds. If a piece of paper is heated in the bulb, a dark colored oil condenses upon the sides of the tube, which has a strong empyreumatic odor. A piece of litmus paper indicates that this oil is acid, as it is quickly changed to red by contact with it. A black residue is now left in the tube, and upon examination we will find that it is charcoal. If, instead of the paper, a piece of animal substance is placed in the bulb, the reddened litmus paper will be converted into its original blue color, while charcoal will be left at the bottom of the tube.

A changing of the substance, however, to a dark color, should not be accepted as an invariable indication of charcoal, as some inorganic bodies thus change color, but the dark substance will not be likely to be mistaken for charcoal. By igniting the suspected substance with nitrate of potassa, it can quickly be ascertained whether it is organic or not, for if the latter, the vivid deflagration will indicate it.

If the substance contains water, it will condense upon the cold portion of the tube, and may be there examined as to whether it is acid or alkaline. If the former, the matter under examination is, perhaps, vegetable ; if the latter, it is of an animal nature. The water may be that fluid absorbed, or it may form a portion of its constitution.

If the substance contain *sulphur*, the sublimate upon the cold part of the tube may be recognized by its characteristic appearance, especially if the substance should be a sulphide of tin, copper, antimony, or iron. The hyposulphites, and several other sulphides, also give off sulphur when heated. The volatile metals, mercury and arsenic, will, however, sublime without undergoing decomposition. As the sulphide of arsenic may be mistaken, from its color and appearance, for sulphur, it must be examined especially for the purpose of determining that point.

Selenium will likewise sublime by heat as does sulphur. This is the case if selenides are present. Selenium gives off the smell of decayed horse-radish.

When the persalts are heated they are reduced to protosalts, with the elimination of a part of their acid. This will be indicated by the blue litmus paper.

If some of the neutral salts containing a volatile acid be present, they will become decomposed. For instance, the red nitrous acid water of the nitrates will indicate the decomposition of the salt, especially if it be the nitrate of a metalic oxide.

If there is an odor of sulphur, then it is quite probable, if no free sulphur be present, that a hyposulphite is decomposed.

If an oxalate be present, it is decomposed with the evolution of carbonic oxide, which may be inflamed at the mouth of the tube ; but there are oxalates that give off carbonic acid gas, which, of course, will not burn. A cyanide will become decomposed and eliminate nitrogen gas, while the residue is charred. Some cyanides are, however, not thus decomposed, as the dry cyanides of the earths and alkalies.

There are several oxides of metals which will sublime, and may be thus examined in the tube. *Arsenious acid* sublimes with great ease in minute octohedral crystals. The oxides of tellurium and antimony will sublime, the latter in minute glittering needles.

There are several metals which will sublime, and may be examined in the cold portion of the tube. *Mercury* condenses upon the tube in minute globules. These often do not present the metalic appearance until they are disturbed with a glass rod, when they attract each other, and adhere as small globules. Place in the tube about a grain of red precipitate of the drug stores and apply heat, when the oxide will become decomposed, its oxygen will escape while the vaporized mercury will condense upon the cold portion of the tube, and may there be examined with a magnifying glass.

Arsenic, when vaporized, may be known by its peculiar alliaceous odor. Arsenic is vaporized from its metallic state, and likewise from its alloys. Several compounds which contain arsenic will .also sublime, such as the arsenical cobalt. Place in the bulb a small piece of arsenical cobalt or "fly-stone," and apply heat. The sulphide of arsenic will first rise, but soon the arsenic will adhere to the sides of the tube.

The metals tellurium and cadmium are susceptible of solution, but the heat required is a high one. This is best done upon charcoal.

The *perchloride of mercury* sublimes undecomposed in the bulb, previously undergoing fusion.

The *protochloride of mercury* likewise sublimes, but it does not undergo fusion first, as is the case with the corrosive sublimate.

The *ammoniacal salts* all are susceptible of sublimation, which they do without leaving a residue. There are, however, several which contain fixed acids, which latter are left in the bulb. This is particularly the case with the phosphates and borates A piece of red litmus paper will readily detect the escaping ammonia, while its odor will indicate its presence with great certainty. The halogen compounds of mercury, we should have mentioned, also sublime, the red iodide giving a yellow sublimate.

The bulb is also a convenient little instrument for the purpose of heating those substances which phosphoresce, and likewise those salts that decrepitate.

Should the above reactions not be readily discerned, it should not be considered as an indication that the substances are not present, for they are frequently expelled in such combinations that the above reactions will not take place. This is often the case with sulphur, selenium, arsenic, and tellurium. It frequently happens, likewise, that these substances are in such combinations that heat alone will not sublime them ; or else two or more of them may arise together, and thus complicate the sublimate, so that the eye cannot readily detect either substance. Sometimes sulphur and arsenic will coat the tube with a metal-like appearance, which is deceptive. This coating presents a metallic lustre at its lower portion, but changing, as it progresses upward, to a dark brown, light brown, orange or yellow ; this sublimate being due to combinations of arsenic and sulphur, which compounds are volatilized at a lower temperature than metallic arsenic.

If certain reagents are mixed with many substances, changes are effected which would not ensue with heat alone. *Formiate of soda* possesses the property of readily reducing metallic oxides. When this salt is heated, it gives off a quantity of carbonic oxide gas. This gas, when in the presence of a metallic oxide, easily reduces the metal, by withdrawing its oxygen from it, and being changed into carbonic oxide. If a little fly-stone is mixed with some formiate of soda, and heated in the bulb, the arsenic is reduced, volatilized, and condenses in the cool portion of the tube. By this method, the smallest portion of a grain of the arsenical compound may be thus examined with the greatest readiness. If the residue is now washed, by which the soda is got rid of, the metallic arsenic may be obtained in small spangles. If the compound examined be the sulphide of antimony, the one-thousandth part can be readily detected, and hence this method is admirably adapted to the examination of medicinal antimonial compounds. The arsenites of silver and copper are reduced by the formiate of soda to their metals, mixed with metallic arsenic. The mercurial salts are all reduced with the metal plainly visible as a bright silvery ring on the cool portion of the tube. The chloride and nitrate of silver are completely reduced, and may be obtained after working out the soda, as bright metallic spangles. The salts of antimony and zinc are thus reduced; also the sulphate of cadmium. The sublimate of the latter, although in appearance not unlike that of arsenic, can easily be distingushed by its brighter color. It is, in fact, the rich yellow of this sublimate which has led artists to adopt it as one of their most valued pigments.

2. EXAMINATIONS IN THE OPEN TUBE.

The substance to be operated upon should be placed in the tube, about half an inch from the end, and the flame applied at first very cautiously, increasing gradually to the required temperature. The tube, in all these *roasting* operations, as they are termed, should be held in an inclined position. The nearer perpendicular the tube is held, the stronger is the draught of air that passes through it. If but little heat is required in the open tube operation, the spirit-lamp is the best method of applying the heat. But if a greater temperature is required, then recourse must be had to the blowpipe. Upon the angle of inclination of the tube depends the amount of air that passes through it, and therefore, the rapidity of the draught may be easily regulated at the will of the operator. The inclination of the tube may, as a general rule, be about the angle represented in Fig. 14.

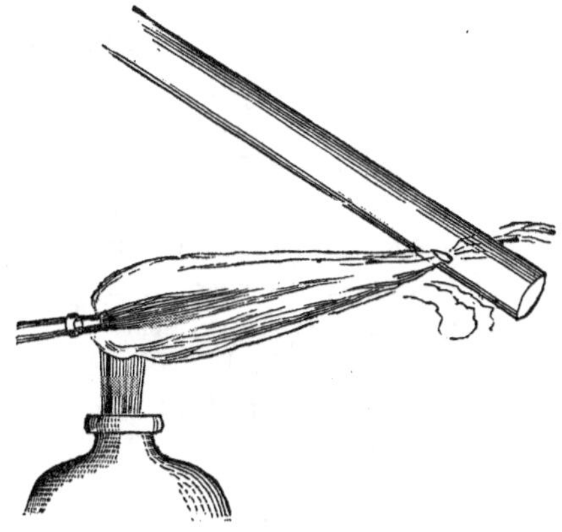

Fig. 14.

The length of the tube must be about six inches, so that the portion upon which the substance rested in a previous examination may be cut off. The portion of the tube left will answer for several similar operations.

When the substance is under examination, we should devote our attention to the nature of the sublimates, and to that of the *odors* of the gases. If sulphur be in the substance experimented upon, the characteristic odor of sulphurous acid gas will readily indicate the sulphur. If metallic sulphides, for instance, are experimented upon, the sulphurous acid gas eliminated will readily reveal their presence. As it is a property of this gas to bleach, a piece of Brazil-wood test paper should be held in the mouth of the tube, when its loss of color will indicate the presence of the sulphurous acid. It often happens, too, that a slight deposition of sulphur will be observed upon the cool portion of the tube. This is particularly the case with those sulphides which yield sublimates of sulphur when heated in the bulb.

Selenium undergoes but slight oxidation, but it becomes readily volatilized, and may be observed on the cool portion of the tube. At the same time the nose, if applied close to the end of the tube, will detect the characteristic odor of rotten horse-radish. Arsenic also gives its peculiar alliaceous odor, which is so characteristic that it can be easily detected. A few of the arsenides produce this odor. The *sublimates* should be carefully observed, as they indicate often with great certainty the presence of certain substances ; for instance, that of arsenic. The sublimate, in this case, presents itself as the arsenious acid, or the metallic arsenic itself. If it be the former, it may be discerned by aid of the magnifying glass as beautiful glittering octohedral crystals. If the latter, the metallic lustre will reveal it.

But it will be observed that while some of the arsenides are sublimed at a comparatively low temperature, others require a very high one.

Antimony gives a white sublimate when its salts are roasted, as the sulphide, or the antimonides themselves, or the oxide of this metal. This white sublimate is not antimonious acid, but there is mixed with it the oxide of antimony with which the acid is sublimed. As is the case with arsenious acid, the antimonious acid may, by dexterous heating, be driven from one portion of the tube to another.

Tellurium, or its acid and oxide, may be got as a sublimate in the tube. The tellurious acid, unlike the arsenious and antimonious acids, cannot be driven from one portion of the tube to another, but, on the contrary, it fuses into small clear globules, visible to the naked eye sometimes, but quite so with the aid of the magnifying glass.

Lead, or its chloride, sublimes like tellurium, and, like that substance, fuses into globules or drops.

Bismuth, or its sulphide, sublimes into an orange or brownish globules, when it is melted, as directed above, for tellurium. The color of the bismuth and lead oxides are somewhat similar, although that of the latter is paler.

If any mineral containing *fluorine* is fused, first with the microcosmic salt bead, then put into the tube, and the flame of the blowpipe be directed *into* the tube upon the bead, hydrofluoric acid is disengaged and attacks the inside of the tube. The fluoride of calcium, or fluorspar, may be used for this experiment.

During the roasting, a brisk current of air should be allowed to pass through the tube, whereby unoxidized matter may be prevented from volatilization, and the clogging up of the substance under examination be prevented.

3. EXAMINATIONS UPON CHARCOAL.

In making examinations upon charcoal, it is quite necessary that the student should make himself familiar with the different and characteristic appearances of the deposits upon the charcoal. In this case I have found the advice given by Dr. Sherer to be the best; that is, to begin with the examination of the pure materials first, until the eye becomes familiarized with the appearances of their incrustations upon charcoal.

The greater part of the metals fuse when submitted to the heat of the blowpipe, and if exposed to the outer flame, they oxidize. These metals, termed the noble metals, do not oxidize, but they fuse. The metals platinum, iridium, rhodium, osmium and palladium do not fuse. The metal osmium, if exposed to the flame of oxidation, fuses and is finally dissipated as osmic acid. In the latter flame, the salts of the noble metals are reduced to the metallic state, and the charcoal is covered with the bright metal.

We shall give a brief description of the appearance of the principal elementary bodies upon being fused with charcoal. This plan is that deemed the most conducive to the progress of the student, by Berzelius, Plattner, and Sherer. Experience has taught us that this method is the most efficient that could have been devised as an initiatory exercise for the student, ere he commences a more concise and methodical method of analysis. In these reactions upon charcoal, we shall follow nearly the language of Plattner and Sherer.

SELENIUM is not difficult of fusion, and gives off brown fumes in either the oxidation or reduction flame. The deposit upon the charcoal is of a steel-grey color, with a slightly metallic lustre. The deposit however that fuses outside of this steel-grey one is of a dull violet color, shading off to a light brown. Under the flame of oxidation this deposit is easily driven from one portion of the charcoal to another, while the application of the reducing flame volatilizes it with the evolution of a beautiful blue light. The characteristic odor of decayed horse-radish distinguishes the volatilization of this metal.

TELLURIUM.—This metal fuses with the greatest readiness, and is reduced to vapor under both flames with fumes, and coats the charcoal with a deposit of tellurous acid. This deposit is white near the centre, and is of a dark yellow near the edges. It may be driven from place to place by the flame of oxidation, while that of reduction volatilizes it with a green flame. If there be a mixture of selenium present, then the color of the flame is bluish-green.

ARSENIC.—This metal is volatilized without fusing, and covers the charcoal both in the oxidizing and reducing flames with a deposit of arsenious acid. This coating is white in the centre, and grey towards the edges, and is found some distance from the assay. By the most gentle application of the flame, it is immediately volatilized, and if touched for a moment with the reducing flame, it disappears, tinging the flame pale blue. During volatilization a strong garlic odor is distincly perceptible, very characteristic of arsenic, and by which its presence in any compound may be immediately recognized.

ANTIMONY.—This metal fuses readily, and coats the charcoal under both flames with antimonious acid. This incrustation is of a white color where thick, but of a bluish tint where it is thin, and is found nearer to the assay than that of arsenic. When greatly heated by the flame of oxidation, it is driven from place to place without coloring the flame, but when volatilized by the flame of reduction, it tinges the flame blue. As antimonious acid is not so volatile as arsenious acid, they may thus be easily distinguished from one another.

When metallic antimony is fused upon charcoal, and the metallic bead raised to a red heat, if the blast be suspended, the fluid bead remains for some time at this temperature, giving off opaque white fumes, which are at first deposited on the surrounding charcoal, and then upon the bead itself, covering it with white, pearly crystals. The phenomenon is dependent upon the fact, that the heated button of antimony, in absorbing oxygen from the air, developes sufficient heat to maintain the metal in a fluid state, until it becomes entirely covered with crystals of antimonious acid so formed.

BISMUTH.—This metal fuses with ease, and under both flames covers the charcoal with a coating of oxide, which, while hot, is of an orange-yellow color, and after cooling, of a lemon-yellow color, passing, at the edges, into a bluish white. This white coating consists of the carbonate of bismuth. The sublimate from bismuth is formed at a less distance from the assay than is the case with antimony. It may be driven from place to place by the application of either flame ; but in so doing, the oxide is first reduced by the heated charcoal, and the metallic bismuth so formed is volatilized and reoxidized. The flame is uncolored.

LEAD.—This metal readily fuses under either flame, and incrusts the charcoal with oxide at about the same distance from the assay as is the case with bismuth. The oxide is, while hot, of a dark lemon-yellow color, but upon cooling, becomes of a sulphur yellow. The carbonate which is formed upon the charcoal, beyond the oxide, is of a bluish-white color. If the yellow incrustation of the oxide be heated with the flame of oxidation, it disappears, undergoing changes similar to those of bismuth above mentioned. Under the flame of reduction, it, however, disappears, tinging the flame blue.

CADMIUM.—This metal fuses with ease, and, in the flame of oxidation, takes fire, and burns with a deep yellow color, giving off brown fumes, which coat the charcoal, to within a small distance of the assay, with oxide of cadmium. This coating exhibits its characteristic reddish-brown color most clearly when cold. Where the coating is very thin, it passes to an orange color. As oxide of cadmium is easily reduced, and the metal very volatile, the coating of oxide may be driven from place to place by the application of either flame, to neither of which does it impart any color. Around the deposit of oxide, the charcoal has occasionally a variegated tarnish.

ZINC.—This metal fuses with ease, and takes fire in the flame of oxidation, burning with a brilliant greenish-white light, and forming thick white fumes of oxide of zinc, which coat the charcoal round the assay. This coating is yellow while hot, but when perfectly cooled, becomes white. If heated with the flame of oxidation, it shines brilliantly, but is not volatilized, since the heated charcoal is, under these circumstances, insufficient to effect its reduction. Even under the reducing flame, it disappears very slowly.

TIN.—This metal fuses readily, and, in the flame of oxidation, becomes covered with oxide, which, by a strong blast, may be easily blown off. In the reducing flame, the fused metal assumes a white surface, and the charcoal becomes covered with oxide. This oxide is of a pale yellow color while hot, and is quite brilliant when the flame of oxidation is directed upon it. After cooling, it becomes white. It is found immediately around the assay, and cannot be volatilized by the application of either flame.

MOLYBDENUM.—This metal, in powder, is infusible before the blowpipe. If heated in the outer flame, it becomes gradually oxidized, and incrusts the charcoal, at a small distance from the assay, with molybdic acid, which, near the assay, forms transparent crystalline scales, and is elsewhere deposited as a fine powder. The incrustation, while hot, is of a yellow color, but becomes white after cooling. It may be volatilized by heating with either flame, and leaves the surface of the charcoal, when perfectly cooled, of a dark-red copper color, with a metallic lustre, due to the oxide of molybdenum, which has been formed by the reducing action of the charcoal upon the molybdic acid. In the reducing flame, metallic molybdenum remains unchanged.

SILVER.—This metal, when fused alone, and kept in this state for some time, under a strong oxidizing flame, covers the charcoal with a thin film of dark reddish-brown oxide. If the silver be alloyed with lead, a yellow incrustation of the oxide of that metal is first formed, and afterwards, as the silver becomes more pure, a dark red deposit is formed on the charcoal beyond. If the silver contains a small quantity of antimony, a white incrustation of antimonious acid is formed, which becomes red on the surface if the blast be continued. And if lead and antimony are both present in the silver, after the greater part of these metals have been volatilized, a beautiful crimson incrustation is produced upon the charcoal. This result is sometimes obtained in fusing rich silver ores on charcoal.

SULPHIDES, CHLORIDES, IODIDES, AND BROMIDES.

In blowpipe experiments, it rarely occurs that we have to deal with pure metals, which, if not absolutely non-volatile, are recognized by the incrustation they form upon charcoal. Some compound substances, when heated upon charcoal, form white incrustations, resembling that formed by antimony, and which, when heated, may, in like manner, be driven from place to place. Among these are certain sulphides, as sulphide of potassium, and sulphide of sodium, which are formed by the action of the reducing flame upon the sulphates of potassa and soda, and are, when volatilized, reconverted into those sulphates, and as such deposited on the charcoal. No incrustation is, however, formed, until the whole of the alkaline sulphate has been absorbed into the charcoal, and has parted with its oxygen. As sulphide of potassium is more volatile than sulphide of sodium, an incrustation is formed from the former sooner than from the latter of these salts, and is considerably thicker in the former case. If the potash incrustation be touched with the reducing flame, it disappears with a violet-colored flame; and if a soda incrustation be treated in like manner, an orange-yellow flame is produced.

Sulphide of lithium, formed by heating the sulphate in the reducing flame, is volatilized in similar manner by a strong blast, although less readily than the sulphide of sodium. It affords a greyish white film, which disappears with a crimson flame when submitted to the reducing flame.

Besides the above, the sulphides of bismuth and lead give, when heated in either flame, two different incrustations, of which the more volatile is of a white color, and consists in the one case of sulphate of lead, and in the other of sulphate of bismuth. If either of these be heated under the reducing flame, it disappears in the former case with a bluish flame, in the latter unaccompanied by any visible flame. The incrustation formed nearest to the assay consists of the oxide of lead or bismuth, and is easily recognized by its color when hot and after cooling. There are many other metallic sulphides, which, when heated by the blowpipe flame, cover the charcoal with a white incrustation, as sulphide of antimony, sulphide of zinc, and sulphide of tin. In all these cases, however, the incrustation consists of the metallic oxide alone, and either volatilizes or remains unchanged, when submitted to the oxidizing flame.

Of the metallic chlorides there are many which, when heated on charcoal with the blowpipe flame, are volatilized and re-deposited as a white incrustation. Among these are the chlorides of potassium, sodium, and lithium, which volatilize and cover the charcoal immediately around the assay with a thin white film, after they have been fused and absorbed into the charcoal, chloride of potassium forms the thickest deposit, and chloride of lithium the thinnest, the latter being moreover of a greyish-white color. The chlorides of ammonium, mercury, and antimony volatilize without fusing.

The chlorides of zinc, cadmium, lead, bismuth, and tin first fuse and then cover the charcoal with two different incrustations, one of which is a white volatile chloride, and the other a less volatile oxide of the metal.

Some of the incrustations formed by metallic chlorides disappear with a colored flame when heated with the reducing flame ; thus chloride of potassium affords a violet flame, chloride of sodium an orange one, chloride of lithium a crimson flame, and chloride of lead a blue one. The other metals mentioned above volatilize without coloring the flame.

The chloride of copper fuses and colors the flame of a beautiful blue. Moreover, if a continuous blast be directed upon the salt, a part of it is driven off in the form of white fumes which smell strongly of chlorine, and the charcoal is covered with incrustations of three different colors. That which is formed nearest to the assay is of a dark grey color, the next, a dark yellow passing into brown, and the most distant of a bluish white color. If this incrustation be heated under the reducing flame, it disappears with a blue flame.

Metallic iodides and bromides behave upon charcoal in a similar manner to the chlorides. Those principally deserving of mention are the bromides and iodides of potassium and sodium. These fuse upon charcoal, are absorbed into its pores, and volatilize in the form of white fumes, which are deposited upon the charcoal at some distance from the assay. When the saline films so formed are submitted to the reducing flame, they disappear, coloring the flame in the same manner as the corresponding chlorides.

4. EXAMINATIONS IN THE PLATINUM FORCEPS.

Before the student attempts to make an examination in the platinum forceps or tongs, he should first ascertain whether or not it will act upon the platinum. If the substance to be examined shall act chemically upon the platinum, then it should be examined on the charcoal, and the color of the flame ascertained as rigidly as possible. The following list of substances produce the color attached to them.

A. VIOLET.

Potash, and all its compounds, with the exception of the phosphate and the borate, tinge the color of the flame violet.

B. BLUE.

Chloride of copper, ...Intense blue.
Lead, ...Pale clear blue.
Bromide of copper, ...Bluish green.
Antimony, ...Bluish green.
Selenium, ...Blue.
Arsenic, ...English green.

C. GREEN.

Ammonia, ...Dark green.
Boracic acid, ...Dark green.
Copper, ...Dark green.
Tellurium, ...Dark green.
Zinc, ...Light green.
Baryta, ...Apple green.
Phosphoric acid, ...Pale green.
Molybdic acid, ...Apple green.
Telluric acid, ...Light green.

D. YELLOW.

Soda, ...Intense yellow.
Water, ...Feeble yellow.

E. RED.

Strontia, ...Intense crimson.
Lithia, ...Purplish red.
Potash, ...Violet red.
Lime, ...Purplish red.

The student may often be deceived in regard to the colors: for instance, if a small splinter of almost any mineral be held at the point of the flame of oxidation, it will impart a very slight yellow to the flame. This is caused, doubtless, by the water contained in the mineral. If the piece of platinum wire is used, and it should be wet with the saliva, as is frequently done by the student, then the small quantity of soda existing in that fluid will color the flame of a light yellow hue.

A. THE VIOLET COLOR.

The salts of potash, with the exception of the borate and the phosphate, color the flame of a rich violet hue. This color is best discovered in the outer flame of the blowpipe, as is the case with all the other colors. The flame should be a small one, with a lamp having a small wick, while the orifice of the blowpipe must be quite small. These experiments should likewise be made in a dark room, so that the colors may be discerned with the greatest ease. In investigating with potash for the discernment of color, it should be borne in mind that the least quantity of soda will entirely destroy the violet color of the potash, by the substitution of its own strong yellow color. If there be not more than the two hundredth part of soda, the violet reaction of the potash will be destroyed. This is likewise the case with the presence of lithia, for its peculiar red color will destroy the violet of the potash. Therefore in making investigations with the silicates which contain potash, the violet color of the latter can only be discerned when they are free from soda and lithia.

B. THE BLUE COLOR.

(*a.*) *The Chloride of Copper.*—Any of the chlorides produce a blue color in the blowpipe flame, or any salt which contains chlorine will show the blue tint, as the color in this case is referable to the chlorine itself. There are, however, some chlorides which, in consequence of the peculiar reactions of their bases, will not produce the blue color, although in these cases the blue of the chlorine will be very likely to blend itself with the color produced by the base. The chloride of copper communicates an intense blue to the flame, when fused on the platinum wire. If the heat be continued until the chlorine is driven off, then the greenish hue of the oxide of copper will be discerned.

(*b.*) *Lead.*—Metallic lead communicates to the flame a pale blue color. The oxide reacts in the same manner. The lead-salts, whose acids do not interfere with the color, impart also a fine blue to the flame, either in the platina forceps, or the crooked wire.

(*c.*) *Bromide of Copper.*—This salt colors the flame of a bluish-green color, but when the bromine is driven off, then we have the green of the oxide of copper.

(*d.*) *Antimony.*—This metal imparts a blue color to the blowpipe flame, but if the metal is in too small a quantity, then the color is a brilliant white. If antimony is fused on charcoal, the fused metal gives a blue color. The white sublimate which surrounds the fused metal, being subjected to the flame of oxidation, disappears from the charcoal with a bluish-green color.

(*e.*) *Selenium.*—If fused in the flame of oxidation, it imparts to the flame a deep blue color. The incrustation upon charcoal gives to the flame the same rich color.

(*f.*) *Arsenic.*—The arseniates and metallic arsenic itself impart to the blowpipe flame a fine blue color, provided that there is no other body present which may have a tendency to color the flame with its characteristic hue. The sublimate of arsenious acid which surrounds the assay, will give the same blue flame, when dissipated by the oxidation flame. The platinum forceps will answer for the exhibition of the color of arsenic, even though the salts be arseniates, whose bases possess the property of imparting their peculiar color to the flame, such as the arseniate of lime

C. THE GREEN COLOR.

(*a.*) *Ammonia.*—The salts of ammonia, when heated before the blowpipe, and just upon the point of disappearing, impart to the flame a feeble though dark green color. This color, however, can only be discerned in a dark room.

(*b.*) *Boracic Acid.*—If any one of the borates is mixed with two parts of a flux composed of one part of pulverized fluor-spar, and four and a half parts of bisulphate of potash, and after being melted, is put upon the coil of a platinum wire, and held at the point of the blue flame, soon after fusion takes place a dark green color is discerned, but it is not of long duration. The above process is that recommended by Dr. Turner. The green color of the borates may be readily seen by dipping them, previously moistened with sulphuric acid, into the upper part of the blue flame, when the color can be readily discerned. If soda be present, then the rich green of the boracic acid is marred by the yellow of the soda. Borax, or the biborate of soda (NaO, $2BO_3$) may be used for this latter reaction, but if it be moistened with sulphuric acid, the green of the boracic acid can then be seen. If the borates, or minerals which contain boracic acid, are fused on charcoal with carbonate of potash, then moistened with sulphuric acid and alcohol, then the bright green of the boracic acid is produced, even if the mineral contains but a minute portion of the boracic acid.

(*c.*) *Copper.* Nearly all the ores of copper and its salts, give a bright green color to the blowpipe flame. Metallic copper likewise colors the flame green, being first oxidized. If iodine, chlorine, and bromine are present, the flame is considerably modified, but the former at least intensifies the color. Many ores containing copper also color the flame green, but the internal portion is of a bright blue color if the compound contains lead, the latter color being due to the lead. The native sulphide and carbonate of copper should be moistened with sulphuric acid, while the former should be previously roasted. If hydrochloric acid is used for moistening the salts, then the rich green given by that moistened with the sulphuric acid is changed to a blue, being thus modified by the chlorine of the acid. Silicates containing copper, if heated in the flame in the platinum forceps, impart a rich green color to the outer flame. In fact, if any substance containing copper be submitted to the blowpipe flame, it will tinge it green, provided there be no other substance present to impart its own color to the flame, and thus modify or mar that of the copper.

(*d.*) *Tellurium.*—If the flame of reduction is directed upon the oxide of tellurium placed upon charcoal, a green color is imparted to it. If the telluric acid be placed upon platinum wire in the reduction flame, the oxidation flame is colored green. Or if the sublimate be dissipated by the flame of oxidation, it gives a green color. If selenium be present, the green color is changed to a blue.

(*e.*) *Zinc.*—The oxide of zinc, when strongly heated, gives a blue flame. This is especially the case in the reducing flame. The flame is a small one, however, and not very characteristic, as with certain preparations of zinc the blue color is changed to a bright white. The soluble salts of zinc give no blue color.

(*f.*) *Baryta.*—The soluble salts of baryta, moistened, and then submitted to the reduction flame, produce a green color. The salt should be moistened, when the color will be strongly marked in the outer flame. The insoluble salts do not produce so vivid a color as the soluble salts, and they are brighter when they have previously been moistened. The carbonate does not give a strong color, but the acetate does, so long as it is not allowed to turn to a carbonate. The chloride, when fused on the platinum wire, in the point of the reduction flame, imparts a fine green color to the oxidation flame. This tint changes finally to a faint dirty green color. The sulphate of baryta colors the flame green when heated at the point of the reduction flame. But neither the sulphate, carbonate, nor, in fact, any other salt of baryta, gives such a fine green color as the chloride. The presence of lime does interfere with the reaction of baryta, but still does not destroy its color.

(*g.*) *Phosphoric Acid.*—The phosphates give a green color to the oxidation flame, especially when they are moistened with sulphuric acid. This is best shown with the platinum forceps. The green of phosphoric, or the phosphates, is much less intense than that of the borates or boracic acid, but yet the reaction is a certain one, and is susceptible of considerable delicacy, either with the forceps, or still better upon platinum wire. Sulphuric acid is a great aid to the development of the color, especially if other salts be present which would be liable to hide the color of the phosphoric acid. In this reaction with phosphates, the water should be expelled from them previous to melting them with sulphuric acid. They should likewise be pulverized. Should soda be present it will only exhibit its peculiar color after the phosphoric acid shall have been expelled; therefore, the green color of the phosphoric acid should be looked for immediately upon submitting the phosphate to heat.

(*h.*) *Molybdic Acid.*—If this acid or the oxide of molybdenum be exposed upon a platinum wire to the point of the reduction flame, a bright green color is communicated to the flame of oxidation. Take a small piece of the native sulphide of molybdenum, and expose it in the platinum tongs to the flame referred to above, when the green color characteristic of this metal will be exhibited.

(*i.*) *Telluric Acid.*—If the flame of reduction is directed upon a small piece of the oxide of tellurium placed upon charcoal, a bright green color is produced. Or if telluric acid be submitted to the reduction flame upon the loop of a platinum wire, it communicates to the outer flame the bright green of tellurium. If the sublimate found upon the charcoal in the first experiment be submitted to the blowpipe flame, the green color of tellurium is produced while the sublimate is volatilized. If selenium be present the green color is changed to a deep blue one.

D. YELLOW.

The salts of soda all give a bright yellow color when heated in the platinum loop in the reduction flame. This color is very persistent, and will destroy the color of almost any other substance. Every mineral of which soda is a constituent, give this bright orange-yellow reaction. Even the silicate of soda itself imparts to the flame of oxidation the characteristic yellow of soda.

E. RED.

(*a*.) *Strontia*.—Moisten a small piece of the chloride of strontium, put it in the platinum forceps and submit it to the flame of reduction, when the outer flame will become colored of an intense red. If the salt of strontia should be a soluble one, the reaction is of a deeper color than if an insoluble salt is used, while the color is of a deeper crimson if the salt is moistened. If the salt be a soluble one, it should be moistened and dipped into the flame, while if it be an insoluble salt, it should be kept dry and exposed beyond the point of the flame. The carbonate of strontia should be moistened with hydrochloric acid instead of water, by which its color similates that of the chloride of strontium when moistened with water. In consequence of the decided red color which strontia communicates to flame, it is used by pyrotechnists for the purpose of making their "crimson fire."

(*b*.) *Lithia*.—The color of the flame of lithia is slightly inclined to purple. The chloride, when placed in the platinum loop, gives to the outer flame a bright red color, sometimes with a slight tinge of purple. Potash does not prevent this reaction, although it may modify it to violet; but the decided color of soda changes the red of lithia to an orange color. If much soda be present, the color of the lithia is lost entirely. The color of the chloride of lithium may be distinctly produced before the point of the blue flame, and its durability may be the means of determining it from that of lithium, as the latter, under the same conditions, is quite evanescent. The minerals which contain lithia, frequently contain soda, and thus the latter destroys the color of the former.

(*c.*) *Potash.*—The salts of potash, if the acid does not interfere, give a purplish-red color before the blowpipe ; but as the color is more discernibly a purple, we have classed it under that color.

(*d.*) *Lime.*—The color of the flame of lime does not greatly differ from that of strontia, with the exception that it is not so decided. Arragonite and calcareous spar, moistened with hydrochloric acid, and tried as directed for strontia, produce a red light, not unlike that of strontia. The chloride of calcium gives a red tinge, but not nearly so decided as the chloride of strontium. The carbonate of lime will produce a yellowish flame for a while, until the carbonic acid is driven off, when the red color of the lime may be discerned.

If the borate or phosphate of lime be used, the green color of the acids predominates over the red of the lime. Baryta also destroys the red color of the lime, by mixing its green color with it. There is but one silicate of lime which colors the flame red, it is the variety termed tabular spar.

5. EXAMINATIONS IN THE BORAX BEAD.

In order to examine a substance in borax, the loop of the platinum wire should, after being thoroughly cleaned, and heated to redness, be quickly dipped into the powdered borax, and then quickly transferred to the flame of oxidation, and there fused. If the bead is not large enough to fill the loop of the wire, it must be subjected again to the same process. By examining the bead, both when hot and cold, by holding it up against the light, it can be soon ascertained whether it is free from dirt by the transparency, or the want of it, of the bead.

In order to make the examination of a substance, the bead

should be melted and pressed against it, when enough will adhere to answer the purpose. This powder should then be fused in the oxidation flame until it mixes with, and is thoroughly dissolved by the borax bead.

The principal objects to be determined now are: the color of the borax bead, both when heated and when cooled; also the rapidity with which the substance dissolves in the bead, and if any gas is eliminated.

If the color of the bead is the object desired, the quantity of the substance employed must be very small, else the bead will be so deeply colored, as in some cases to appear almost opaque, as, for instance, in that of cobalt. Should this be the case, then, while the bead is still red hot, it should be pressed flat with the forceps; or it may, while soft, be pulled out to a thin thread, whereby the color can be distinctly discovered.

Some bodies, when heated in the borax bead, present a clear bead both while hot and cold; but if the bead be heated with the intermittent flame, or in the flame of reduction, it becomes opalescent, opaque or milk-white. The alkaline earths are instances of this kind of reaction, also glucina oxide of cerium, tantalic and titanic acids, yttria and zirconia. But if a small portion of silica should be present, then the bead becomes clear. This is likewise the case with some silicates, provided there be not too large a quantity present, that is: over the quantity necessary to saturate the borax, for, in that case, the bead will be opaque when cool.

If the bead be heated on charcoal, a small tube or cavity must be scooped out of the charcoal, the bead placed in it, and the flame of reduction played upon it. When the bead is perfectly fused, it is taken up between the platinum forceps and pressed flat, so that the color may be the more readily discerned. This quick cooling also prevents the protoxides, if there be any present, from passing into a higher degree of oxidation.

The bead should first be submitted to the oxidation flame, and any reaction carefully observed. Then the bead should be submitted to the flame of reduction. It must be observed that the platinum forceps should not be used when there is danger of a metallic oxide being reduced, as in this case the metal would alloy with the platinum and spoil the forceps. In this case charcoal should be used for the support. If, however, there be oxides present which are not reduced by the borax, then the platinum loop may be used. Tin is frequently used for the purpose of enabling the bead to acquire a color for an oxide in the reducing flame, by its affinity for oxygen. The oxide, thus being reduced to a lower degree of oxidation, imparts its peculiar tinge to the bead as it cools.

The arsenides and sulphides, before being examined, should be roasted, and then heated with the borax bead. The arsenic of the former, it should be observed, will act on the glass tube in which the sublimation is proceeding, if the glass should contain lead.

It should be recollected that earths, metallic oxides, and metallic acids are soluble in borax, except those of the easily reducible metals, such as platinum or gold, or of mercury, which too readily vaporize. Also the metallic sulphides, after the sulphur has been driven off. Also the salts of metals, after their acids are driven off by heat. Also the nitrates and carbonates, after their acids are driven off during the fusion. Also the salts of the halogens, such as the chlorides, iodides, bromides, etc., of the metals. Also the silicates, but with great tardiness. Also the phosphates and borates that fuse in the bead without suffering decomposition. The metallic sulphides are insoluble in borax, and many of the metals in the pure state.

There are many substances which give clear beads with borax both while hot and cold, but which, upon being heated with the intermittent oxidation flame, become enamelled and opaque. The intermittent flame may be readily attained, not by varying the force of the air from the mouth, but by raising and depressing the bead before the point of the steady oxidating flame. The addition of a little nitrate of potash will often greatly facilitate the production of a color, as it oxidizes the metal. The hot bead should be pressed upon a small crystal of the nitrate, when the bead swells, intumesces, and the color is manifested in the surface of the bead.

6. EXAMINATIONS IN MICROCOSMIC SALT.

Microcosmic salt is a better flux for many metallic oxides than borax, as the colors are exhibited in it with more strength and character. Microcosmic salt is the phosphate of soda and ammonia. When it is ignited it passes into the biphosphate of soda, the ammonia being driven off. This biphosphate of soda possesses an excess of phosphoric acid, and thus has the property of dissolving a great number of substances, in fact almost any one, with the exception of silica. If the substances treated with this salt consist of sulphides or arsenides, the bead must be heated on charcoal. But if the substance experimented upon consists of earthly ingredients or metallic oxides, the platinum wire is the best. If the latter is used a few additional turns should be given to the wire in consequence of the greater fluidity of the bead over that of borax. The microcosmic salt bead possesses the advantage over that of borax, that the colors of many substances are better discerned in it, and that it separates the acids, the more volatile ones being dissipated, while the fixed ones combine with a portion of the base equally with the phosphoric acid, or else do not combine at all, but float about in the bead, as is the case particularly with silicic acid. Many of the silicates give with borax a clear bead, while they form with microcosmic salt an opalescent one.

It frequently happens, that if a metallic oxide will not give its peculiar color in one of the flames, that it will in the other, as the difference in degree with which the metal is oxidized often determines the color. If the bead is heated in the reducing flame, it is well that it should be cooled rapidly to prevent a reoxidation. Reduction is much facilitated by the employment of metallic tin, whereby the protoxide or the reduced metal may be obtained in a comparatively brief time.

The following tables, taken from Plattner and Sherer, will present the reactions of the metallic oxides, and some of the metallic acids, in such a clear light, that the student cannot very easily be led astray, if he gives the least attention to them. It frequently happens that a tabular statement of reactions will impress facts upon the memory when long detailed descriptions will fail to do so. It is for this purpose that we subjoin the following excellent tables.

TABLE I.

A. BORAX.	B. MICROCOSMIC SALT.
1. Oxydizing flame.	1. Oxydizing flame.
2. Reducing "	2. Reducing "

A. BORAX.

1. Oxydizing flame

Color of Bead.	Substances which produce this color in the hot bead.		Substances which produce this color in the cold bead.	
Colorless.	Silica	In all proportions.	Silica	
	Alumina		Alumina	
	Oxide of Tin		Oxide of Tin	
	Telluric Acid		Telluric Acid	With intermittent flame opaque white.
	Baryta		Baryta	
	Strontia		Strontia	
	Lime		Lime	
	Magnesia		Magnesia	
	Glucina		Glucina	
	Yttria		Yttria	
	Zirconia		Zirconia	
	Thoria		Thoria	
	Oxide of Lanthanum		Oxide of Lanthanum	
			" " Silver	
	Tantalic Acid		Tantalic Acid	
	Niobic "		Niobic "	
	Pelopic "		Pelopic	
	Titanic "		Titanic	
	Tungstic "	In small quantity only.	Tungstic	
	Molybdic "		Molybdic	
	Oxide of Zinc		Oxide of Zinc	
	" " Cadmium	In large quantity yellow.	" ' Cadmium	
	" " Lead		" " Lead	
	" " Bismuth		" " Bismuth	
	" " Antimony		" " Antimony	

Yellow, orange red, and reddish-brown.	Titanic Acid, yellow Tungstic " " Molybdic " dark-yellow Oxide of Zinc, pale-yellow " " Cadmium, pale-yellow " " Lead, yellow " " Bismuth, orange " " Antimony, yellow " " Cerium, red " " Iron, dark-red " " Uranium, red " " Silver Vanadic Acid, yellow Oxide of Chromium, dark-red (Titanic Acid to Antimony:) When in large quantity. Otherwise colorless.	Oxide of Cerium with interm. flame opaque white. Oxide of Iron, yellow Oxide of Uranium with interm. flame opaque yellow. Oxide of Silver in large proportion, with interm. flame opaline. Vanadic Acid, yellow. Oxide of Nickel, reddish-brown. " " Manganese, red to violet.
Violet or Amethyst.	Oxide of Nickel " " Manganese " " Didymium	Oxide of Didymium.
Blue.	Oxide of Cobalt	Oxide of Cobalt. " " Copper, blue to greenish-blue.
Green.	Oxide of Copper	Oxide of Chromium, with yellowish tinge.

A. BORAX.

2. Reducing flame.

Color of Bead.	Substances which produce this color in the hot bead.		Substances which produce this color in the cold bead.	
Colorless.	Silica		Silica	
	Alumina		Alumina	
	Oxide of Tin		Oxide of Tin	
	Baryta		Baryta	With an intermittent flame opaque-white.
	Strontia		Strontia	
	Lime		Lime	
	Magnesia		Magnesia	
	Glucina		Glucina	
	Yttria		Yttria	
	Zirconia		Zirconia	
	Thoria		Thoria only when saturated	
	Oxide of Lanthanum		Oxide of Lanthanum	
	" " Cerium		" " Cerium	
	Tantalic Acid		Tantalic Acid	
	Oxide of Didymium		Oxide of Didymium	
	" " Manganese		" " Manganese	
	Niobic Acid	In small proportions.	Niobic Acid	In small proportions.
	Pelopic		Pelopic	
	Oxide of Silver		Oxide of Silver	After long continued blowing. Otherwise grey.
	" " Zinc	After long continued blowing. Otherwise grey.	" " Zinc	
	" " Cadmium		" " Cadmium	
	" " Lead		" " Lead	
	" " Bismuth		" " Bismuth	
	" " Antimony		" " Antimony	
	" " Nickel		" " Nickel	
	Telluric Acid		Telluric Acid	

Yellow to brown.	Titanic Acid Tungstic " Molybdic " Vanadic "		Titanic Acid. Tungstic " Molybdic "	
Blue.	Oxide of Cobalt		Oxide of Cobalt. Titanic Acid with intermittent flame opaque-blue.	
Green.	Oxide of Iron " " Uranium " " Chromium		Oxide of Iron, bottle-green. " " Uranium, bottle-green. " " Chromium, emerald-green. Vanadic Acid, emerald-green.	
Opaque-grey. (The opacity generally becomes distinct during cooling.)	Oxide of Silver " " Zinc " " Cadmium " " Lead " " Bismuth " " Antimony " " Nickel Telluric Acid	After short blowing. Otherwise colorless.	Oxide of Silver. " " Zinc " " Cadmium " " Lead " " Bismuth " " Antimony " " Nickel Telluric Acid	After short blowing. Otherwise colorless.
	Niobic Acid Pelopic	After long continued blowing and in considerable proportion.	Niobic Acid Pelopic "	After long continued blowing and in considerable proportion.
Opaque-red and reddish-brown.	Oxide of Copper		Oxide of Copper.	

B. MICROCOSMIC SALT.

1. Oxidizing flame.

Color of Bead.	Substances which produce this color			
	in the hot bead.		in the cold bead.	
Colorless.	Silica (only slightly soluble)	In all proportions.	Silica	
	Alumina		Alumina	
	Oxide of Tin		Oxide of Tin	
	Telluric Acid		Telluric Acid	With an intermittent flame opaque white.
	Baryta		Baryta	
	Strontia		Strontia	
	Lime		Lime	
	Magnesia		Magnesia	
	Glucina		Glucina	
	Yttria		Yttria	
	Zirconia		Zirconia	
	Thoria		Thoria	
	Oxide of Lanthanum		Oxide of Lanthanum	
			" " Cerium.	
	Niobic Acid		Niobic Acid.	
	Pelopic "		Pelopic "	
	Tantalic "		Tantalic "	
	Titanic "		Titanic "	
	Tungstic "		Tungstic "	
	Oxide of Zinc	In small proportions only. In larger quantity yellow.	Oxide of Zinc.	
	" " Cadmium		" " Cadmium.	
	" " Lead		" " Lead.	
	" " Bismuth		" " Bismuth.	
	" " Antimony		" " Antimony.	

Yellow, orange, red and brown.	Tantalic Acid Titanic " Tungstic " Oxide of Zinc " " Cadmium " " Lead " " Bismuth " " Antimony (In large quantity: Tantalic Acid through Oxide of Antimony) " " Silver " " Cerium " " Iron " " Nickel " " Uranium Vanadic Acid Oxide of Chromium	Oxide of Silver. Oxide of Iron. " " Nickel. " " Uranium, yellowish-green. Vanadic Acid.
Violet or Amethyst.	Oxide of Manganese " " Didymium	Oxide of Manganese. " " Didymium.
Blue.	Oxide of Cobalt	Oxide of Cobalt. " " Copper, to greenish-blue.
Green.	Molybdic Acid, yellowish-green Oxide of Copper	Molybdic Acid, pale yellowish-green. Oxide of Uranium, yellowish-green. " " Chromium, emerald-green.

B. MICROCOSMIC SALT.

2. Reducing flame.

Color of Bead.	Substances which produce this color in the hot bead.		in the cold bead.	
Colorless.	Silica (only slightly soluble)		Silica (only slightly soluble).	
	Alumina		Alumina.	
	Oxide of Tin		Oxide of Tin.	
	Baryta		Baryta	With an intermittent flame opaque-white.
	Strontia		Strontia	
	Lime		Lime	
	Magnesia		Magnesia	
	Glucina		Glucina	
	Yttria		Yttria	
	Zirconia		Zirconia	
	Thoria		Thoria only when saturated	
	Oxide of Lanthanum		Oxide of Lanthanum	
	" " Cerium		" " Cerium.	
	" " Didymium		" " Didymium.	
	" " Manganese		" " Manganese.	
	Tantalic Acid	After long continued blowing. Otherwise grey.	Tantalic Acid.	
	Oxide of Silver		Oxide of Silver	After long continued blowing. Otherwise grey.
	" " Zinc		" " Zinc	
	" " Cadmium		" " Cadmium	
	" " Lead		" " Lead	
	" " Bismuth		" " Bismuth	
	" " Antimony		" " Antimony	
	" " Nickel		" " Nickel	
	Telluric Acid		Telluric Acid	

Yellow, red, and brown.	Oxide of Iron, red Titanic Acid, yellow Pelopic Acid, brown Ferruginous Titantic Acid, blood red " Niobic " " " Pelopic " " " Tungstic " " Vanadic Acid, brownish Oxide of Chromium, reddish	Oxide of Iron. Pelopic Acid. Ferruginous Titanic Acid. " Niobic " " Pelopic " " Tungstic "
Violet or Amethyst.	Niobic Acid in large proportion	Niobic Acid in large proportion. Titanic Acid.
Blue.	Oxide of Cobalt Tungstic Acid Niobic Acid in very large proportion	Oxide of Cobalt. Tungstic Acid. Niobic Acid in very large proportion.
Green.	Oxide of Uranium Molybdic Acid	Oxide of Uranium. Molybdic Acid. Vanadic " Oxide of Chromium.
Opaque-grey. (The opacity generally becomes distinct during cooling.)	Oxide of Silver " " Zinc " " Cadmium " " Lead " " Bismuth " " Antimony " " Nickel Telluric Acid	Oxide of Silver. " " Zinc. " " Cadmium. " " Lead. " " Bismuth. " " Antimony. " " Nickel. Telluric Acid.
Opaque-red and reddish-brown.	Oxide of Copper	Oxide of Copper.

TABLE II.

Metallic Oxide.	Behavior with Borax on Platinum wire		Behavior with Mic. Salt on Platinum wire	
	in the oxidizing flame.	in the reducing flame.	in the oxidizing flame.	in the reducing flame.
1. Oxide of Cerium, C^2O^3.	Dissolves into a red or dark yellow glass (similar to that produced by iron). During cooling, the color diminishes in intensity and becomes finally yellow. If much oxide be dissolved, an opaque bead may be obtained with an intermittent flame, and a still larger quantity renders it opaque spontaneously.	The color of the bead becomes paler, so that a bead, which is yellow in the oxidizing flame, is rendered colorless. With a large quantity of oxide the bead becomes white and crystalline on cooling.	As with borax. During the process of cooling the color entirely disappears.	Both, when hot and cold, the bead is colorless, by which character oxide of cerium may be distinguished from oxide of iron. The glass remains clear even when containing a large quantity of the oxide.
2. Oxide of Lanthanum, LaO.	Dissolves into a colorless glass, which, when sufficient oxide is present, may be rendered opaque with an intermittent flame, and becomes so spontaneously	As in the oxidizing flame.	As with borax.	No reaction.

	on cooling, when a still larger amount is dissolved.			
3. Oxide of Didymium, DO.	Dissolves to a clear dark amethystine glass.	No reaction.	As with borax.	No reaction.
4. Oxide of Manganese, Mn^2O^3.	Affords an intense amethyst color, which on cooling becomes violet. A large quantity of the oxide produces an apparently black bead, which however, if pressed flat, is seen to be transparent.	The colored bead becomes colorless. With a large amount of the oxide, this reaction is best obtained upon charcoal, and is facilitated by the addition of tin foil.	With a considerable quantity of oxide an amethyst color is obtained, but never so dark as in borax. With but little oxide a colorless bead is obtained, in which, however, the amethyst-color may be brought out by adding a little nitre. While the bead is kept fused, it froths and gives off bubbles of gas.	The colored bead immediately loses its color, either on platinum wire or on charcoal. After the reduction the fluid bead remains still.

Metallic Oxides.	Behavior in Borax on Platinum wire		Behavior in Mic. Salt on Platinum wire	
	in the oxidizing flame.	in the reducing flame.	in the oxidizing flame.	in the reducing flame.
5. Oxide of Iron, Fe^2O^3.	With a small proportion of oxide, the glass is of a yellow color, while warm, and colorless when cold; with a larger proportion, red, while warm, and yellow, when cold; and with a still larger amount, dark-red, while warm, and dark-yellow, when cold.	Treated alone on platinum wire, the glass becomes of a bottle-green color (F^3O^4), and if touched with tin, it becomes of a pale sea-green. On charcoal with tin, it assumes at first a bottle-green color, which by continued blowing changes to a sea-green (FeO).	With a certain amount of oxide, the glass is of a yellowish-red color, which on cooling changes to yellow, then green, and finally becomes colorless. With a large addition of oxide, the color is, when warm, dark red, and passes, while cooling, into brownish-red, dark green, and finally brownish-red. During the cooling process, the colors change more rapidly than with borax.	With a small proportion of oxide there is no reaction. With a larger amount the bead is red, while warm, and becomes on cooling successively yellow, green, and russet. With the addition of tin the glass becomes, during cooling, first green and then colorless.
6. Oxide of Cobalt, CoO.	Colors the glass of an intense smalt blue both whilst hot and	As in the oxidizing flame.	As with borax, but less intensively colored. During cooling the	As in the oxidizing flames.

	when cold. When much oxide is present, the color is so deep as to appear black.		color becomes somewhat paler.	
7. Oxide of Nickel NiO.	Colors intensely. A small amount of oxide affords a glass which, while warm, is violet, and becomes of a pale reddish-brown on cooling. A larger addition produces a dark violet color in the warm and reddish-brown in the cold bead.	The oxide is reduced and the metallic particles give the bead a turbid grey appearance. If the blast be continued the metallic particles fall together without fusing, and the glass becomes colorless. This reaction is readily obtained with tin upon charcoal, and the reduced nickel fuses to a bead with the tin.	Dissolves into a reddish glass which becomes yellow on cooling. With a large addition of the oxide, the glass is brownish while hot, and orange when cold.	On platinum wire the nickeliferous bead undergoes no change. Treated with tin upon charcoal, it becomes at first opaque and grey, and after long continued blowing the reduced nickel forms a bead, and the glass remains colorless.

Metallic Oxides.	Behavior in Borax on Platinum wire		Behavior in Mic. Salt on Platinum wire	
	in the oxidizing flame.	in the reducing flame.	in the oxidizing flame.	in the reducing flame.
8. Oxide of Zinc, ZnO.	Dissolves easily into a clear colorless glass, which, when much oxide is present, may be rendered opaque and flocculent by an intermittent flame, and becomes so spontaneously with a still larger addition. When a considerable quantity is dissolved, a glass is obtained which is pale yellow, while hot, and colorless when cold.	On platinum wire the saturated glass becomes at first opaque and grey, but by a sustained blast is again rendered clear. On charcoal the oxide is gradually reduced; the metal is volatilized and incrusts the charcoal with oxide.	As with borax.	As with borax.
	When in very large proportion, dissolves to a clear yellow glass, which becomes nearly colorless on cooling. When the oxide is	Upon charcoal ebullition takes place and the oxide is reduced. The	When in very large proportion dissolves to a clear glass, having a	On charcoal the oxide is slowly and imperfectly reduced. The reduced metal forms the characteristic incrustation on the charcoal, but the deposit

9. Oxide of Cadmium, CdO.	present in any considerable quantity, the glass can be rendered opaque with an intermittent flame, and, with a larger addition, it becomes so spontaneously on cooling.	metallic cadmium is volatilized and incrusts the charcoal with its characteristic deep yellow oxide.	yellow tinge, while hot, which disappears on cooling, and when perfectly saturated, becomes milk-white.	is thin and does not exhibit its color clearly until quite cold. The addition of tin hastens the reaction.
10. Oxide ot Lead, PbO.	Dissolves readily to a clear yellow glass, which loses its color upon cooling, and when containing much oxide can be rendered dull under an intermittent flame. With a still larger addition ot oxide it becomes opaline yellow on cooling.	The plumbiferous glass spreads out on charcoal, becomes turbid, bubbles up, until the whole of the oxide is reduced, when it again becomes clear. It is, however, difficult to bring the lead together into a bead.	As with borax, but a larger addition of oxide, required to produce a yellow color in the warm bead	On charcoal the plumbiferous glass becomes grey and dull. With an over dose of oxide a part is volatilized and forms an incrustation on the charcoal beyond the bead. The addition of tin does not render the glass opaque, but somewhat more dull and grey than in its absence.

Metallic Oxides.	Behavior in Borax on Platinum wire		Behavior in Mic. Salt on Platinum wire	
	in the oxidizing flame.	in the reducing flame.	in the oxidizing flame.	in the reducing flame.
11. Oxide of Tin, SnO^2.	In small quantity dissolves slowly into a clear colorless glass, which, when cold, remains clear, and cannot be rendered opaque with an intermittent flame. If a saturated bead, which has been allowed to cool, be reheated to incipient redness, it loses its rounded form and exhibits imperfect crystallization.	A glass containing but little oxide undergoes no change. If much of the latter be present, a part may be reduced upon charcoal.	In small quantity dissolves very slowly to a colorless glass, which remains clear on cooling.	The glass undergoes no change, either on charcoal or platinum wire.
	Dissolves readily to a clear glass which with a small amount of the oxide is yellow, while warm, and becomes	A glass becomes at first grey and turbid, then begins to effervesce, which action continues during the reduction of	Dissolves in small quantity to a clear colorless glass. A larger addition affords a glass which, while warm, is yellow, and becomes colorless	On charcoal, and especially with the addition of tin, the glass remains

12. Oxide of Bismuth, BiO^3.	colorless on cooling. With a larger addition, the glass is, in the hot state, of a deep orange color, which changes to yellow and finally becomes opaline in process of cooling.	the oxide, and it finally becomes perfectly clear. If tin be added, the glass becomes at first grey from the reduced bismuth, but, when the metal is collected into a bead, the glass is again clear and colorless.	on cooling. When in sufficient proportion the glass may be rendered opaque under an intermittent flame, and a still larger addition of oxide renders the bead spontaneously opaque on cooling.	colorless and clear, while warm, but becomes on cooling of a dark grey color and opaque.
13. Oxide of Uranium, U^2O^3.	Behaves similarly to oxide of iron, with the exception that the color of the former is somewhat paler. When sufficiently saturated, the glass may be rendered of an opaque yellow by an intermittent flame.	Affords the same color as the oxide of iron. The green glass obtained in this flame, if sufficiently saturated, can be rendered black by an intermittent flame, but it has under these circumstances no enameline appearance. On charcoal, with the addition of tin, the glass takes a dark green color.	Dissolves to a clear yellow glass, which assumes a yellowish-green color on cooling.	The glass assumes a beautiful green color, which becomes more brilliant as the bead cools. The addition of tin upon charcoal produces no further change.

Metallic Oxides.	Behavior in Borax on Platinum wire		Behavior in Mic. Salt on Platinum wire	
	in the oxidizing flame.	in the reducing flame.	in the oxidizing flame.	in the reducing flame.
14. Oxide of Copper, CuO.	Produces an intense coloration. If in small quantity, the glass is green, while warm, and becomes blue on cooling. If in large proportion, the green color is so intense as to appear black. When cool, this becomes paler, and changes to a greenish blue.	If not too saturated, the cupriferous glass soon becomes nearly colorless, but immediately on solidifying assumes a red color and becomes opaque. By long continued blowing on charcoal, the copper in the bead is reduced and separates out as a small metallic bead, leaving the glass colorless. With the addition of tin, the glass becomes of an opaque dull-red on cooling.	With an equal proportion of oxide, this salt is not so strongly colored as borax. A small amount imparts a green color in the warm and a blue in the cold. With a very large addition of oxide, the glass is opaque in the hot state, and after cooling of a greenish-blue.	A tolerably saturated glass assumes a dark green color under a good flame, and on cooling becomes of an opaque brick-red, the moment it solidifies. A glass containing but a small proportion of the oxide becomes equally red and opaque on cooling, if treated with tin upon charcoal.
15. Oxide of Mercury, HgO.	No reaction.	No reaction.	No reaction.	No reaction.

16. Oxide of Silver, AgO.	The oxide is partly dissolved and partly reduced. In small quantity, it colors the glass yellow while warm, the color disappearing on cooling. In larger quantity, the glass is yellow while warm, but during cooling becomes paler to a certain point, and then again deeper. If reheated slightly, the glass becomes opalescent.	On charcoal the argentiferous glass becomes at first grey from the reduced metal, but afterwards, when the silver is collected into a bead, it becomes clear and colorless.	Both the oxide and the metal afford a yellowish glass, which, when containing much oxide becomes opaline, exhibiting a yellow color by daylight and a red one by artificial light.	As in borax.
17. Oxide of Platinum, PtO^2. 18. Oxide of Palladium, PdO^2. 19. Oxide of Rhodium, R^2O^3. 20. Oxide of Iridium, Ir^2O^3.	Are reduced without being dissolved. The reduced metal, being infusible, cannot however be collected into a bead.	As in the oxidizing flame.	As in borax.	As in borax.

Metallic Oxides.*	Behavior in Borax on Platinum wire		Behavior in Mic. Salt on Platinum wire	
	in the oxidizing flame.	in the reducing flame.	in the oxidizing flame.	in the reducing flame.
21. Oxide of Ruthenium, Ru^2O^3. 22. Oxide of Osmium, OsO^2.				
23. Oxide of Gold, Au^2O^3.	Is reduced without being dissolved and can be collected into a bead on charcoal.	As in the oxidizing flame.	As in borax.	As in borax.
	Dissolves readily to a clear glass, which, when but little acid is present, is colorless, but when in larger proportion, yellow, and, on cooling,	In small proportion, it renders the glass yellow, in larger quantity dark-	Dissolves readily to a clear glass, which, when	The glass obtained in the oxidizing flame becomes yellow in the hot state, but on cooling assumes a beautiful violet color. If too saturated, this color is so deep as to appear opaque, but is

24. Titanic Acid, TiO^2.	colorless. When sufficiently saturated, it may be rendered opaque with an intermittent flame, and with a still larger addition of the acid becomes so spontaneously on cooling.	yellow or brown. A saturated bead assumes a blue enamel-like appearance under an intermittent flame.	sufficiently saturated, is yellow while hot, and becomes colorless on cooling.	not enameline. If the titanic acid contain iron, the glass becomes on cooling of a brownish-yellow or red color. The addition of tin neutralizes the iron, and the glass then becomes violet.
25. Tantalic Acid, TaO^3.	Dissolves readily to a clear colorless glass, which, when sufficiently saturated, may be rendered opaque with an intermittent flame, and with a larger addition of the acid becomes spontaneously enameline on cooling.	As in the oxidizing flame.	Dissolves readily to a clear glass, which, when it contains a large proportion of the acid, is yellow while warm, but becomes colorless on cooling.	The glass obtained in the oxidizing flame undergoes no change, nor does it, according to *H. Rose*, alter by the addition of sulphate of iron.

Metallic Oxides.	Behavior in Borax on Platinum wire		Behavior in Mic. Salt on Platinum wire	
	in the oxidizing flame.	in the reducing flame.	in the oxidizing flame.	in the reducing flame.
26. Niobic Acid, Ni^2O^3.	Behaves in a similar manner to tantalic acid, but the glass requires a very large dose of the acid to render it opaque under an intermittent flame. With an increased amount of the acid, the glass is clear and yellow, while warm, but becomes on cooling turbid, and when quite cold is white.	The glass obtained in the oxidizing flame and which has become opalescent on cooling, is rendered clear in the reducing flame. With a larger addition of the acid, it becomes dull, and of a bluish-grey color on cooling, and a still larger amount renders it opaque and bluish grey.	Dissolves in large quantity to a clear colorless glass.	If the acid be not present in too large a proportion, the glass remains unchanged. An additional amount of the acid renders it violet, and a still larger quantity affords a beautiful pure blue color, similar to that produced by tungstic acid. If to such a bead some sulphate of iron be added, the glass becomes blood-red. The addition of peroxide of iron renders the glass deep yellow while warm, the color becoming paler on cooling.

27. Pelopic Acid, Pp^2O^3.	Behaves similarly to the preceding.	A bead containing sufficient of the acid to render it spontaneously opaque on cooling, has a greyish color.	Dissolves even in large quantity to a colorless glass.	With a sufficient dose of the acid, the bead becomes brown with a violet tinge. This reaction is readily obtained upon charcoal. Sulphate of iron renders the bead blood-red.
28. Oxide of Antimony, SbO^3.	Even when in large proportion, dissolves to a clear glass, which is yellow when warm, but almost entirely loses its color on cooling. On charcoal, the antimonious acid may be almost expelled, so that tin produces no further change.	A bead, that has only been treated for a short time in the oxidizing flame, when submitted to the reducing flame becomes grey and turbid from the reduced antimony. This soon volatilizes and the glass again becomes clear. The addition of tin renders the glass ash-grey or black, according to the amount of oxide it contains.	Dissolves with ebullition to a glass of a pale yellow color while warm.	On charcoal the saturated glass becomes at first dull, but as soon as the reduced antimony is volatilized, it again becomes clear. With tin, the glass is at first rendered grey by the reduced antimony, but by continued blowing is restored to clearness. Even when the glass contains but little oxide, tin produces this reaction.

Metallic Oxides.	Behavior in Borax on Platinum wire		Behavior in Mic. Salt on Platinum wire	
	in the oxidizing flame.	in the reducing flame.	in the oxidizing flame.	in the reducing flame.
29. Tungstic Acid, WO^3.	Dissolves readily to a clear colorless glass. In large proportion it renders the borax yellow, while warm, and with a still greater addition the bead may be made opaque with an intermittent flame. If more be then added, this reaction takes place spontaneously.	When the oxide is present in small quantity, the glass undergoes no change. With a larger proportion, the glass is deep yellow while warm, and yellowish-brown when cold. This reaction takes place upon charcoal, with a small quantity of the acid. Tin produces a dark coloration, when the acid is not present in too great a quantity.	Dissolves to a clear glass, which, when saturated, is yellow in the hot state.	The glass is of a pure blue. If the tungstic acid contain iron, the glass becomes blood-red on cooling, similar to titanic acid. In this case, tin restores the blue color, or, if iron be in considerable quantity, renders it green.
	Dissolves readily and in large quantity. When but little is dissolved, the glass is yellow while hot and colorless when cold.	The glass, which has been treated in the oxidizing flame, becomes, when the acid is not present in too large a quantity, brown, and	Dissolves to a clear glass, which, when sufficient acid is present, is	The glass becomes of a bottle-green color, which on cooling, changes to a

30. Molydbic Acid, MO^3.	When in larger quantity yellow while warm and opaline when cold, and a further addition of acid renders it yellow when warm, the color, on cooling, changing first to a pale enamel blue, and then to an enamel white.	when in large quantity, perfectly opaque. In a strong flame, oxide of molybdenum is formed which is visible in the yellow glass in the form of black flakes. If the glass appear opaque, it should be flattened with the forceps.	of a yellowish-green color when warm, and becomes nearly colorless on cooling. On charcoal, the glass becomes dark, and when cool has a beautiful green color.	brilliant green, similar to that produced by oxide of chromium. The reaction on charcoal is precisely similar. Tin renders the color somewhat darker.
31. Vanadic Acid, VaO^3.	Dissolves to a clear glass, which is colorless when only a small quantity of acid is present, and yellow when containing a larger proportion.	The yellow color of the glass changes to a brown when warm and a chrome-green on cooling.	As with borax.	As with borax.

Metallic Oxides.	Behavior in Borax on Platinum wire		Behavior in Mic. Salt on Platinum wire	
	in the oxidizing flame.	in the reducing flame.	in the oxidizing flame.	in the reducing flame.
32. Oxide of Chromium, Cr^2O^3	Affords an intense color, but dissolves slowly. A small proportion colors the glass yellow when warm, and yellowish green when cold; a larger addition produces a dark red color when warm, which, on cooling, becomes yellow and finally a brilliant green with a tinge of yellow.	A small quantity of the oxide renders the glass beautifully green both when warm and when cold. A larger addition changes it to a darker emerald green. Tin produces no change in the color.	Dissolves to a clear glass which has a pink tinge while warm, but on cooling becomes dusky green, and finally brilliantly green.	As in the oxidizing flame, except that the colors are somewhat darker. Tin produces no further change.
33. Arsenious Acid, AsO^3.	No reaction.	No reaction.	No reaction.	No reaction.
34. Tellurous Acid, TeO^2.	Dissolves to a clear colorless glass which, when treated on charcoal, becomes grey and dull from particles of reduced tellurium.	As in the oxidizing flame.	As with borax.	As with borax.

7. EXAMINATIONS WITH CARBONATE OF SODA.

The carbonate of soda is pulverized and then kneaded to a paste with water; the substance to be examined, in fine powder, is also mixed with it. A small portion of this paste is placed on the charcoal, and gradually heated until the moisture is expelled, when the heat is brought to the fusion of the bead, or as high as it can be raised. Several phenomena will take place, which must be closely observed. Notice whether the substance fuses with the bead, and if so, whether there is intumescence or not. Or, whether the substance undergoes reduction; or, whether neither of these reactions takes place, and, on the contrary, the soda sinks into the charcoal, leaving the substance intact upon its surface. If intumescence takes place, the presence of either tartaric acid, molybdic acid, silicic, or tungstic acid, is indicated. The silicic acid will fuse into a bead, which becomes clear when it is cold. Titanic acid will fuse into the bead, but may be easily distinguished from the silicic acid by the bead remaining opaque when cold.

Strontia and baryta will flow into the charcoal, but lime will not. The molybdic and tungstic acids combine with the soda, forming the respective salts. These salts are absorbed by the charcoal. If too great a quantity of soda is used, the bead will be quite likely to become opaque upon cooling, while, if too small a quantity of soda is used, a portion of the substance will remain undissolved. These can be equally avoided by either the addition of soda, or the substance experimented upon, as may be required.

As silica and titanic acid are the only two substances that produce a clear bead, the student, if he gets a clear bead, may almost conclude that he is experimenting with silica, titanic acid being a rare substance. When soda is heated with silica, a slight effervescence will be the first phenomenon noticed. This is the escape of the carbonic acid of the carbonate of soda, while the silicic acid takes its place, forming a glass with the soda. As titanic acid will not act in the same manner as silica, it can be easily distinguished by its bead not being perfectly pellucid. If the bead with which silica is fused should be tinted of a hyacinth or yellow color, this may be attributed to the presence of a small quantity of sulphur or a sulphate, and this sometimes happens from the fact of the flux containing sulphate of soda. The following metals, when exposed with carbonate of soda to the reducing flame, are wholly or partially reduced, viz. the oxides of all the noble metals, the oxides and acids of tungsten, molybdenum, arsenic, antimony, mercury, copper, tellurium, zinc, lead, bismuth, tin, cadmium, iron, nickel, and cobalt. Mercury and arsenic, as soon as they are reduced, are dissipated, while tellurium, bismuth, lead, antimony, cadmium, and zinc, are only partially volatilized, and, therefore, form sublimates on the charcoal. Those metals which are difficult of reduction should be fused with oxalate of potassa, instead of the carbonate of soda. The carbonic oxide formed from the combustion of the acid of this salt is very efficient in the reduction of these metals. Carbonate of soda is very efficient for the detection of minute quantities of manganese. The mixture of the carbonate of soda with a small addition of nitrate of potassa, and the mineral containing manganese, must be fused on platinum foil. The fused mass, when cooled, presents a fine blue color.

1. The following minerals, according to Griffin, produce beads with soda, but do not fuse when heated alone: quartz, agalmatolyte, dioptase, hisingerite, sideroschilosite, leucite, rutile, pyrophyllite, wolckonskoite.

2. The following minerals produce only slags with soda: allophane, cymophane, polymignite, æschynite, œrstedtite, titaniferous iron, tantalite, oxides of iron, yttro-tantalite, oxides of manganese, peroxide of tin (is reduced), hydrate of alumina, hydrate of magnesia, spinel, gahnite, worthite, carbonate of zinc, pechuran, zircon, thorite, andalusite, staurolite, gehlenite, chlorite spar, chrome ochre, uwarowite, chromate of iron, carbonates of the earths, carbonates of the metallic oxides, basic

phosphate of yttria, do. of alumina, do. of lime, persulphate of iron, sulphate of alumina, aluminite, alumstone, fluoride of cerium, yttrocerite, topaz, corundum, pleonaste, chondrodite.

3. The following minerals produce beads with a small quantity of soda, but produce slags if too much soda is added : phenakite, pierosmine, olivine, cerite, cyanite, talc, gadolinite, lithium-tourmaline.

1. The following minerals, when fused alone, produce beads. Of these minerals the following produce beads with soda : the zeolites, spodumene, soda-spodumene, labrador, scapolite, sodalite (Greenland), elæolite, mica from primitive lime-stone, black talc, acmite, krokidolite, lievrite, cronstedtite, garnet, cerine, helvine, gadolinite, boracic acid, hydroboracite, tincal, boracite, datholite, botryolite, axinite, lapis lazuli, eudialyte, pyrosmalite, cryolite.

2. The following minerals produce beads with a small quantity of soda, but if too much is added they produce slags : okenite, pectolite, red silicate of manganese, black hydro-silicate of manganese, idocrase, manganesian garnets, orthite, pyrorthite, sordawalite, sodalite, fluorspar.

3. The following minerals produce a slag with soda : brevicite, amphodelite, chlorite, fahlunite, pyrope, soap-stone (Cornish) red dichroite, pyrargillite, black potash tourmaline, wolfram, pharmacolite, scorodite, arseniate of iron, tetraphyline, hetepozite, uranite, phosphate of iron, do. of strontia, do. of magnesia, polyhalite, hauyne.

4. The following metals are reduced by soda : tungstate of lead, molybdate of lead, vanadate of lead, chromate of lead, vauquelinite, cobalt bloom, nickel ochre, phosphate of copper, sulphate of lead, chloride of lead, and chloride of silver.

The following minerals fuse on the edges alone, when heated in the blow-pipe flame :

1. The following produce beads with soda : steatite, meerschaum, felspar, albite, petalite, nepheline, anorthite, emerald, euclase, turquois, sodalite (Vesuvius).

2. The following minerals produce beads with a small quan-

5*

tity of soda, but with the addition of more produce slags: tabular spar, diallage, hypersthene, epidote, zoisite.

3. The following minerals produce slags only with soda: stilpnosiderite, plombgomme, serpentine, silicate of manganese (from Piedmont), mica from granite, pimelite, pinite, blue dichroite, sphene, karpholite, pyrochlore, tungstate of lime, green soda tourmaline, lazulite, heavy spar, gypsum.

The reactions of substances, when fused with soda in the flame of oxidation may be of use to the student. A few of them are therefore given. Silica gives a clear glass.

The oxide of tellurium and telluric acid gives a clear bead when it is hot, but white after it is cooled.

Titanic acid gives a yellow bead when hot.

The oxide of chromium gives also a clear yellow glass when hot, but is opaque when cold.

Molybdic acid gives a clear bead when hot, but is turbid and white after cooling.

The oxides and acids of antimony give a clear and colorless bead while hot, and white after cooling.

Vanadic acid is absorbed by the charcoal, although it is not reduced.

Tungstic acid gives a dark yellow clear bead while hot, but is opaque and yellow when cold.

The oxides of manganese give to the soda bead a fine characteristic green color. This is the case with a very small quantity. This reaction is best exhibited on platinum foil.

Oxide of cobalt gives to the bead while hot a red color, which, upon being cooled, becomes grey.

The oxide of copper gives a clear green bead while hot.

The oxide of lead gives a clear colorless bead while hot, which becomes, upon cooling, of a dirty yellow color and opaque.

The following metals, when they are fused with soda on charcoal, in the flame of reduction, produce volatile oxides, and leave an incrustation around the assay, viz. bismuth, zinc, lead, cadmium, antimony, selenium, tellurium, and arsenic.

Bismuth, under the reduction flame, yields small particles of metal, which are brittle and easily crushed. The incrustation is of a flesh color, or orange, when hot, but gets lighter as it cools. The sublimate may be driven about the charcoal from place to place, by either flame, but is finally dissipated. While antimony and tellurium, in the act of dissipation, give color to the flame, bismuth does not, and may thus be distinguished from them.

Zinc deposits an incrustation about the assay, which is yellow while hot, but fades to white when cold. The reduction flame dissipates this deposit, but not that of oxidation. All the zinc minerals deposit the oxide incrustation about the assay, which, when moistened with a solution of cobalt and heated, changes to green.

Lead is very easily reduced, in small particles, and may be easily distinguished by its flattening under the hammer, unlike bismuth. It leaves an incrustation around the assay resembling that of bismuth, in the color of it, and in the peculiar manner in which it lies around the assay.

Cadmium deposits a dull reddish incrustation around the assay. Either of the flames dissipate the sublimate with the greatest readiness.

Antimony reduces with readiness. At the same time it yields considerable vapor, and deposits an incrustation around the assay. This deposit can be driven about on the charcoal by either of the flames. The flame of reduction, however, produces the light blue color of the antimony.

Selenium is deposited on the charcoal as a grey metallic-looking sublimate, but sometimes appearing purple or blue. If the reduction flame is directed on this deposit, it is dissipated with a blue light.

Tellurium is deposited on the charcoal as a white sublimate, sometimes changing at the margin to an orange or red color. The oxidation flame drives the deposit over the charcoal, while the reduction-flame dissipates it with a greenish color.

Arsenic is vaporized rapidly, while there is deposited around the assay a white incrustation of arsenious acid. This deposit will extend to some distance from the assay, and is readily volatilized, the reducing flame producing the characteristic alliaceous color.

The following metals, or their compounds, are reduced when fused with soda on charcoal, in the flame of reduction. They are reduced to metallic particles, but give no incrustation, viz. nickel, cobalt, iron, tin, copper, gold, silver, platinum, tungsten, and molybdenum.

The particles of iron, nickel, and cobalt, it should be borne in mind, are attracted by the magnet.

The following substances are neither fused nor reduced in soda, viz. alumina, magnesia, lime, baryta, strontia, the oxide of uranium, the oxides of cerium, zirconia, tantalic acid, thorina, glucina, and yttria. Neither are the alkalies, as they sink into the charcoal. The carbonates of the earths, strontia, and baryta fuse.

Part III.

SPECIAL REACTIONS; OR, THE BEHAVIOR OF SUBSTANCES BEFORE THE BLOWPIPE.

Analytical chemistry may be termed the art of converting the unknown constituents of substances, by means of certain operations, into new combinations which we recognize through the physical and chemical properties which they manifest.

It is, therefore, indispensably necessary, not only to be cognizant of the peculiar conditions by which these operations can be effected, but it is absolutely necessary to be acquainted with the forms and combinations of the resulting product, and with every modification which may be produced by altering the conditions of the analysis.

We shall first give the behavior of simple substances before the blowpipe; and the student should study this part thoroughly, by repeating each reaction, so that he can acquire a knowledge of the color, form, and physical properties in general, of the resulting combination. There is nothing, perhaps, which will contribute more readily to the progress of the pupil, than thorough practice with the reactions recommended in this part of the work, for when once the student shall have acquired a practical eye in the discernment of the peculiar appearances of substances after they have undergone the decompositions produced by the strong heat of the blowpipe flame, together with the reactions incident to these changes, then he will have greatly progressed in his study, and the rest will be comparatively simple.

A. METALLIC OXIDES.

GROUP FIRST.—THE ALKALIES: POTASSA, SODA, AMMONIA, AND LITHIA.

The alkalies, in their pure, or carbonated state, render reddened litmus paper blue. This is likewise the case with the sulphides of the alkalies. The neutral salts of the alkalies, formed with the strong acids, do not change litmus paper, but the salts formed with the weak acids, render the red litmus paper blue; for instance, the alkaline salts with boracic acid. Fused with borax, soda, or microcosmic salt, they give a clear bead. The alkalies and their salts melt at a low red heat. The alkalies cannot be reduced to the metallic state before the blowpipe. They are not volatile when red hot, except the alkali ammonia, but they are volatile at a white heat.

(*a.*) *Potassa* (KO).—It is not found free, but in combination with inorganic and organic acids, as well in the animal as in the vegetable organism, as in the mineral kingdom. In the pure, or anhydrous state, or as the carbonate, potassa absorbs moisture, and becomes fluid, or is deliquescent, as it is termed. By exposing potassa, or its easily fusible salts (except the phosphate or borate), upon platinum wire, to the point of the blue flame, there is communicated to the external flame a violet color, in consequence of a reduction and reoxidation. This color, though characteristic of all the potassa compounds, is scarcely visible with the phosphate or borate salts of that alkali. The admixture of a very little soda ($\frac{1}{300}$th) destroys the color imparted by the potassa, while the flame assumes a yellow color, characteristic of the soda. The presence of lithia changes the violet color of the potash into red. The silicates of potassa must exist in pretty large proportion before they can be detected by the violet color of the flame, and those minerals must melt easily at the edges. The presence of a little soda in these instances conceals the reaction in the potassa entirely.

If alcohol is poured over potassa compounds which are powdered, and then set on fire, the external flame appears violet-colored, particularly when stirred with a glass rod, and when the alcohol is really consumed. The presence of soda in lithia will, in this case likewise, hide by their own characteristic color, that of the potassa.

The salts of potassa are absorbed when fused upon charcoal. The sulphur, bromine, chlorine, and iodine compounds of potassa give a white, but easily volatile sublimate upon the charcoal, around the place where the fused substance reposed. This white sublimate manifests itself only when the substance is melted and absorbed within the charcoal, and ceases to be visible as soon as it is submitted to the reducing flame, while the external flame is colored violet; sulphate of potassa, for instance, is reduced by the glowing charcoal into the sulphide. This latter is somewhat volatile, but by passing through the oxidation flame, it is again oxidized into the sulphate. This, being less volatile, sublimes upon the charcoal, but by exposing it again to the flame of reduction, it is reduced and carried off to be again oxidized by its passage through the oxidation flame.

Potassa and its compounds give, with soda, borax or microcosmic salt, as well when hot as cold, colorless beads, unless the acid associated with the alkali should itself produce a color. When borax is fused with some pure boracic acid, and sufficient of the oxide of nickel is added, so that the beads appear of a brown color after being cooled, and then the bead thus produced fused with the substance suspected to contain potassa, in the oxidation flame, the brown color is changed to blue. The presence of the other alkalies does not prevent this reaction. As it is not possible to detect potassa compounds with unerring certainty by the blowpipe flame, the

the wet method should be resorted to for the purpose of confirming it.

The *silicates of potassa* must be prepared as follows, for analytical purposes by the wet way. Mix one part of the finely powdered substance with two parts of soda (free from potassa), and one part of borax. Fuse the mixture upon charcoal in the oxidation flame to a clear, transparent bead. This is to be exposed again with the pincers to the oxidation flame, to burn off the adhering coal particles. Then pulverize and dissolve in hydrochloric acid to separate the silica; evaporate to dryness, dissolve the residue in water, with the admixture of a little alcohol, and test the filtrate with chloride of platinum for potassa.

(*b.*) *Soda* (NaO).—This is one of the most abundant substances, although seldom found free, but combined with chlorine or some other less abundant compound. Soda, its hydrate and salts manifest in general the same properties as their respective potash compounds ; but the salts of soda mostly contain crystal water, which leaves the salts if they are exposed to the air, and the salts effervesce.

By exposing soda or its compounds upon a platinum wire to the blue flame, a reddish-yellow color is communicated to the external flame, which appears as a long brilliant stream and considerably increased in volume. The presence of potash does not prevent this reaction of soda. If there is too large a quantity of potash, the flame near to the substance is violet-colored, but the edge of the flame exhibits the characteristic tint of the soda. The presence of lithia changes the yellow color to a shade of red.

When alcohol is poured over powdered soda compounds and lighted, the flame exhibits a reddish-yellow color, particularly if the alcohol is stirred up with a glass rod, or if the alcohol is nearly consumed.

Fused upon charcoal, soda compounds are absorbed by the coal. The sulphide, chloride, iodide, and bromide of soda yield a white sublimate around the spot where the substance is laid, but this sublimate is not so copious as that of the potash compounds, and disappears when touched with the reduction flame, communicating a yellow color to the external flame. The presence of soda in compounds must likewise be confined by reactions in the wet way.

(*c.*) *Ammonia* (NH^4O).—In the fused state, and at the usual temperature, ammonia is a pungent gas, and exerts a reaction upon litmus paper similar to potash and soda. Ammonium is considered by chemists as a metal, from the nature of its behavior with other substances. It has not been isolated, but its existence is now generally conceded by all chemists. The ammonia salts are volatile, and many of them sublimate without being decomposed.

The salts of ammonia, on being heated in the point of the blue flame, produce a feeble green color in the external flame, just previous to their being converted into vapor. But this color is scarcely visible, and presents nothing characteristic. When the ammonia salts are mixed with the carbonate of soda, and heated in a glass tube closed at one end, carbonate of ammonia is sublimed, which can be readily recognized by its penetrating smell of spirits of hartshorn.

This sublimate will render blue a slip of red litmus paper. This can be easily done by moistening the litmus paper, and then inserting the end of it in the tube. By holding a glass rod, moistened with dilute hydrochloric acid, over the mouth of the tube, a white vapor is instantly rendered visible (sal ammoniac).

(*d.*) *Lithia* (LiO).—In the pure state, lithia is white and crystalline, not easily soluble in water, and does not absorb moisture. It changes red litmus to blue, and at a low red heat it melts. Lithia or its salts, exposed to the point of the blue flame, communicates a red color to the external or oxidation flame, in consequence of a reduction, sublimation, and re-oxidation of the lithia. An admixture of potash communicates to this flame a reddish-violet color, and the presence of soda that of a yellowish-red or orange. If the soda, however, is in too great proportion, then its intense yellow hides the red of the lithia. In the latter case the substance under test must be only imperfectly fused in the oxidation flame, and then dipped in wax or tallow. By exposing it now to the reduction flame, the red color imparted to the external flame by the lithia becomes visible, even if a considerable quantity of soda be present. A particular phenomenon appears with the phosphate of lithia, viz., the phosphoric acid itself possesses the property of communicating to the flame a bluish-green color. By its combination with lithia it still exhibits its characteristic color, while the latter presents likewise its peculiar tint. Then we perceive a green flame in the centre of the flame, while the red color of lithia surrounds it.

The *silicates*, which contain only a little lithia, produce only a slight hue in the flame, and often none at all. We have to mix one part of the silicate with two parts of a mixture composed of one part of fluorspar and one and a half parts of bisulphate of potassa. Moisten the mass with water so that the mass will adhere, and then melt it upon a platinum wire in the reduction flame, when that of oxidation will present the red color of lithia.

The *Borates of lithia* produce at first a green color, but it soon yields to the red of lithia. When alcohol is poured over lithia or its compounds, and inflamed, it burns with a deep red color, particularly if the fluid is stirred up with a glass rod, or when the alcohol is nearly consumed. This color presents the same modifications as the corresponding ones communicated to the blowpipe as mentioned above.

The salts of lithia are absorbed by charcoal when fused upon it. The sulphide, bromide, iodide, and chloride of lithia produce upon the charcoal a greyish-white sublimate, although not so copiously as the corresponding compounds of potash and soda. This sublimate disappears when touched by the reduction flame, while the oxidation flame gives the characteristic color of lithia.

SECOND GROUP.—THE ALKALINE EARTHS, BARYTA, STRONTIA, LIME, AND MAGNESIA.

In the pure state, the alkaline earths are caustic, cause red litmus paper to become blue, and are more or less soluble in water. Their sulphides are also soluble. The carbonates and phosphates of the alkaline earths are insoluble in water. By igniting the carbonates, their carbonic acid is expelled, and the alkaline earths are left in the caustic state. The alkaline earths are not volatile, and their organic salts are converted, by ignition, into carbonates.

(*a.*) *Baryta.* (BaO).—This alkaline earth does not occur free in nature, but combined with acids, particularly with carbonic and sulphuric acids. In the pure state, baryta is of a greyish-white color, presents an earthy appearance, and is easily powdered. When sparingly moistened with water, it slakes, becomes heated, and forms a dry, white powder. With still more water it forms a crystalline mass, the hydrate of baryta, which is completely soluble in hot water. Pure baryta is infusible ; the hydrate fuses at a red heat, without the loss of its hydratic water; if caustic baryta is exposed for too great a length of time to the flame, it absorbs water, originated by the combustion, and becomes a hydrate, when it will melt. Salts of baryta, formed with most acids, are insoluble in water ; for instance, the salts with sulphuric, carbonic, arsenic, phosphoric, and boracic acids. The salts of baryta, soluble in water, are decomposed by ignition, except the chloride.

Carbonate of baryta loses its carbonic acid at a red heat, becomes caustic, and colors red litmus paper blue.

By exposing baryta or its compounds upon a platinum wire, or a splinter of the substance held with the platinum tongs, to the point of the blue flame, a pale apple-green color is communicated to the external flame. This color appears at first very pale, but soon becomes more intense. This color is most visible if the substance is operated with in small quantities. The chloride of barium produces the deepest color. This color is less intense if the carbonate or sulphate is used. The presence of strontia, lime, or magnesia, does not suppress the reaction of the baryta, unless they greatly predominate.

When alcohol is poured over baryta or its salts, and inflamed, a feeble green color is communicated to the flame, but this color should not be considered a characteristic of the salt.

Baryta and its compounds give, when fused with carbonate of soda upon platinum foil, a clear bead. Fused with soda upon charcoal, it is absorbed. The sulphate fuses at first to a clear bead, which soon spreads, and is absorbed and converted while boiling into a hepatic mass. If this mass is taken out, placed upon a piece of polished silver and moistened with a little water, a black spot of sulphide of silver is left after washing off the mass with water.

Borax dissolves baryta and its compounds with a hissing noise, as well in the flame of oxidation as in that of reduction. There is formed a clear bead which, with a certain degree of saturation, is clear when cold, but appears milk-white when overcharged, and of an opal, enamel appearance, when heated intermittingly, or with a vacillating flame, that changes frequently from the oxidating to the reducing flame. Baryta and its compounds produce the same reactions with microcosmic salt

Baryta and its compounds fuse when exposed to ignition in the oxidizing flame. Moistened with the solution of nitrate of cobalt, and heated in the oxidation flame, it presents a bead, colored from brick-red to brown, according to the quantity used. This color disappears when cold, and the bead falls to a pale grey powder after being exposed awhile to the air. When heated again, the color does not appear until fusion is effected. If carbonate of soda is fused upon platinum wire with so much of the sesquioxide of manganese that a green bead is produced, this bead, when fused with a sufficient quantity of baryta, or its compounds, after cooling, will appear of a bluish-green, or light blue color.

(*b.*) *Strontia* (SrO).—Strontia and its compounds are analogous to the respective ones of baryta. The hydrate of strontia has the same properties as the hydrate of baryta, except that it is less soluble in water. The carbonate of strontia fuses a little at a red heat, swells, and bubbles up like cauliflower. This produces, in the blowpipe flame, an intense and splendid light, and now produces an alkaline reaction upon red litmus paper. The sulphate of strontia melts in the oxidation flame upon platinum foil, or upon charcoal, to a milk-white globule. This fuses upon charcoal, spreads and is reduced to the sulphide, which is absorbed by the charcoal. It now produces the same reactions upon polished silver as the sulphate of baryta under the same conditions. By exposing strontia and its compounds upon platinum wire, or as a splinter with the platinum tongs, to the point of the blue flame, the external flame appears of an intense crimson color. The deepest red color is produced by the chloride of strontium, particularly at the first moment of applying the heat. After the salt is fused, the red color ceases to be visible in the flame, by which it is distinguished from the chloride of lithium. The carbonate of strontia swells up and produces a splendid white light, while the external flame is colored of a fine purple-red. The color produced by the sulphate of strontia is less intense. The presence of baryta destroys the reaction of the strontia, the flame presenting the light green color of the baryta.

If alcohol is poured over powdered strontia and inflamed, the flame appears purple or deep crimson, particularly if the fluid is stirred with a glass rod, and when the alcohol is nearly consumed.

The insoluble salts of strontia do not produce a very intense color. Baryta does not prevent the reaction of the soluble salts of strontia, unless it exists greatly in excess. In the presence of baryta, strontia can be detected by the following process: mix some of the substance under examination with some pure graphite and water, by grinding in an agate mortar. Place the mixture upon charcoal, and expose it for a while to the reduction flame. The substance becomes reduced to sulphide of barium and sulphide of strontium, when it should be dissolved in hydrochloric acid. The solution should be evaporated to dryness, redissolved in a little water, and enough alcohol added that a spirit of 80 per cent. is produced. Inflame the spirit, and if strontia is present, the flame is tinged of a red color. This color can be discerned more distinctly by moistening some cotton with this spirit and inflaming it.

If strontia or its compounds are fused with a green bead of carbonate of soda and sesquioxide of manganese, as described under the head of baryta, a bead of a brown, brownish-green, or dark grey color is produced. Carbonate of soda does not dissolve pure strontia. The carbonate and sulphate of strontia melt with soda upon platinum foil to a bead, which is milk-white when cold, but fused upon charcoal they are absorbed. Strontia or its compounds produce with borax, or microcosmic salt, the same reactions as baryta. When they are moistened with nitrate of cobalt, and ignited in the oxidizing flame, a black, or grey infusible mass is produced.

(*c.*) *Lime, Oxide of Calcium* (CaO).—Lime does not occur free in nature, but in combination with acids, chiefly the carbonic and sulphuric. The phosphate occurs principally in bones. The hydrate and the salts of lime are in their properties similar to those of the two preceding alkaline earths. In the pure state, the oxide of calcium is white; it slakes, produces a high temperature, and falls into a white powder when sprinkled with a little water. It is now a hydrate, and has greatly increased in volume. The hydrate of lime is far less soluble in water than either those of baryta or strontia, and is less soluble in hot water than in cold. Lime, its hydrate and sulphide of calcium, have a strong alkaline reaction upon red litmus paper. Lime and its hydrate are infusible, but produce at a strong red heat a very intense and splendid white light, while the hydrate loses its water. The carbonate of lime is also infusible, but at a red heat the carbonic acid is expelled, and the residue becomes caustic, appears whiter, and produces an intenser light. The sulphate of lime melts with difficulty, and presents the appearance of an enamelled mass when cold. By heating it upon charcoal it fuses in the reducing flame, and is reduced to a sulphide. This has a strong hepatic odor, and exerts an alkaline reaction upon red litmus paper. By exposing lime, or its compounds, upon platinum wire—or as a small splinter of the mineral in the platinum tongs—to the point of the blue flame, a purple color, similar to that of lithia and strontia, is communicated to the external flame, but this color is not so intense as that produced by strontia, and appears mixed with a slight tinge of yellow. This color is most intense with the chloride of calcium, while the carbonate of lime produces at first a yellowish color, which becomes red, after the expulsion of the carbonic acid. Sulphate of lime produces the same color, but not so intense. Among the silicates of lime only the tablespar ($3CaO, 2SiO^3$) produces a red color. Fluorspar ($CaFl$) produces a red as intense as pure lime, and fuses into a bead. Phosphate and borate of lime produce a green flame which is only characteristic of their acids. The presence of baryta communicates a green color to the flame. The presence of soda produces only a yellow color in the external flame.

If alcohol is poured over lime or its compounds and inflamed, a red color is communicated to the flame. The presence of baryta or soda prevents this reaction. Lime and its compounds do not dissolve much by fusion with carbonate of soda. If this fusion is effected on charcoal, the carbonate of soda is absorbed, and the lime remains as a half-globular infusible mass on the charcoal. This is what distinguishes lime from baryta and strontia, and is a good method of separating the former from the latter. Lime and its compounds fuse with borax in the oxidizing and reducing flames to a clear bead, which remains clear when cold, but when overcharged with an excess or heated intermittingly, the bead appears, when cold, crystalline and uneven, and is not so milk-white as the bead of baryta or strontia, produced under the same circumstances. The carbonate of lime is dissolved with a peculiar hissing noise. Microcosmic salt dissolves a large quantity of lime into a clear bead, which is milky when cold. When the bead has been overcharged with lime, by a less excess, or by an intermittent flame, we will perceive in the bead, when cold, fine crystals in the form of needles. Lime and its compounds form by ignition with nitrate of cobalt, a black or greyish-black infusible mass.

(*d.*) *Magnesia* (MgO).—Magnesia occurs in nature in several minerals. It exists in considerable quantity combined with carbonic, sulphuric, phosphoric, and silicic acids, etc. Magnesia and its hydrate are white and very voluminous, scarcely soluble in hot or cold water, and restores moistened red litmus paper to its original blue color. Magnesia and its hydrate are infusible, the latter losing its water by ignition. The carbonate of magnesia is infusible, loses its carbonic acid at a red heat, and shrinks a little. It now exerts upon red litmus paper an alkaline reaction. The sulphate of magnesia, at a red heat, loses its water and sulphuric acid, is entirely infusible, and gives now an alkaline reaction. The artificial Astrachanit (NaO, SO^3+MgO, SO^3+4HO) fuses easily. When fused on charcoal, the greater part of the sulphate of soda is absorbed, and there remains an infusible mass.

Magnesia and its compounds do not produce any color in the external flame, when heated in the point of the blue flame. The most of the magnesia minerals yield some water when heated in a glass tube closed at one end.

Magnesia, in the pure state, or as the hydrate, does not fuse with soda. Some of its compounds are infusible likewise with soda, and swell up slightly, while others of them melt with soda to a slightly opaque mass. Some few (such as the borate of magnesia) give a clear bead with soda, though it becomes slightly turbid by cooling when saturated with magnesia, and crystallizes in large facets.

Magnesia and its compounds give beads with borax and microcosmic salt similar to those of lime. By igniting magnesia or its compounds very strongly in the oxidizing flame, moistening with nitrate of cobalt, and re-igniting in the oxidation flame, they present, after a continued blowing, a pale flesh-color, which is more visible when cold. It is indispensable that the magnesia compounds should be completely white and free of colored substances, or the color referred to cannot be discerned. In general the reactions of magnesia before the blowpipe are not sufficient, and it will be necessary to confirm its presence or absence by aid of reagents applied in the wet way.

THIRD GROUP.—THE EARTHS, ALUMINA, GLUCINA, YTTRIA, THORINA, AND ZIRCONIA.

The substances of this group are distinguished from the preceding by their insolubility in water, in their pure or hydrated state—that they have no alkaline reaction upon litmus paper, nor form salts with carbonic acid. The earths are not volatile, and, in the pure state, are infusible. They cannot be reduced to the metallic state before the blowpipe. The organic salts are destroyed by ignition, while the earths are left in the pure state, mixed with charcoal, from the organic acids. The most of their neutral salts are insoluble in water; the soluble neutral salts change blue litmus paper to red, and lose their acids when ignited.

(*a.*) *Alumina* (Al^2O^3).—This earth is one of our most common minerals. It occurs free in nature in many minerals, as sapphire, etc.; or in combination with sulphuric acid, phosphoric acid, and fluorine, and chiefly silicates. Pure alumina is a white crystalline powder, or yellowish-white, and amorphous when produced by drying the hydrate, separated chemically from its salts. Alumina is quite unalterable in the fire; the hydrate, however, losing its water at a low red heat. The neutral salts of alumina, with most acids, are insoluble in water. Those soluble in it have an acid reaction upon litmus paper, changing the blue into red.

The sulphates of alumina eliminate water when heated in a glass tube closed at one end. By ignition, sulphurous acid (SO^2) is given off, which can be recognized by its smell, and by its acid reaction upon blue litmus paper, when a small strip of it moistened is brought within the orifice of the tube; an infusible residue is left in the tube.

The greater part of the alumina compounds give off water with heat; the most of them are also infusible, except a few phosphates and silicates.

Pure alumina does not fuse with carbonate of soda. The sulphates, when exposed upon charcoal with soda to the reducing flame, leave a hepatic residue. The phosphates melt with a little soda, with a hissing noise, to a semi-transparent mass, but they are infusible with the addition of soda, and give only a tough mass. This is the case, likewise, with the silicates of alumina. Fluoride of aluminium melts with carbonate of soda to a clear bead, spreads by cooling, and appears then milk-white. Borax dissolves the alumina compounds slowly in the oxidizing and reducing flames to a clear bead, which is also clear when cold, or heated intermittingly with a vacillating flame. The bead is turbid, as well in the heat as the cold, when an excess of alumina is present. When the alumina compound is added to excess in the powdered form, the bead appears crystalline upon cooling, and melts again with great difficulty.

Alumina and its compounds are slowly dissolved in the microcosmic salt to a bead, clear in both flames, and when hot or cold. When alumina is added to excess, the undissolved portion appears semi-transparent. Alumina melts with bisulphate of potash into a mass soluble in water. When the powdered alumina compounds are strongly ignited in the oxidizing flame, then moistened with nitrate of cobalt, and re-ignited in the oxidizing flame, an infusible mass is left, which appears, when cooled, of an intense blue color. The presence of colored metallic oxides, in considerable quantity, will alter or suppress this reaction. The silicates of the alkalies produce, in a very strong heat, or continued heat, with nitrate of cobalt, a pale blue color. The blue color produced by alumina is only distinctly visible by daylight; by candle-light it appears of a dirty violet color.

(*b.*) *Glucina.* (G^2O^3).—Glucina only occurs in a few rare minerals, in combination with silica and alumina. It is white and insoluble in the pure state, and its properties generally are similar to those of alumina. The most of its compounds are infusible, and yield water by distillation. Carbonate of soda does not dissolve glucina by ignition. Silicate of glucina melts with carbonate of soda to a colorless globule. Borax and microcosmic salt dissolve glucina and its compounds to a colorless bead which, when overcharged with glucina, or heated with the intermittent flame appears, after cooling, turbid or milk-white. Glucina yields, by ignition with nitrate of cobalt, a black, or dark grey infusible mass.

(*c.*) *Yttria* (YO) occurs only in a few rare minerals, and usually in company with terbium and erbium. Its reactions before the blowpipe are similar to the preceding, but for its detection in compounds it will be necessary to resort to analysis in the wet way.

(*d.*) *Zirconia* (Zr^2O^3).—This substance resembles alumina in appearance, though it occurs only in a few rare minerals. It is in the pure state infusible, and at a red heat produces such a splendid and vivid white light that the eyes can scarcely endure it. Its other reactions before the blowpipe are analogous to glucina. Microcosmic salt does not dissolve so much zirconia as glucina, and is more prone to give a turbid bead. Zirconia yields with nitrate of cobalt, when ignited, an infusible black mass. To recognize zirconia in compounds we must resort to fluid analysis.

(*e.*) *Thorina* (ThO).—This is the rarest among the rare minerals. In the pure state it is white and infusible, and will not melt with the carbonate of soda. Borax dissolves thorina slowly to a colorless, transparent bead, which will remain so when heated with the intermittent flame. If overcharged with the thorina, the bead presents, on cooling, a milky hue. Microcosmic salt dissolves the thorina very tardily. By ignition with nitrate of cobalt, thorina is converted into an infusible black mass.

CLASS II.

FOURTH GROUP.—CERIUM, LANTHANIUM, DIDYMIUM, COLUMBIUM, NIOBIUM, PELOPIUM, TITANIUM, URANIUM, VANADIUM, CHROMIUM, MANGANESE.

The substances of this group cannot be reduced to the metallic state, neither by heating them *per se*, nor by fusing them with reagents. They give by fusion with borax or microcosmic salt, colored beads, while the preceding groups give colorless beads.

(*a.*) *Cerium* (Ce).—This metal occurs in the oxidated state in a few rare minerals, and is associated with lanthanium and didymium, combined with fluorine, phosphoric acid, carbonic acid, silica, etc. When reduced artificially, it forms a grey metallic powder.

(*a.*) *Protoxide of Cerium* (CeO).—It exists in the pure state as the hydrate, and is of a white color. It soon oxidizes and becomes yellow, when placed in contact with the air. When heated in the oxidation flame, it is converted into the sesquioxide, and then is changed into light brick-red color. In the oxidation flame it is dissolved by borax into a clear bead, which appears of an orange or red while hot, but becomes yellow upon cooling. When highly saturated with the metal, or when heated with a fluctuating flame, the bead appears enamelled as when cold. In the reduction flame it is dissolved by borax to a clear yellow bead, which is colorless when cold. If too much of the metal exists in the bead, it then appears enamelled when cooled.

Microcosmic salt dissolves it, in the oxidation flame, to a clear bead, which is colored dark yellow or orange, but loses its color when cold. In the reduction flame the bead is colorless when either hot or cold. Even if highly saturated with the metal, the bead remains colorless when cold. By fusing it with carbonate of soda upon charcoal in the reduction flame, the soda is absorbed by the charcoal, while the protoxide of the metal remains as a light grey powder.

(*B.*) *Sesquioxide of Cerium* (Ce^2O^3).—This oxide, in the pure state, is a red powder. When heated with hydrochloric acid, it produces chlorine gas, and is dissolved to a salt of the protoxide. It is not affected by either the flame of oxidation or of reduction; when fused with borax or microcosmic salt, it acts like the protoxide. It does not fuse with soda upon charcoal. In the reduction flame it is reduced to the protoxide, which remains of a light grey color, while the soda is absorbed by the charcoal.

(*b.*) *Lanthanium* (La.)—This metal is invariably associated with cerium. It presents, in its metallic state, a dark grey powder, which by compression acquires the metallic lustre.

The *oxide of lanthanium* (LaO) is white, and its salts are colorless. Heated upon charcoal, it does not change either in the oxidation flame or that of reduction. With borax, in the flame of oxidation or reduction, it gives a clear colorless bead. This bead, if saturated, and when hot, presents a yellow appearance, but is clouded or enamelled when cold. With microcosmic salt the same appearance is indicated. It does not fuse with carbonate of soda, but the soda is absorbed by the charcoal, while the oxide remains of a grey color.

(*c.*) *Didymium* (D).—This metal occurs only in combination with the preceding ones, and it is therefore, like them, a rare one.

Oxide of Didymium (DO).—This oxide is of a brown color, while its salts present a reddish-violet or amethyst color. The oxide is infusible in the oxidation flame, and in that of reduction it loses its brown color and changes to grey. With borax in the oxidation flame, it fuses to a clear dark red or violet bead, which retains its clearness when highly saturated with the oxide, or if heated with a fluctuating flame.

The reactions with microcosmic salt are the same as with borax.

It does not melt with carbonate of soda upon charcoal, but the oxide remains with a grey color, while the soda is absorbed by the charcoal.

(*d.*) *Columbium*, (*Tantalum*—Ta).—This rare metal occurs quite sparingly in the minerals *tantalite*, *yttrotantalite*, etc., as columbic acid. In the metallic state, it presents the appearance of a black powder, which, when compressed, exhibits the metallic lustre. When heated in the air it is oxidized into columbic acid, and is only soluble in hydrofluoric acid, yielding hydrogen. It is oxidized by fusion with carbonate of soda or potash.

Columbic Acid (Ta^2O^3) is a white powder, and is infusible. When heated in the flame of oxidation or reduction, it appears of a light yellow while hot, but becomes colorless when cold. With borax, in the flames of oxidation and reduction, it fuses to a clear bead, which appears by a certain degree of saturation, of a yellow color so long as it continues hot, but becomes colorless when cold. If overcharged, or heated with an intermittent flame, it presents an enamel white when cool.

It melts with microcosmic salt quite readily in both of the flames, to a clear bead, which appears, if a considerable quantity of columbic acid be present, of a yellow color while hot, but colorless when cold, and does not become clouded if the intermittent flame be applied to it.

With carbonate of soda it fuses with effervescence to a bead which spreads over the charcoal. Melted with more soda, it becomes absorbed by the charcoal.

It yields, moistened with a solution of nitrate of cobalt, and exposed to the oxidation flame after continued blowing, an infusible mass, presenting while hot a light grey color, but after being cooled that of a light red, similar to the color presented by magnesia under the same circumstances. But if there be some alkali mixed with it, a fusion at the edges will be manifest, and it will yield by cooling a bluish-black mass.

(*e.*) *Niobium* (Ni).—This metal occurs as niobic acid in columbite (tantalite). Niobic acid is in its properties similar to columbic acid. It is white and infusible. By heating it either in the flames of reduction or oxidation, it presents as long as it continues hot, a greenish-yellow color, but becomes white when cool. Borax dissolves it in the oxidation flame quite readily to a clear bead, which, with a considerable quantity of niobic acid, is yellow when hot, but transparent and colorless when cold. A saturated bead is clear when either hot or cold, but becomes opaque when heated intermittingly.

In the flame of reduction, borax is capable of dissolving more of the niobic acid, so that a bead overcharged and opaque in the oxidation flame appears quite clear when heated in the flame of reduction. A bead overcharged in the flame of reduction, appears by cooling dim and bluish-grey.

Microcosmic salt dissolves in the flame of oxidation a great quantity of it to a clear bead, which is yellow while hot, but colorless when cold.

In the flame of reduction, and in presence of a considerable quantity of niobic acid, the bead appears while hot of a light dirty blue color, and when cold, of a violet hue ; but by the addition of more niobic acid, the bead, when hot, is of a dirty dark blue color, and when cold, of a transparent blue. In the presence of the oxides of iron, the bead is, while hot, of a brownish-red color, but changing when cool to a dark yellow.

This acid fuses with an equal quantity of carbonate of soda upon charcoal, to a bead which spreads very quickly, and is then infusible. When fused with still more soda, it is absorbed.

When moistened with nitrate of cobalt, and heated in the flame of oxidation, it yields an infusible mass which appears grey when hot, and dirty green when cold ; but if the heat has been too strong, it is fused a little at the edges, which present a dark bluish-grey color.

Pelopium (Pe).—This metal occurs as an acid in the mineral columbite (tantalite), and is very similar to the two preceding metals.

(*f.*) *Pelopic Acid* (PeO^3).—This acid is white, and appears yellow when heated, but resumes its white color when cold. Borax dissolves it in the oxidation flame to a clear colorless bead, which appears, when overcharged and heated intermittingly, emanel-white when cold. This is likewise the case in the flame of reduction, but when overcharged the color is light grey, when the bead is cooled.

Microcosmic salt dissolves it in the flame of oxidation, to a clear yellow bead, which loses its color when cold. In the reduction flame, when the bead is highly saturated, a violet-brown color is produced. In presence of the oxides of iron, the reactions are like those of niobic acid. With carbonate of soda, the reactions are similar to those of niobic acid. By heating with nitrate of cobalt, it yields a light grey infusible mass.

(*g.*) *Titanium* (Ti).—This metal occurs occasionally in the slags of iron works, in the metallic state, as small cubical crystals of a red color. It is a very hard metal, and very infusible. Titanic acid occurs in nature crystallized in *anatase, arkansite, brookite,* and *rutile.* Titanium is harder than agate, entirely infusible, and loses only a little of its lustre, which can be regained by fusion with borax. It does not melt with carbonate of soda, borax, or microcosmic salt, and is insoluble in every acid except the hydrofluoric. By ignition with saltpetre it is converted into titanic acid, which combines with the potassium, forming the titanate of potassium.

Titanic Acid (TiO^2) is white, insoluble, and, when heated, it appears yellow while hot, but resumes upon cooling its white color.

Borax dissolves it in the oxidation flame to a clear yellow bead, which when cool is colorless. When overcharged, or heated with the intermitting flame, it is enamel-white after being cooled. In the reduction flame, the bead appears yellow, if the acid exists in small quantity, but if more be added, then it is of an orange, or dark yellow, or even brown. The saturated bead, when heated intermittingly, appears when cold of an enamelled blue. By addition of the acid, and by heating the bead on charcoal in the reduction flame, it becomes dark yellow while hot, but dark blue, or black and opaque when cold. This bead appears, when heated intermittingly, of a light blue, and when cold, enamelled.

Microcosmic salt fuses with it in the oxidation flame to a clear colorless bead, which appears yellow only in the presence of a quantity of titanic acid, though by cooling it loses its color. In the reduction flame this bead exhibits a yellow color when hot, but is red while cooling, and when cold of a beautiful bluish-violet. If the bead is overcharged, the color becomes so dark that the bead appears opaque, though not presenting an enamel appearance. By heating the bead again in the oxidation flame the color disappears. The addition of some tin promotes the reduction. If the titanic acid contains oxide of iron, or if some is added, the bead appears, when cold, brownish-yellow, or brownish-red.

By fusion with carbonate of soda, titanic acid is dissolved with effervescence to a clear dark yellow bead, which crystallizes by cooling, whereby so much heat is eliminated, that the bead, at the instant of its crystallization, glows with great brightness. A reduction to a metal cannot, however, be effected. By ignition with a solution of nitrate of cobalt in the oxidation flame, it yields an infusible yellowish-green mass.

(*h.*) *Uranium* (U).—This rare metal occurs in the form of protoxide along with other oxides, in the mineral *pitch-blende;* as peroxide in *uranite* and *uran-mica,* associated with phosphoric acid and lime.

In the metallic state it presents the appearance of a dark grey mass, which is infusible, and remains unchanged when under water, or when exposed to dry air, but, when heated in the oxidation flame, it becomes oxidized, with lively sparkling, to a dark green mass, composed of the protoxide and peroxide.

The *protoxide of uranium* (UO) is black, uncrystalline, or forms a brown powder. When exposed to heat it is converted partially into peroxide, when it has a dark green color.

The *peroxide of uranium* (U^2O^3) is of an orange color, while its hydrate is of a fine yellow color, and in the form of a powder. The salts are yellow.

By heating it in the oxidation flame, it acquires a dark green color, and is partly reduced to protoxide. In the reduction flame it presents a black appearance, and is there completely reduced to protoxide.

Borax dissolves it in the oxidation flame to a clear dark yellow bead, which is colorless when cold, if the metal is not present in great quantity. If more of the metal, or peroxide, be added, the bead changes to orange when hot, and light yellow when cold. When heated with the intermittent flame, it requires a large quantity of the peroxide to produce an enamel appearance in the cooled bead.

In the flame of reduction the bead becomes of a dirty green color, being partly reduced to protoxide, and appears, with a certain degree of saturation, black, when heated intermittingly, but never enamelled. The bead appears on charcoal, and with the addition of tin, of a dark green color.

It fuses with microcosmic salt in the oxidation flame to a clear yellow bead, which is greenish-yellow when cold. In the reduction flame it produces a beautiful green bead, which increases when cold.

When fused upon charcoal with the addition of tin, its color is darker. Carbonate of soda does not dissolve it, although with a very small portion of soda it gives indications of fusion, but with still more of the soda it forms a yellow, or light-brown mass, which is absorbed by the charcoal, but it is not reduced to the metallic state.

(*i.*) *Vanadium* (V).—This very rare mineral is found in small quantity in iron-ores, in Sweden, and as vanadic acid in a few rare minerals. The metal presents the appearance of an iron-grey powder, and sometimes that of a silver-white mass. It is not oxidized either by air or water, and is infusible.

Vanadic Acid (VO^3) fuses upon platinum foil to a deep orange liquid, which becomes crystalline after cooling. When fused upon charcoal, one part of it is absorbed, while the rest remains upon the charcoal and is reduced to protoxide similar in appearance to graphite.

A small portion of it fuses with borax in the oxidation flame to a clear colorless bead, which appears, with the addition of more vanadic acid, of a yellow color, but changes to green when cold.

In the reduction flame the bead is brown while hot, but changes, upon cooling, to a beautiful sapphire-green. At the moment of crystallization, and at a degree of heat by which at daylight no glowing of the heated mass is visible it begins to glow again. The glow spreads from the periphery to the centre of the mass, and is caused by the heat liberated by the sudden crystallization of the mass. It now exhibits an orange color, and is composed of needle crystals in a compact mass.

Microcosmic salt and vanadic acid fuse in the oxidation flame to a dark yellow bead which, upon cooling, loses much of its color.

In the reduction flame the bead is brown while hot, but, upon cooling, acquires a beautiful green color.

Vanadic acid fuses with carbonate of soda upon charcoal, and is absorbed.

(*k.*) *Chromium* (Cr) occurs in the metallic state only in a very small quantity in meteoric iron, but is frequently found in union with oxygen, as oxide in chrome iron ore, and as chromic acid in some lead ores.

In the metallic state it is of a light grey color, with but little metallic lustre, very hard, and not very fusible. Acids do not act upon it, except the hydrofluoric; fused with nitre, it forms chromate of potassa. It is unaltered in the blowpipe flame.

Sesquioxide of Chromium (Cr^2O^3).—This oxide forms black crystals of great hardness, and is sometimes seen as a green powder. Its hydrate (Cr^2O^3+6HO) is of a bluish-grey color. It forms with acids two classes of isomeric salts, some of which are of a green color, and the others violet-red or amethyst. The neutral and soluble salts have an acid reaction upon blue litmus paper, and are decomposed by ignition.

Sesquioxide of chromium in the oxidation and reduction flames is unchangable. When exposed to heat, the hydrate loses its water, and gives a peculiarly beautiful flame. In the oxidation flame borax dissolves the sesquioxide of chromium slowly to a yellow bead (chromic acid) which is yellowish green when cold. Upon the addition of more of the oxide, the bead is dark red while hot, but changes to green as it becoms cold.

In the reduction flame the bead is of a beautiful green color, both while hot and when cold. It is here distinguished from vanadic acid, which gives a brownish or yellow bead while hot.

With microcosmic salt it fuses in the oxidation flame to a clear yellow bead, which appears, as it cools, of a dirty-green color, but upon being cool is of a fine green color. If there be a superabundance of the oxide, so that the microcosmic salt cannot dissolve it, the bead swells up, and is converted into a foamy mass, in consequence of the development of gases.

In the reduction flame it fuses to a fine green bead. The addition of a little tin renders the green still deeper.

Sesquioxide of chromium fuses with carbonate of soda upon platinum foil to a brown or yellow bead, which, upon cooling, appears of a lighter color and transparent (chromate of sodium).

When fused with soda upon charcoal, the soda is absorbed, and the green oxide is left upon it, but is never reduced to the metallic state.

Chromic Acid (CrO^3) crystallizes in the form of deep ruby red needles. It is decomposed into sesquioxide and oxygen when heated. This decomposition is attended with a very lively emission of light, but this is not the case if the chromic acid has been attained by the coöperation of an aqueous solution, unless the reduction is effected in the vapor of ammonia. Before the blowpipe chromic acid produces the same reactions as the sesquioxide.

(*l.*) *Manganese* (Mn).—This metal occurs in considerable abundance, principally as oxides, less frequently as salts, and sometimes in combination with sulphur and arsenic. It is found in plants, and passes with them into the animal body. In the metallic state, it is found frequently in cast iron and steel. It is a hard, brittle metal, fusible with difficulty, and of a light grey color. It tarnishes upon exposure to the air and under water, and falls into a powder.

Protoxide of Manganese exists as a green powder ; as hydrate separated by caustic alkalies, it is white, but oxidizes very speedily upon exposure to the air. The protoxide is the base of the salts of manganese. These salts, which are soluble in water, are decomposed when heated in the presence of the air—except the sulphate (MnO, SO^3), but if the latter is exposed to ignition for awhile, it then ceases to be soluble in water, or at least only sparingly so.

Sesquioxide of Manganese (Mn^2O^3) Occurs very sparingly in nature as small black crystals (*Braunite*) which give, when ground, a brown powder. When prepared by chemical process, it is in the form of a black powder. The hydrate occurs sometimes in nature as black crystals (*manganite*). By digestion with acids, it is dissolved into salts of the protoxide. With hydrochloric acid, it yields chlorine.

The *prot-sesquioxide of manganese* ($MnO + Mn^2O^3$) occurs sometimes in black *crystals* (*hausmannite*). Prepared artificially, it is in the form of a brown powder.

Peroxide of Manganese (MnO^2) occurs in considerable abundance as a soft black amorphous mass, or crystallized as pyrolusite, also reniform and fibrous. It is deprived of a part of its oxygen when exposed to ignition. It eliminates a considerable quantity of chlorine from hydrochloric acid, and is thereby converted into chloride of manganese (ClMn).

Most of the manganese compounds which occur in nature yield water when heated in a glass tube closed at one end. The sesquioxide and peroxide give out oxygen when strongly heated, which can be readily detected by the increased glow which it causes, if a piece of lighted wood or paper is brought to the mouth of the tube. The residue left in the tube is a brown mass ($MnO + Mn^2O^3$).

When exposed to ignition with free access of air, all manganese oxides are converted into ($MnO + Mn^2O^3$), but without fusion. Such, at least, is the statement of some of the German chemists, although it will admit perhaps of further investigation.

Manganese oxides fuse with borax in the oxidation flame to a clear and intensely colored bead, of a violet hue while hot, but changing to red as it cools. If a considerable quantity of the oxide is added, the bead acquires a color so dark as to become opaque. If such be the case, we have to press it flat, by which its proper color will become manifest.

In the reduction flame the bead is colorless. A very dark colored bead must be fused upon charcoal with the addition of some tin. The bead must be cooled very suddenly, for if it cools too slowly, it then has time to oxidize again. This may be effected by pushing it off the platinum wire, or the charcoal, and pressing it flat with the forceps.

The oxides of manganese fuse with microcosmic salt in the oxidation flame, to a clear brownish-violet bead, which appears reddish-violet while cooling. This bead does not become opaque when overcharged with manganese. As long as it is kept in fusion a continued boiling or effervescence takes place, produced by the expulsion of oxygen, in consequence of the fact that the microcosmic salt cannot dissolve much sesquioxide, while the rest is reduced to protoxide, is re-oxidated, and instantly again reduced. If the manganese is present in such a minute quantity as not to perceptibly tinge the bead, the color may be made to appear by the contact of a crystal of nitre while hot. The bead foams up upon the addition of the nitre, and the foam appears, after cooling, of a rose-red or violet color. In the reduction flame the bead sometimes becomes colorless.

The oxides of manganese fuse with carbonate of soda upon

platinum foil or wire, to a clear green bead, which appears bluish-green and partially opaque when cold (manganate of soda $NaO+MnO^3$). A very minute trace of manganese will produce this green color. The oxides of manganese cannot be reduced upon charcoal with carbonate of soda before the blowpipe. The soda is absorbed, and ($MnO+Mn^2O^3$) is left.

GROUP FIFTH.—IRON, COBALT, NICKEL.

The oxides of this group are reduced to the metallic state when fused with carbonate of soda upon charcoal in the reduction flame. Metals when thus reduced form powders, are not fusible or volatile in the blowpipe flame, but they are attracted by the magnet.

Furthermore, these oxides are not dissolved by carbonate of soda in the oxidation flame, but they produce colored beads with borax and microcosmic salt.

(*a.*) *Iron.*—It occurs in great abundance in nature. It is found in several places in America in the metallic state, and it likewise occurs in the same state in meteors. It occurs chiefly as the oxide (red hematite, brown hematite, magnetic oxide, etc.), and frequently in combination with sulphur. Iron also forms a constituent of the blood.

Metallic iron is of a grey color, and presents the metallic lustre vividly when polished. It is very ductile, malleable, and tenacious. It is very hard at common temperatures, but soft and yielding at a red heat.

In dry and cold air, iron does not oxidize, but when the air is dry and moist, it oxidizes rapidly. This likewise takes place with great rapidity when the metal is heated to redness. When submitted to a white heat iron burns with brilliant scintillations.

Protoxide of Iron (FeO).—This oxide does not occur pure in nature, but in union with the peroxide of iron and other substances. It presents the form of a black powder, and has some metallic lustre, is brittle, and fuses at a high temperature to a vitreous looking mass. It is attracted by the magnet, and of course is susceptible of becoming magnetic itself. It forms with water a hydrate, but this passes so rapidly into a state of higher oxidation, that it is difficult to keep it in the pure state.

Magnetic Oxide of Iron ($FeO+Fe^2O^3$).—This peculiar oxide is of a dark color, and is magnetic, so that tacks or small nails adhere to it when brought in contact with it. It is the variety of the oxide termed "loadstone." It is found frequently crystallized in octahedrons in Scandinavia and other places. Magnetic oxide of iron is produced when red-hot iron is hammered.

Sesquioxide of Iron (Fe^2O^3).—This oxide is found native in great abundance as red hematite and specular iron, crystallized in the rhombic form. In the crystalline state it is of a blackish-grey color, and possessed of the metallic lustre. When powdered, it forms a brownish-red mass. When artificially prepared, it presents the appearance of a blood-red powder. It is not magnetic, and has less affinity for acids than the protoxide. Its hydrate is found native as brown hematite.

By exposing the peroxide of iron to the oxidation flame, it is not acted upon, but in the reduction flame it becomes reduced to the magnetic oxide.

The oxides of iron are dissolved by borax in the oxidation flame to a clear dark-yellow or dark-red bead, which appears lighter while cooling, and yellowish when cold. In the presence of a very small quantity of iron, the bead appears colorless when cold. If the iron is increased, the bead is opaque while cooling, and of a dirty dark-yellow color when cold. In the reduction flame, and fused upon platinum wire, the bead appears dark green ($FeO+Fe^2O^3$). By the addition of some tin, and fused upon charcoal, the bead appears bluish-green, or not unlike that of sulphate of iron.

Microcosmic salt dissolves the oxides of iron in the oxidation flame to a clear bead, which, by the addition of a considerable quantity of iron, becomes of an orange color while hot, but gets lighter while cooling, presenting finally a greenish hue, and gradually becoming lighter, till, when cold, it is colorless. If the iron is increased, the hot bead presents a dark red color, but while cooling a brownish-red, which changes to a dirty-green, and, when cold, to a brownish-red color. The decrease of the color during the transition from the hot to the cold state is still greater in the bead formed by the microcosmic salt.

In the reduction flame no change is visible if the quantity of iron be small. By the addition of more iron, the hot bead appears red, and while cooling, changes to yellow, then green, and, when cold, is of a dull red. By fusing the bead on charcoal with a small addition of tin, it exhibits, while cooling, a bluish-green color, but, when cold, is colorless.

The oxides of iron are not dissolved in the oxidation flame by fusion with carbonate of soda. By ignition with soda upon charcoal in the reduction flame, they are absorbed and reduced to the metallic state. Cut out this portion of the charcoal; grind it with the addition of some water in an agate mortar, for the purpose of washing off the carbon particles, when the iron will remain as a grey magnetic powder.

(*b.*) *Cobalt* (Co) occurs in combination with arsenic and sulphur, and associated with nickel and iron. It is found occasionally in combination with selenium, and there are a traces of it in meteoric iron. In the metallic state it is of a light, reddish-grey color, rather brittle, and only fusible at a strong white heat; at common temperatures it is unalterable by air or water. At a red heat, it oxidizes slowly and decomposes water; at a white heat it burns with a red flame. Cobalt is soluble in dilute sulphuric or hydrochloric acid by the aid of heat, whereby hydrogen is eliminated. These solutions have a fine red color.

Protoxide of Cobalt (CoO).—It is an olive-green powder, but, by exposure to the air, it becomes gradually brown. Its hydrate is a rich red powder. The solntion of its salts is red, but the aqueous solution is often blue.

When heated in the oxidation flame, the protoxide is converted into the black proto-sesquioxide ($CoO + Co^2O^3$). In the reduction flame it shrinks and is reduced without fusion to the metallic state. It is now attracted by the magnet and acquires lustre by compression.

Borax dissolves it in the oxidation flame, and produces a clear, intensely colored blue bead, which remains transparent and of the same beautiful blue when cold. This blue is likewise manifest even if the bead be heated intermittingly. If the cobalt exists in considerable quantity, the color of the bead is so intense as to appear almost black.

This reaction of cobalt is so characteristic and sensitive that it can detect a minute trace.

With microcosmic salt the same reaction is exhibited, but not so sensitive, nor is the bead so intensely colored when cold as that with borax.

By fusion with carbonate of soda upon a platinum wire, with a very small portion of cobalt, a bright red colored mass is produced which appears grey, or slightly green when cold. By fusion upon platinum foil the fused portion floats down from the sides, and the foil is coated around the undissolved part, with a thin, dark-red sublimate. When fused upon charcoal, and in the reduction flame, it is reduced with soda to a grey powder, which is attracted by the magnet, and exhibits the metallic lustre by compression.

Sesquioxide of Cobalt (Co^2O^3).—It is a dark brown powder. Its hydrate ($2HO + Co^2O^3$) is a brown powder. It is soluble only in acetic acid as the acetate of the sesquioxide. All other acids dissolve its salts to protoxide, the hydrochloric acid producing chloric gas. By ignition in the oxidation flame, it is converted into the proto-sesquioxide ($CoO + Co^2O^3$) and produces with reagents before the blowpipe the same reactions as the protoxide.

(*c.*) *Nickel* (Ni).—This metal occurs invariably associated with cobalt, and in analogous combinations, chiefly as the arsenical nickel. In the metallic state it is greyish, silver-white, has a high lustre, is hard, and malleable both cold and hot. At common temperatures, it is unalterable either in dry or moist air. When ignited, it tarnishes. It is easily dissolved by nitric acid, but very slowly by dilute sulphuric or hydrochloric acid, producing hydrogen.

Protoxide of Nickel (NiO).—It is in the form of small greyish-black octahedrons, or a dark, greenish-grey powder. Its hydrate is a green powder. Both are unalterable in the air, and are soluble in nitric, sulphuric, and hydrochloric acids, to a green liquid. The protoxide is the base of the salts of nickel, which in the anhydrous state are yellow, and when hydrated are green. The soluble neutral salts change blue litmus paper to red. By ignition in the oxidation flame, protoxide of nickel is unaltered. In the reduction flame and upon charcoal, it becomes reduced, and forms a grey adherent powder, which is infusible, and presents the metallic lustre by compression, and is magnetic. Borax dissolves it in the oxidation flame very readily to a clear bead, of a reddish-violet or dark yellow color, but yellow or light red when cold. If there is but a small quantity of the oxide present, it is colorless. If more of the oxide be present, the bead is opaque and dark brown, and appears, while cooling, transparent and dark red. By the addition of a salt of potassa (the nitrate or carbonate) a blue or a dark purple colored bead is produced. The borax bead, in the reduction flame, is grey, turbid, or completely opaque from the reduced metallic particles. After a continued blast, the bead becomes colorless, although the particles are not fused. If the nickel contains cobalt, it will now be visible with its peculiar blue color. Upon charcoal, and by the addition of some tin, the reduction of the oxide of nickel is easily effected, while the reduced nickel fuses with the tin.

The oxide of nickel is dissolved by microcosmic salt in the oxidation flame to a clear bead, which appears reddish while hot, but yellow and sometimes colorless when cooling. If a considerable quantity of nickel be present the heated bead is of a brown color, but orange when cooled. In the reduction flame, and upon platinum wire, the color of the bead is orange when cold; but upon charcoal, and with the addition of a little tin, the bead appears grey and opaque. After being submitted to the blowpipe flame all the nickel is reduced, and the bead becomes colorless.

Carbonate of soda does not affect it in the oxidation flame, but in the reduction flame and upon charcoal, it is absorbed and reduced, and remains, after washing off the carbon, as a white metallic powder, which is infusible, and has a greater attraction for the magnet than iron.

Sesquioxide of Nickel (Ni^2O^3).—It is in the form of a black powder, and does not combine with other substances, unless it is reduced to the protoxide. It exhibits before the blowpipe the same behavior as the protoxide.

GROUP SIXTH.—ZINC, CADMIUM, ANTIMONY, TELLURIUM.

The substances of this group can be reduced upon charcoal by fusion with carbonate of soda, but the reduced metals are volatilized, and cover the charcoal with sublimates.

(*a.*) *Zinc* (Zn).—This metal is found in considerable abundance, but never occurs in the pure metallic state, but in combination with other substances, chiefly as sulphide in zinc blende, as carbonate in calamine, and as the silicate in the kieselzinc ore; also, with sulphuric acid, the "vitriol of zinc."

Zinc is of a bluish-white color and metallic lustre, is crystalline and brittle when heated 400°F., but malleable and ductile between 200° and 300°. It will not oxidize in dry air, but tarnishes if exposed to air containing moisture, first becomes grey, and then passes into the white carbonate. It decomposes in water at a glowing heat. It is dissolved by diluted acids, while hydrogen is eliminated. It melts at about 775°, and distills when exposed to a white heat in a close vessel. When heated over 1000° in the open air, it takes fire, and burns with a bluish-white light, and with a thick white smoke of oxide of zinc.

Oxide of Zinc (ZnO).—In the pure state, oxide of zinc is a white powder, infusible, and not volatile. It is readily soluble in acids after being heated strongly. Its soluble neutral salts, when dissolved in water, change blue litmus paper to red. Its salts, with organic acids, are decomposed by ignition, and the carbonate of zinc remains.

The oxide of zinc turns yellow by being ignited in the oxidation flame, but it is only visible by daylight; this color changes to white when cold. It does not melt, but produces a strong light, and it is not volatile.

It disappears gradually in the flame of reduction, while a white smoke sublimates upon the charcoal. This sublimate is yellow while hot, but changes to white when cold. The cause of this is, that the oxide is reduced, is volatilized, and re-oxidized, by going through the external flame in the form of a metallic vapor.

Borax dissolves oxide of zinc in the flame of oxidation easily to a clear bead, which is yellow while hot, and colorless when cold. The bead becomes, by the addition of more oxide, enamelled, while cooling. If the bead is heated with the intermittent flame, it is milk-white when cold. When heated in the flame of reduction upon platinum wire, the bead at first appears opaque, and of a greyish color, but becomes clear again after a continued blast.

When heated upon charcoal in the reduction flame, it is reduced to a metal; but, at the same moment, is volatilized, and sublimes as oxide of zinc upon the charcoal, about one line's distance from the assay. This is likewise the case with the microcosmic salt, except that it is more easily volatilized in the reduction flame.

Carbonate of soda does not dissolve the oxide of zinc in the flame of oxidation. In the reduction flame and upon charcoal, the oxide of zinc is reduced to the metallic state, and is volatilized with a white vapor of the zinc oxide, which sublimes on the charcoal and exhibits a yellow color while hot, and which changes to white when cold. By a strong heat the reduced zinc burns with a white flame.

Moistened with a solution of cobalt oxide, and heated strongly in the flame of oxidation, zinc oxide becomes of a yellowish-green color while hot, and changes to a beautiful green color when cold.

(*b.*) *Cadmium* (Cd).—This is one of the rare metals. It occurs in combination with sulphur in *greenockite*, and in some ores of zinc. It was detected first in the year 1818, and presents itself as a tin-white metal of great lustre, and susceptible of a fine polish. It has a fibrous structure, crystallizes easily in regular octahedrons, presenting often the peculiar arborescent appearance of the fern. It is soft, but harder and more tenacious than tin; it can be bent, filed, and easily cut: it imparts to paper a color like that of lead. It is very malleable and ductile, and can be hammered into thin leaves. It is easily fused, and melts before it glows (450°). At a temperature not much over the boiling point of mercury, it begins to boil, and distills, the vapor of the metal possessing no peculiar odor. It is unalterable in the air for a long time, but at length it tarnishes and presents a greyish-white, half metallic color. This metal easily takes fire when heated in the air, and burns with a brownish-yellow vapor, while it deposits a yellow sublimate upon surrounding bodies. It is easily soluble in acids with the escape of hydrogen, the solutions being colorless. Its salts, soluble in water, are decomposed by ignition in free air. Its soluble neutral salts change blue litmus paper to red. The salts, insoluble in water, are readily dissolved in acids.

Oxide of Cadmium (CdO).—This oxide is of a dark orange color. It does not melt, and is not volatile, not even at a very high temperature. Its hydrate is white, loses in the heat its hydratic water, and absorbs carbonic acid from the air when it is kept in open vessels.

Cadmium oxide is unaltered when exposed upon platinum wire in the flame of oxidation. When heated upon charcoal in the flame of reduction it disappears in a very short time, while the charcoal is coated with a dark orange or yellow powder, the color of which is more visible after it is cooled. The portions of this sublimate furthest from the assay present a visible iridescent appearance. This reaction of cadmium is so characteristic and sensitive that minerals (for instance, calamine, carbonate of zinc) which contains from one to five per cent. of carbonate of cadmium, will give a dark yellowish ring of cadmium oxide, a little distance from the assay, after being exposed for a few moments to the flame of reduction. This sublimate is more visible when cold, and is produced some time previous to the reduction of the zinc oxide. If a vapor of the latter should appear, it indicates that it has been exposed too great a length of time to the flame.

Borax dissolves a considerable quantity of cadmium oxide upon a platinum wire to a clear yellow bead, which, when cold, is almost colorless. If the bead is nearly saturated with the cadmium oxide, it appears milk-white when intermittingly heated. If the bead is completely saturated, it retains its opalescent appearance. Upon charcoal, and in the flame of reduction, the bead intumesces, the cadmium oxide becomes reduced to metal; this becomes volatilized and re-oxidized, and sublimes upon the charcoal as the yellow cadmium oxide.

In the oxidation flame, microcosmic salt dissolves a large quantity of it to a clear bead, which, when highly saturated and while hot, is yellowish colored, but colorless when cold. By complete saturation, the bead is enamel-white when cold.

Upon charcoal, in the flame of reduction, the bead is slowly and only partially reduced, a scanty sublimate being produced on the charcoal. The addition of tin promotes the reduction.

Carbonate of soda does not dissolve cadmium oxide in the oxidation flame. In the reduction flame, upon charcoal, it is reduced to metal, and is volatilized to a red-brown or dark-red sublimate of cadmium oxide upon the charcoal, at a little distance from the assay the charcoal presenting the characteristic iridescent appearance. This reaction is still more sensitive if the cadmium oxide is heated *per se* in the reduction flame.

Antimony (Sb).—This metal is found in almost every country. It principally occurs as the tersulphide (SbS^3), either pure or combined with other sulphides, particularly with basic sulphides. Sometimes it occurs as the pure metal, and rarer in a state of oxidation as an antimonious acid and as the oxysulphide.

In the pure state, antimony has a silver-white color, with much lustre, and presents a crystalline structure. The commercial and impure metal is of a tin-white color, and may frequently be split in parallel strata. It is brittle and easily pulverized. It melts at a low red heat (810°), is volatilized at a white heat, and can be distilled. At common temperatures it is not affected by the air. At a glowing heat it takes fire, and burns with a white flame, and with white fumes, forming volatile antimonious acid. Common acids oxidize antimony, but dissolve it slightly. It is soluble in aqua regia (nitro-hydrochloric acid).

Sesquioxide of Antimony (Sb^2O^3).—In the pure state this oxide is a white powder, is fusible at a dull red heat to a yellow liquid, which, after cooling, is greyish-white and crystalline. If it is heated excluded from the air, it can be volatilized completely; it sublimes in bright crystals having the form of needles. It occurs sometimes in nature as white and very bright crystals. It takes fire when heated in the open air, and burns with a white vapor to antimonious acid. It fuses with the ter-sulphide of antimony to a red bead. It is distinguished from the other oxides of antimony by the readiness with which it is reduced to the metallic state upon charcoal, and by its easy fusibility and volatility.

The sesquioxide is the base of some salts—for instance, the tartar emetic. It is not soluble in nitric acid, but is soluble in hydrochloric acid. This solution becomes milky by the addition of water. A part of the salts of the sesquioxide of antimony are decomposed by ignition. The haloid salts are easily volatilized, without decomposition. Its soluble neutral salts change blue litmus paper to red, and are converted, by admixture of water, into insoluble basic and soluble acid salts.

Antimonious acid (antimoniate of sesquioxide of antimony, $Sb^2O^3 + Sb^2O^5$) is of a white color, but, when heated, of a light yellow color, but changes to white again when cold. It is infusible and unaltered by heat. It forms a white hydrate, and both are insoluble in water and nitric acid. It is partly soluble in hydrochloric acid, with the application of heat. The addition of water causes a precipitate in this solution.

Antimonic Acid (Sb^2O^6).—In the pure state this acid is a light yellow-colored powder. Its hydrate is white, and is insoluble in water and nitric acid. It is sparingly soluble in hot concentrated hydrochloric acid. It forms salts with every base, some of which are insoluble, and others sparingly so. Notwithstanding that antimonic acid is insoluble in water, it expels the carbonic acid from the solutions of the carbonates of the alkalies. Antimonic acid and its hydrate changes moistened blue litmus paper to red.

Behavior of Antimony and its Oxides before the Blowpipe.

Metallic Antimony fuses easily upon charcoal. When heated to glowing, and then removed from the flame, it continues to glow for awhile, and produces a thick white smoke. The vapor crystallizes gradually, and coats the assay with small crystals which iridesce like mother of pearl (sesquioxide of antimony). It is not volatile at the temperature of melted glass. Ignited in an open glass tube, it burns slowly with a white vapor, which condenses upon the cool part of the tube, and exhibits some indications of crystallization. This vapor consists of the sesquioxide, and can be driven by heat from one place to another, without leaving a residue. If the metallic antimony contains sulphide of antimony, there is a corresponding portion of antimonious acid produced, which remains as a white sublimate after the sesquioxide is removed.

7

Sesquioxide of antimony melts easily, and sublimes as a white vapor. It may be prepared by precipitating and drying. When heated, it takes fire previous to melting, glows like tinder, and is converted into antimonious acid, which is now infusible. When heated upon charcoal in the flame of reduction, it is reduced to the metallic state, and partly volatilized. A white vapor sublimates upon the charcoal, while the external flame exhibits a greenish-blue color. Antimonious acid is infusible, produces a strong light, and is diminished in volume when heated in the external flame, during which time a dense white vapor sublimes upon the charcoal. It is not, however, in this manner reduced to the metallic state like the sesquioxide.

Antimonic acid, when first heated, becomes white, and is converted into antimonious acid. Hydrated antimonic acid, which is originally white, appears at first yellow while giving off water, and then becomes white again, while oxygen is expelled, and it is converted into antimonious acid.

The oxides of antimony produce, with blowpipe reagents, the following reactions : borax dissolves oxides of antimony in the oxidation flame in considerable quantity to a clear bead, which is yellow while hot, but colorless when cold. If the bead is saturated, a part of the oxide is volatilized as a white vapor. Upon charcoal, in the oxidation flame, it is completely volatilized, and the charcoal is covered with a white sublimate. Heated upon charcoal in the reducing flame, the bead is of a greyish color, and partially, if not wholly opaque, from the presence of reduced metallic particles. A continued heat will volatilize them, and the bead becomes clear. The addition of tin promotes the reduction.

Microcosmic salt dissolves the compounds of antimony in the flame of oxidation with intumescence, to a clear light-yellow colored bead, which when cold is colorless. Heated upon charcoal in the reduction flame, the bead is first turbid, but soon becomes transparent. The addition of tin renders the bead greyish while cooling, but a continued blast renders it transparent. Soda dissolves the compounds of antimony upon platinum wire in the oxidation flame, to a clear colorless bead, which is white when cold.

Upon charcoal, both in the oxidation and reduction flames, the antimony compounds are readily reduced to the metal, which is immediately volatilized, and produces a white incrustation of oxide of antimony upon the charcoal. If the antimony compounds are heated upon charcoal in the flame of reduction, with a mixture of carbonate of soda and cyanide of potassium (KCy), there are produced small globules of metallic antimony. At the same time, a part of the reduced metal is volatilized (this continues after the assay is removed from the flame) and re-oxidized. A white incrustation appears upon the charcoal, and the metallic globules are covered with small white crystals. If this white sublimate upon the charcoal is moistened with a solution of cobalt-oxide, and exposed to the reduction flame, a part of it is volatilized, while the other part passes into higher oxidation, and remains, after cooling, of a dirty dark-green color.

(*d.*) *Tellurium* (Te).—This is one of the rare metals. It occurs very seldom in the metallic state, but often with bismuth, lead, silver, and gold. Tellurium, in the pure state, is silver-white, very bright, of a foliated or lamellar structure, brittle, and easily triturated. It is inclined to crystallize. It is soluble in concentrated sulphuric acid without oxidation. The solution is of a fine purple color, and gives a precipitate with the addition of water.

Tellurium in the Metallic form.—By the aid of heat it is oxidized in sulphuric acid, a portion of the oxygen of the acid oxidizing the metal, while sulphurous acid gas escapes. This solution is colorless, and is tellurous acid, dissolved in sulphuric acid. It melts at a low red heat, and volatilizes at a higher temperature. If tellurium is heated with free access of air, it takes fire, and burns with a blue color, the flame being greenish at the edges, while a thick white vapor escapes, which has a feeble acidulous odor.

Tellurous Acid (TeO^2) is of a fine, granulous, crystalline or white earthy mass, which is partly soluble in water. The solution has a strong metallic taste, and an acid reaction upon litmus paper. Heated in a tube closed at one end until it begins to glow, it fuses to a yellow liquid which is colorless, crystalline, and opaque when cold. Beads of it remain usually transparent like glass. Heated upon platinum wire in the flame of oxidation, it melts, and is volatilized as a white vapor. When heated upon charcoal in the oxidation flame, it melts, and is reduced to the metallic state, but volatilizes and a sublimate of white tellurous acid is formed upon the charcoal. The edge of this deposit is usually red or dark-yellow.

Heated upon charcoal in the flame of reduction, it is rapidly reduced, the external flame exhibiting a bluish-green color.

Borax dissolves it in the oxidation flame upon platinum wire to a clear colorless bead which turns grey when heated upon charcoal, through the presence of reduced metallic particles. Upon charcoal, in the reduction flame, the bead is grey, caused by the reduced metal. After a continued blast, tellurium is completely volatilized, and the bead appears clear again, while a white sublimate is deposited upon the charcoal.

With microcosmic salt, the same reactions are produced.

With carbonate of soda, tellurous acid fuses upon platinum wire to a clear colorless bead, which is white when cold. Upon charcoal it is reduced, and forms *tellur-sodium*, which is absorbed by the charcoal, and metallic tellurium, which is volatilized, and deposits upon the charcoal a white incrustation (tellurous acid).

If tellurous acid, finely powdered charcoal, and carbonate of soda are mixed together, and the mixture be well ignited in a closed tube, until fusion is effected, and a few drops of boiled water are brought into the tube, they are colored purple, indicating the presence of *tellur-sodium.*

Telluric Acid (TeO^3) forms six-sided prismatic crystals. It has not an acid, but rather a metallic taste. It changes blue litmus paper to red ; is slowly soluble in water, and rather sparingly. Exposed to a high temperature, but not until glowing, the crystalline acid loses its water, and acquires an orange color, but still it preserves its crystalline form, although no longer soluble in water, and is in fact so much changed in its properties as to present the instance of an isomeric modification.

If telluric acid is heated gently in a closed tube, it loses water and turns yellow. Heated still more strongly, it becomes milk-white, oxygen is expelled, and it is converted into tellurous acid. The presence of oxygen can be recognized by the more lively combustion which an ignited splinter of wood undergoes when held in it. Telluric acid produces the same reactions with the blowpipe reagents as tellurous acid.

SEVENTH GROUP.—LEAD, BISMUTH, TIN.

The oxides of these metals are also reduced to the metallic state by fusion with soda upon charcoal in the flame of reduction, but they are volatilized only after a continued blast, and a sublimate is thrown upon the charcoal.

(*a.*) *Lead* (Pb).—This metal occurs in considerable quantity in nature, chiefly as galena or lead-glance (sulphide of lead). Likewise, but more rarely, as a carbonate; also as a sulphate, and sometimes combined with other acids and metals.

In the metallic state, lead is of a bluish-grey color, high lustre, and sp. gr. 11·4. It is soft, and communicates a stain to paper. It is malleable, ductile, but has very little tenacity. It melts at about 612°. Exposed to the air it soon tarnishes, being covered with a grey matter, which some regard as a suboxide (Pb^2O), and others as simply a mixture of lead and protoxide. At a glowing heat it is oxidized to a protoxide, and at a white heat it is volatilized. It is insoluble in most acids. It is, however, soluble in nitric acid, but without decomposing water.

(*L.*) *Protoxide of Lead* (PbO).—It is an orange-colored powder, which melts at a glowing temperature, and forms a lamellar mass after cooling. Protoxide of lead absorbs oxygen from the atmosphere while melting, which is given off again by cooling. Being exposed for a longer while to the air, it absorbs carbonic acid and water, and becomes white on the surface. It is soluble in nitric acid and caustic alkalies. It forms with most acids insoluble salts. It is slightly soluble in pure water, but not in water which contains alkaline salts. This hydrate is white.

(β.) *Red Oxide of Lead* (PbO^2,PbO).—It forms a puce-colored powder. It is insoluble in caustic alkalies. Hydrochloric acid dissolves it and forms a yellow liquid, which is soon decomposed into chloride of lead and chlorine. It is reduced by ignition to the protoxide.

(γ.) *Peroxide of Lead* (PbO^2).—It is a dark-brown powder. It yields with hydrochloric acid the chloride of lead and chlorine gas. When heated it liberates oxygen, and is reduced to the protoxide.

Lead combinations give the following reactions before the blowpipe : Metallic lead tarnishes when heated in the oxidation flame, and is instantly covered with a grey matter, consisting of the protoxide and the metal. It fuses quickly, and is then covered with a yellowish-brown protoxide until all the lead is converted into the protoxide, which melts to a yellow liquid. In the reduction flame and upon charcoal, it is volatilized, while the charcoal becomes covered with a yellow sublimate of oxide. A little distance from the assay, this sublimate appears white (carbonate of lead). Protoxide of lead melts in the flame of oxidation to a beautiful dark yellow bead. In the flame of reduction, and upon charcoal, it is reduced with intumescence to metallic lead, which is volatilized by a continued blast, and sublimates on charcoal, as mentioned above.

Red oxide of lead turns black when heated in the glass tube closed at one end, and liberates oxygen, which is easily detected by the introduction of an ignited splinter, when a more lively combustion of the wood proves the presence of uncombined oxygen. The red oxide in this case is reduced to the protoxide.

Heated upon platinum foil, it first turns black, is reduced to the protoxide, and melts into a dark yellow liquid. In the reduction flame, upon charcoal, it is reduced to the metal with intumescence. After a continued blast, a yellow sublimate of protoxide is produced upon the charcoal, and at a little distance off, around this sublimate, a white one of carbonate of lead is produced. This sublimate disappears when touched by the flame of reduction, while it communicates an azure blue-tinge to the external flame. This is likewise the case with the peroxide of lead.

The different oxides of lead produce with the blowpipe reagents the same reactions.

Borax dissolves lead compounds with the greatest readiness upon platinum wire in the oxidation flame to a transparent bead, which is yellow when hot, but colorless after being cooled. With the addition of more of the lead oxide, it becomes opalescent. When heated by the intermittent flame, and with still more of the oxide, it acquires a yellow enamel after cooling. Heated upon charcoal, in the flame of reduction, the bead spreads and becomes opaque. After a continued blast, all the oxide is reduced with effervescence to metallic lead, which melts and runs towards the edges of the bead, while the bead again becomes transparent.

Microcosmic Salt dissolves oxides of lead upon platinum wire in the flame of oxidation easily to a clear, colorless bead, which appears, when highly saturated, yellow while hot. A saturated bead becomes enamel-like after cooling. The bead appears in the flame of reduction, and upon charcoal, of a greyish color and dull. By the addition of more oxide, a yellow sublimate of protoxide is produced upon the charcoal. By the addition of tin, the bead appears of a darker grey, but it is never quite opaque.

Carbonate of Soda dissolves oxide of lead in the flame of oxidation upon platinum wire quite readily to a transparent bead, which becomes yellow when cooling, and is opaque. Upon charcoal in the flame of reduction, it is rapidly reduced to metallic lead, which yields, after a continued blast, a yellow sublimate of oxide upon the charcoal.

(*b.*) *Bismuth* (Bi).—This metal occurs mostly in the metallic state, and less frequently as the sulphide. In the pure metallic state, it is of a reddish-white color and great lustre. It crystallizes in cubes. It is brittle, and may be readily pulverized. It melts at 476°, and is volatilized at a white heat. It is soluble in nitric acid, and forms the nitrate of bismuth.

(*a.*) *Oxide of Bismuth* (Bi^2O^3).—This oxide is a light yellow powder, fusible at a red heat, insoluble in caustic potash and ammonia. It is the base of the salts of bismuth. Its hydrate is white, and easily soluble in acids. The addition of water causes these solutions to become milky, because they are decomposed into a soluble acidulous and an insoluble basic salt of bismuth.

(*β.*) *Peroxide of Bismuth* (BiO^2) is a dark-colored powder, completely soluble in boiling nitric acid, and yielding oxygen; produces, with hydrochloric acid, chlorine gas. It can be heated up to the temperature of 620° without being decomposed; but, exposed to a temperature of 630° it yields oxygen. Mixed with combustible substances, it glows with brightness.

(*γ.*) *Bismuthic Acid* (Bi^2O^6) is a brown powder similar to the peroxide, but is converted by boiling nitric acid into a green, scarcely soluble substance (Bi^2O^3, Bi^2O^5). Its hydrate is of a red color.

BLOWPIPE REACTIONS.—Metallic bismuth is converted, when exposed upon platinum wire to the flame of oxidation, into a dark brown oxide, which turns light yellow while cooling. It is slowly volatilized when heated, and a yellow sublimate of oxide is produced upon the charcoal.

Oxide of bismuth melts upon platinum foil in the flame of oxidation very easily into a dark-brown liquid, which changes to a light yellow while cooling. By too strong a heat, it is reduced and penetrates the platinum foil.

Upon charcoal, in the flame of oxidation and of reduction, it is reduced to metallic bismuth, which melts into one or more globules. By a continued blast they are slowly volatilized, and produce a yellow sublimate of oxide upon the charcoal, beyond which a white sublimate of carbonate of bismuth is visible. These sublimates disappear in the flame of reduction, but without communicating any color to it.

Borax dissolves oxide of bismuth upon platinum wire, in the flame of oxidation, easily to a clear yellow bead, which appears colorless after cooling. By the addition of more oxide, the hot bead becomes orange. It turns more yellow while cooling, and when cool is opalescent. Upon charcoal in the flame of reduction, the bead becomes turbid and greyish colored. The oxide is reduced with intumescence to the metallic state, and the bead becomes clear again. The addition of tin promotes the reduction.

Microcosmic Salt dissolves oxide of bismuth upon platinum wire, in the flame of oxidation, to a yellow bead, which becomes colorless after cooling. By the addition of more oxide, the bead is yellowish-brown while hot, and colorless after cooling, but not quite transparent. This bead becomes enamelled when heated by the intermittent flame ; also, by the addition of still more of the oxide, after it is cooled.

Upon charcoal, in the flame of reduction, and particularly with the addition of tin, the bead is colorless and transparent while hot, but while cooling becomes of a dark-gray color and opaque.

Oxide of bismuth is reduced, by fusion with carbonate of soda, as well in the oxidating as in the reducing flame, instantly to metallic bismuth.

As the above mentioned higher oxides of bismuth are converted by ignition into oxide of the metal and free oxygen, they have the same behavior before the blowpipe.

As bismuth occurs mostly in the metallic form, it is necessary to know how to distinguish it from metals similar to it. Its brittleness distinguishes it from lead, zinc and tin, as they are readily flattened by a stroke of the hammer, while bismuth is broken to pieces. Bismuth, in this latter respect, might perhaps be mistaken for antimony or tellurium; but, by the following examination, it is easy to separate bismuth from antimony or tellurium.

1. Neither bismuth nor antimony sublimates when heated in a glass tube closed at one end. At a temperature which is about to fuse the glass, tellurium yields a small quantity of a white vapor (some tellurium is oxidized to tellurous acid by the oxygen of the air in the tube). After that, a grey metallic sublimate settles on the sides of the tube.

2. Heated in an open tube, antimony yields a white vapor, which coats the inside of the glass tube, and can be driven by heat from one part of the tube to another without leaving a residue. The metallic globule is covered with a considerable quantity of fused oxide. Tellurium produces, under the same circumstances, an intense vapor, and deposits on the glass a white powder, which melts by heat into globules that run over the glass. The metallic globules are covered by fused, transparent, and nearly colorless oxide, which becomes white while cooling. By a high temperature, and with little access of air, metallic tellurium sublimes with the deposition of a grey powder. Bismuth produces, under similar treatment, scarcely any vapor, unless it is combined with sulphur. The metal is enveloped by fused oxide of a dark yellow color, which appears light yellow after being cooled. It acts upon the glass, and dissolves it.

3. Upon charcoal, exposed to the blowpipe flame, the three metals are volatilized, and yield a sublimate upon the charcoal. That of antimony is white, while those of bismuth and tellurium are dark yellow. By exposing them to the flame of reduction, the sublimate of tellurium disappears and communicates an intense green color to the flame. The antimony incrustation gives a feeble greenish-blue color, while the sublimate of bismuth gives no perceptible color in the light. It is, however, worthy of notice that if the operation takes place in the dark, a very pale blue flame will be seen with the bismuth.

(*c.*) *Tin* (Sn).—This metal does not occur in nature in the metallic state, very seldom in the sulphide, but chiefly in the oxide (tinstone). In the metallic state it is silver-white, possesses a very high lustre, is soft (but harder than lead), ductile, but has not much tenacity, and it is very malleable. The metal when it is cast gives a peculiar creaking noise when twisted or bent, which proceeds from the crystalline structure of the metal. This crystallization is quite clearly manifested by attacking the surface of the metal, or that of tin plate, with acids.

Tin is very slightly tarnished by exposure to the air. It fuses at 442°, and becomes grey, being a mixture of the oxide and the metal. At a high temperature even, tin is but little subject to pass off as vapor. It is soluble in aqua regia, and with the liberation of hydrogen, in hot sulphuric and hydrochloric acids, and in cold dilute nitric acid, without decomposing water, or the production of a gas, while nitrate of tin and nitrate of ammonia are formed. Concentrated nitric acid converts tin into insoluble tin acids.

(*a.*) *Protoxide of Tin* (SnO) is a dark-grey powder. Its hydrate is white, and is soluble in caustic alkalies. When this solution is heated, anhydrous crystalline black protoxide is separated. The soluble neutral salts of tin-protoxide are decomposed by the addition of water, and converted into acid soluble, and basic insoluble salts.

When protoxide of tin is ignited with free access of air, it takes fire and is converted with considerable intensity into the acids, producing white vapors. This is likewise the case if it is touched by a spark of fire from steel. The hydrate of the protoxide of tin can be ingnited by the flame of a candle, and glows like tinder.

(*β.*) *Sesquioxide of Tin* (Sn^2O^3) is a greyish-brown powder. Its hydrate is white, with a yellow tinge. It is soluble in aqua ammonia and in hydrochloric acid; this solution forms with solution of gold the "purple of Cassius."

(*γ.*) *Stannic Acid* (peroxide, SnO^2).—This acid occurs in nature crystallized in quadro-octahedrons, of a brown or an intense black color, and of great hardness (tinstone). Artificially prepared, it is a white or yellowish-white powder. It exists in two distinct or isomeric modifications, one of which is insoluble in acids (natural tin-acid) while the other (tin-acid prepared in the wet way) is soluble in acids. By ignition the soluble acid is converted into the insoluble. Both modifications form hydrates.

Reactions before the Blowpipe.—Metallic tin melts easily. It is covered in the flame of oxidation into a yellowish-white oxide, which is carried off sometimes by the stream of air which propels the flame. In the reduction flame, and upon charcoal, melting tin retains its metallic lustre, while a thin sublimate is produced upon the charcoal. This sublimate is light-yellow while hot, and gives a strong light in the flame of oxidation, and turns white while cooling. This sublimate is found near to the metal, and cannot be volatilized in the oxidation flame. In the flame of reduction it is reduced to metallic tin. Sometimes this incrustation is so imperceptible that it can scarcely be distinguished from the ashes of the charcoal. If such be the case, moisten it with a solution of cobalt, and expose it to the flame of oxidation, when the sublimate will exhibit, after cooling, a bluish-green color.

Protoxide of tin takes fire in the flame of oxidation, and burns with flame and some white vapor into tin acid, or stannic acid. In a strong and continued reduction flame, it may be reduced to metal, when the same sublimate above mentioned is visible. The sesquioxide of tin behaves as the above.

Stannic acid, heated in the flame of oxidation, does not melt and is not volatilized, but produces a strong light, and appears yellowish while hot, but changing as it cools to a dirty-yellow white color. In a strong and continued flame of reduction, it may be reduced likewise to the metallic state, with the production of the same sublimate as the above.

Borax dissolves tin compounds in the flame of oxidation, and upon platinum wire, very tardily, and in small quantity, to a transparent colorless bead, which remains clear after cooling.

and also when heated intermittingly. But if a saturated bead, after being completely cool, is exposed again to the flame of oxidation, at a low red heat, the bead while cooling is opaque, loses its globular form, and exhibits an indistinct crystallization. This is the case too in the flame of reduction, but if the bead is highly saturated, a part of the oxide is reduced.

Microcosmic Salt dissolves the oxides in the flame of reduction very tardily in a small quantity to a transparent colorless bead, which remains clear while cooling. If to this bead sesquioxide of iron is added in proper proportion, the sesquioxide loses its property of coloring the bead, but of course an excess of the iron salt will communicate to the bead its own characteristic color. In the flame of reduction no further alteration is visible.

Tin-oxides combine with carbonate of soda, in the flame of oxidation upon platinum wire, with intumescence to a bulky and confused mass, which is insoluble in more soda. Upon charcoal, in the reduction flame, it is easily reduced to a metallic globule. Certain compounds of tin-oxides, particularly if they contain tantalum, are by fusion with carbonate of soda reduced with difficulty ; but by the addition of some borax, the reduction to the metallic state is easily effected.

Tin-oxides exposed to the oxidation flame, then moistened with a solution of cobalt, and exposed again to the flame of oxidation, will exhibit, after having completely cooled, a bluish-green color.

EIGHTH GROUP.—MERCURY, ARSENIC.

These two metals are volatilized at a temperature lower than that of a red heat, and produce, therefore, no reactions with borax and microcosmic salt. Their oxides are easily reduced to the metallic state.

(*a.*) *Mercury* (Hg).—This metal occurs in nature chiefly combined with sulphur as a bisulphide.

It occurs still more rarely in the metallic form, or combined with silver, selenium, or chlorine.

Mercury, in the metallic state, has a strong lustre, and is liquid at ordinary temperatures, whereby it is distinguished from any other metal. It freezes at 40° and boils at 620°, but it evaporates at common temperatures. Pure mercury is unalterable. Upon being exposed to the air, it tarnishes only by admixture with other metals, turns grey on the surface, and loses its lustre. It is soluble in cold nitric acid and in concentrated hot sulphuric acid, but not in hydrochloric acid.

(χ.) *Protoxide of Mercury* (Hg^2O).—It is a black powder, which is decomposed by ignition into metallic mercury and oxygen. By digestion with certain acids, and particularly with caustic alkalies, it is converted into metallic mercury and peroxide. Some neutral salts of the protoxide are only partly soluble in water, as they are converted into basic insoluble and acid soluble salts.

Protoxide of mercury is completely insoluble in hydrochloric acid. Its neutral salts change blue litmus paper to red.

(β.) *Peroxide of Mercury* (HgO).—This oxide exists in two allotropic modifications. One is of a brick-red color, and the other is orange. Being exposed to heat, they turn black, but regain their respective colors upon cooling. They are decomposed at a high temperature into metallic mercury and oxygen. They yield with acids their own peculiar salts.

Mercury, in the metallic form, can never be mistaken for any other metal in consequence of its fluid condition at ordinary temperatures.

Exposed to the blowpipe flame, it is instantly volatilized. This is also the case with it when combined with other metals. The oxides of mercury are, in the oxidation and reduction flames, instantly reduced and volatilized. They do not produce any alteration with fluxes, as they are volatilized before the bead melts. Heated with carbonate of soda in a glass tube closed at one end, they are reduced to metallic mercury, which is volatilized, and condenses upon a cool portion of the tube as a grey powder. By cautious knocking against the tube, or by rubbing with a glass rod, this sublimate can be brought together into one globule of metallic mercury. Compounds of mercury can be most completely reduced by a mixture of neutral oxalate of potassa and cyanide of potassium. If the substance under examination contains such a small quantity of mercury that it cannot be distinguished by volatilization, a strip of gold leaf may be attached to an iron wire, and introduced during the experiment in the glass tube. The smallest trace of mercury will whiten the gold leaf in spots.

(*b.*) *Arsenic* (As).—This metal occurs in considerable quantity in nature, chiefly combined with sulphur or metals.

Arsenic, in the metallic state, is of a whitish-grey color, high lustre, and is crystalline, of a foliated structure, and is so brittle that it can be pulverized. It does not melt, but is volatilized at 356°. Its vapor has a strong alliaceous odor. Arsenic sublimes in irregular crystals. By exposure to the air it soon tarnishes, and is coated black. Being mixed with nitrate of potassa and inflamed, it detonates with vehemence. Mixed with carbonate of potassa, it is inflamed by a stroke of the hammer, and detonates violently.

Heated in oxygen gas, it is inflamed, and burns with a pale blue flame to arsenious acid.

(*β.*) *Arsenious Acid* (AsO^3).—This acid crystallizes in octahedrons, or, when fused, forms a colorless glass, which finally becomes opaque and enamel-like, or forms a white powder. It sublimes without change or decomposition. When heated for a longer while below the temperature of sublimation, it melts into a transparent, colorless, tough glass. The opaque acid is sparingly soluble in cold water, and still more soluble in hot water. It is converted, by continued boiling, into the transparent acid, which is much more soluble in water. Arsenious acid is easily dissolved by caustic potassa. It is also soluble in hydrochloric acid. This acid occurs associated with antimonious acid, protoxide of tin, protoxide of lead, and oxide of copper. It occurs likewise in very small quantity in ferruginous mineral springs.

(γ.) *Arsenic Acid* (AsO^5) is a white mass, which readily absorbs moisture and dissolves. It will not volatilize at a low red heat, nor will it decompose. Exposed to a strong heat, it is decomposed, yielding oxygen, and passing into arsenious acid.

Reactions before the Blowpipe.

Metallic arsenic, heated in a glass tube closed at one end, yields a black sublimate of a metallic lustre, and at the same time gives out the characteristic alliaceous odor. This is the case too with alloys of arsenic, if there is a maximum quantity of arsenic present.

When heated in a glass tube open at both ends, metallic arsenic is oxidized to arsenious acid, which appears as a white crystalline sublimate on the sides of the glass tube. This deposit will occur at some distance from the assay, in consequence of the great volatility of the arsenic. The sublimate can be driven from one place upon the tube to another, by a very low heat. Alloys of arsenic are converted into basic arseniates of metal oxides, while surplus arsenic is converted into arsenious acid, which sublimes on the tube. If too much arsenic is used for this experiment, a dark-brown incrustation will sublime upon the sides of the tube which will give an alliaceous smell. If this sublimate should be deposited near the assay, then it resembles the white sublimate of arsenious acid.

Heated upon charcoal, metallic arsenic is volatilized before it melts, and incrusts the charcoal in the flame of oxidation as a white deposit of arsenious acid. This sublimate appears sometimes of a greyish color, and takes place at some distance from the assay. When heated slightly with the blowpipe flame, this sublimate is instantly driven away, and being heated rapidly in the reduction flame, it disappears with a light blue tinge, while the usual alliaceous or garlic smell may be discerned.

Arsenious acid sublimes in both glass tubes very readily, as a white crystalline sublimate. These crystals appear to be regular octahedrons when observed under the microscope. Upon charcoal it instantly volatilizes, and when heated, the characteristic garlic smell may be observed.

Arsenic acid yields, heated strongly in a glass tube closed at one end, oxygen and arsenious acid, the latter of which sublimes in the cool portions of the tube. Compounds of arsenic produce, in consequence of their volatility, no reactions with fluxes. Being heated upon charcoal with carbonate of soda, they are reduced to metallic arsenic which may be detected by the alliaceous odor peculiar to all the arsenic compounds when volatilized.

NINTH GROUP.—COPPER, SILVER, GOLD.

These metals are not volatile, neither are their oxides. They are reduced to the metallic state, by fusion with carbonate of soda, when they melt to a metallic grain. The oxides of silver and gold are reduced *per se* to the metallic state by ignition. In the reduction of the oxides of this group, no sublimate is visible upon the charcoal.

(*a.*) *Copper* (Cu).—This metal occurs in the metallic state, also as the protoxide, and as oxides combined with acids in different salts (carbonate of copper as malachite, etc.) The sulphide of copper is the principal ore of copper occurring in nature. In the metallic state, copper is of a red color, has great lustre and tenacity, is ductile and malleable, and crystallizes in octahedrons and cubes. It melts at a bright red heat, is more difficult than silver to fuse, but fuses more readily than gold. It absorbs oxygen while melting. There arises from its surface a fine dust of metallic globules, which are covered with the protoxide. The surface of the metal is likewise covered with the protoxide. Copper exposed to moist air tarnishes, and is converted into hydratic carbonate of copper. When ignited in the open air, it is soon covered with the brownish-red protoxide.

(χ.) *Protoxide of Copper* (Cu^2O).—This oxide occurs in nature, crystallized in octahedrons of a ruby-red color, of a lamellar structure, and transparent. Artificially prepared, it forms a powder of the same color. It is decomposed by dilute acids into salts of peroxide and metal. It is converted by ignition, with free access of air, into peroxide.

(β.) *Oxide of Copper* (CuO).—This oxide is a dark-brown or black powder. It is dissolved by acids, with a blue or green-colored solution. It is soluble in aqua ammonia, and the solution is of a dark blue color.

Reactions before the Blowpipe.—Oxide of copper exposed upon platinum wire to the inmost flame (the blue flame), communicates to the external flame a green color. Heated upon charcoal in the oxidation flame, it melts to a black ball, soon spreads over the charcoal, and is partially reduced.

Exposed to the reduction flame, at a temperature which will not melt copper, it is reduced with a bright metallic lustre, but as soon as the blast ceases, the surface of the metal becomes oxidized, and appears dark brown or black. If the temperature is continued still higher, it melts to a metallic grain.

Borax dissolves the oxide of copper in the flame of oxidation to a clear green-colored bead, even if the quantity of oxide be quite small, but by cooling, the bead becomes blue. In the flame of reduction upon platinum wire, the bead soon becomes colorless, but while cooling presents a red color (protoxide of copper). This bead is opaque, but, if too much of the oxide is added, a part of it is reduced to metal, which is visible by breaking the metallic grain.

Upon charcoal, the oxide is reduced to the metal, and the bead appears colorless after cooling. With the addition of some tin, the bead becomes brownish-red and opaque after cooling.

Microcosmic Salt dissolves oxide of copper in the flame of oxidation to a green bead, not so intensely colored as the borax bead. In the reduction flame the bead, if pretty well saturated, becomes dark-green while hot, and brownish-red when cool, opaque and enamel-like. If the oxide is so little that no reaction is visible, by the addition of some tin, the bead appears colorless while hot, and dark brownish-red and opaque when cold.

Carbonate of Soda dissolves oxide of copper in the oxidation flame upon platinum wire, to a clear, green bead, which loses its color when cooling, and becomes opaque.

Upon charcoal, it is reduced to the metal, the soda is absorbed by the charcoal, and the metallic particles melt with sufficient heat to a grain.

(*b.*) *Silver* (Ag).—This metal occurs in nature in the metallic state, and in combination with other metals, particularly with lead. It also occurs as the sulphide in several mines. It crystallizes in cubes and octahėdrons ; is of a pure white color, great lustre, is very malleable and ductile, and is softer than copper, but harder than gold. It is not oxidizable, neither at common temperatures nor at those which are considerably higher. It is soluble in dilute nitric acid, and in boiling concentrated sulphuric acid.

(χ.) *Protoxide of Silver* (Ag^2O).—It is a black powder. It is converted by acids and ammonia into oxide and metal.

(β.) *Oxide of Silver* (AgO).—It is a greyish-brown or black powder, and is the base of the silver salts. With aqua ammonia, it is converted into the black, fulminating silver.

(γ.) *Superoxide or Binoxide of Silver* (AgO^2).—This oxide occurs in black needles or octahedral crystals of great metallic lustre. It is dissolved by the oxygen acids with the disengagement of oxygen gas.

Behavior before the Blowpipe.—When exposed to the flames of oxidation and reduction, the oxides of silver are instantly reduced to the metallic state.

Borax dissolves silver-oxides upon platinum wire in the

oxidation flame but partially, while the other portion is reduced, the bead appearing opalescent after cooling, in correspondence to the degree of saturation. The bead becomes grey in the flame of reduction, the reduced silver melting to a grain, and the bead is rendered clear and colorless again.

Microcosmic Salt dissolves oxides of silver in the flame of oxidation upon platinum wire to a transparent yellowish bead, which presents, when much of the oxide is present, an opalescent appearance.

In the flame of reduction, the reaction is analogous to that of borax.

By fusion with carbonate of soda in the oxidation and reduction flames, the silver oxides are instantly reduced to metallic silver, which fuses into one or more grains.

(*c*.) *Gold* (Au).—This metal occurs mostly in the metallic state, but frequently mixed with ores, and with other metals. Gold crystallizes in cubes and octahedrons, is of a beautiful yellow color, great lustre, and is the most malleable and ductile of all the metals. It melts at a higher temperature than copper, gives a green colored light when fused, and contracts greatly when cooling. It does not oxidize at ordinary temperatures, nor when heated much above them. It is soluble in nitro-hydrochloric acid (*aqua regia*).

(χ.) *Protoxide of Gold* (Au^2O).—This oxide is a dark violet colored powder which is converted by a temperature of 540° into metallic gold and oxygen. It is only soluble in aqua regia. Treated with hydrochloric acid, it yields the chloride of gold and the metal. With aqua ammonia, it yields the fulminating gold, which is a blue mass and very explosive.

(χ.) *Peroxide of Gold* (Au^2O^3).—This oxide is an olive-green or dark brown powder, containing variable quantities of water. Decomposed at 530°, it yields metallic gold and oxygen.

Reactions before the Blowpipe.—Oxides of gold are reduced, in both the oxidation and reduction flames, to the metal, which fuses to grains

Borax does not dissolve it, but it is reduced to the metallic state in this flux in either flame. The reduced metal fuses upon charcoal to a grain.

Microcosmic Salt presents the same reactions as borax.

When fused with soda, upon charcoal, the soda is absorbed, and the gold remains as a metallic grain.

TENTH GROUP.—MOLYBDENUM, OSMIUM.

These metals are not volatile, and are infusible before the blowpipe; but some of their oxides are volatile, and can be reduced to an infusible metallic powder.

(*a.*) *Molybdenum* (Mo) occurs in the metallic state; also combined with sulphur, or as molybdic acid combined with lead. It is a white, brittle metal, and is unaltered by exposure to the air. When heated until it begins to glow, it is converted into a brown oxide. Heated at a continued dull red heat, it turns blue. At a higher temperature, it is oxidized to molybdic acid, when it glimmers and smokes, and is converted into crystallized molybdic acid upon the surface.

(χ.) *Protoxide of Molybdenum* (MoO).—This oxide is a black powder.

(χ.) *Deutoxide of Molybdenum* (MoO^2).—This oxide is a dark copper-colored crystalline powder.

Reactions before the Blowpipe.—Metallic molybdenum, its protoxide and binoxide, are converted in the oxidation flame into molybdic acid. This acid fuses in the flame of oxidation to a brown liquid, which spreads, volatilizes, and sublimes upon the charcoal as a yellow powder, which appears crystalline in the vicinity of the assay. This sublimate becomes white after cooling. Beyond this sublimate there is visible a thin and not volatile ore of binoxide, after cooling; this is of a dark copper-red color, and presenting a metallic lustre.

Heated in a glass tube, closed at one end, it melts to a brown mass, vaporizes and sublimates to a white powder upon a cool portion of the tube. Immediately above the assay, yellow crystals are visible; these crystals are colorless after cooling, and the fused mass becomes light yellow-colored and crystalline.

Upon platinum foil, in the flame of oxidation, it melts and vaporizes, and becomes light yellow and crystalline after cooling. In the reduction flame it becomes blue, and brown-colored if the heat is increased.

Upon charcoal, in the reduction flame, it is absorbed by the charcoal; and, with an increase of the temperature, it is reduced to the metal, which remains as a grey powder after washing off the particles of charcoal.

Borax dissolves it, in the oxidation flame, upon platinum wire easily, and in great quantity, to a clear yellow, which becomes colorless while cooling. By the addition of more of the molybdenic acid the bead is dark yellow, or red while hot, and opalescent when cold. In the reduction flame, the color of the bead is changed to brown and transparent. By the addition of more of the acid, it becomes opaque.

Microcosmic Salt dissolves it in the oxidation flame, upon platinum wire, to a clear, yellowish-green bead, which becomes colorless after cooling. In the reduction flame the bead is very dark and opaque, but becomes of a bright green after cooling. This is the case likewise upon charcoal.

Carbonate of Soda dissolves it upon platinum wire in the oxidation flame with intumescence, to a clear bead, which appears milk-white after cooling. Upon charcoal the soda and the molybdic acid are absorbed, the latter is reduced to the metallic state, the metal remaining as a grey powder after washing off the particles of charcoal. When molybdic acid, or any other oxide of this metal, is exposed upon platinum wire, or with platinum tongs, to the point of the blue flame, a yellowish-green color is communicated to the external flame. If also any of the compounds of molybdenum are mixed in the form of a powder with concentrated sulphuric acid and alcohol, and the latter inflamed, the flame of the alcohol appears colored green.

(*c.*) *Osmium* (Os).—This metal occurs associated with platinum. It is of a bluish-grey color, and is very brittle. Ignited in the open air, it is oxidized to volatile osmic acid, which is possessed of a pungent smell, and affects the eyes. It communicates a bright white color to the flame of alcohol. Osmium oxide (OsO^2) is converted in the oxidation flame to osmic acid, which is volatilized with a peculiar smell, leaving a sublimate.

In the reduction flame it is reduced to a dark-brown infusible metallic powder. It produces no reactions with fluxes. Carbonate of soda reduces it upon charcoal to an infusible metallic powder, which appears, after washing off the particles of charcoal, of a dark-brown color.

ELEVENTH GROUP.—PLATINUM, PALLADIUM, IRIDIUM, RHODIUM, RUTHENIUM.

These metals are infusible before the blowpipe. They are not volatile, nor are they oxidizable. Their oxides are, in both flames, reduced to a metallic and infusible powder. They give no reactions with fluxes, but are separated in the metallic form. These metals are generally found associated together in the native platinum, also with traces of copper, lead, and iron.

The metal palladium is found native, associated with iridium and platinum. This metal generally occurs in greatest quantity in Brazil.

The metal rhodium is found along with platinum, but in very small quantities.

Iridium occurs in nature associated with osmium, gold, and platinum, in the mines of Russia. Its great hardness has rendered it desirable for the points of gold pens. In South America this metal is found native, associated with platinum and osmium. The latter metal, associated with platinum and iridium, has been found in South America.

As these metals will not oxidize or dissolve, they cannot be separated from each other by the blowpipe with the reagents peculiar to that species of analysis. It is true that colors may be discerned in the beads, but these tints proceed from the presence of small traces of copper, iron, etc.

The ore of osmium and iridium can be decomposed, and the former recognized by its fetid odor. This metal, strongly ignited in a glass tube with nitrate of potash, is converted to the oxide of osmium, which gives an odor not unlike the chloride of sulphur.

As the metals of this group are very rare ones, especially the last four ones, we shall not devote an especial division to each of them. For a more detailed statement of their reactions, the student is referred to the large works upon blowpipe analysis.

CLASS III.

NON-METALLIC SUBSTANCES.

1. *Water*—2. *Nitric Acid*—3. *Carbon*—4. *Phosphorus*—5. *Sulphur* — 6. *Boron* — 7. *Silicon* — 8. *Chlorine*—9. *Bromine*—10. *Iodine*—11. *Fluorine*—12. *Cyanogen*—13. *Seleninm.*

(1.) *Water* (HO).—Pure distilled water is composed of one volume of oxygen, and two volumes of hydrogen gases; or, by weight, of one part of hydrogen to eight parts of oxygen gases. Water is never found pure in nature, but possessing great solvent properties, it always is found with variable proportions of those substances it is most liable to meet with, dissolved in it. Thus it derives various designations depending upon the nature of the substance it may hold in solution, as lime-water, etc.

In taking cognizance of water in relation to blowpipe analysis, we regard it only as existing in minerals. The examination for water is generally performed thus: the substance may be placed in a dry tube, and then submitted to heat over a spirit-lamp. If the water exists in the mineral mechanically it will soon be driven off, but if it exists chemically combined, the heat will fail to drive it off, or if it does, it will only partially effect it. The water will condense upon the cool portions of the tube, where it can be readily discerned. If the water exists chemically combined, a much stronger heat must be applied in order to separate it.

Many substances may be perhaps mistaken for water by the beginner, such as the volatile acids, etc.

(2) *Nitric Acid* (NO^5).—Nitric acid occurs in nature in potash and soda saltpetre. These salts are generally impure, containing lime, as the sulphate, carbonate and nitrate, and also iron in small quantity. The soda saltpetre generally contains a quantity of the chloride of sodium. The salts containing nitric acid deflagrate when heated on charcoal. Substances containing nitric acid may be heated in a glass tube closed at one end, by which the characteristic red fumes of nitrous acid are eliminated. If the acid be in too minute a quantity to be thus distinguished, a portion of the substance may be intimately mixed with some bisulphate of potash, and treated as above. The sulphuric acid of the bisulphate combines with the base, and liberates the nitric acid, while the tube contains the nitrous acid gas.

The nitrate of potassa, when heated in a glass tube, fuses to a clear glass, but gives off no water. When fused on platinum wire, it communicates to the external flame the characteristic violet color. When fused and ignited on charcoal, its surface becomes frothy, indicating the nitric acid.

(3.) *Carbon* (C).—Carbon is found in nature in the pure crystallized state as the diamond. It occurs likewise in several allotropic states as graphite, plumbago, charcoal, anthracite, etc. It exists in large quantities combined with oxygen as carbonic acid.

The diamond, although combustible, requires too high a heat for its combustion to enable us to burn it with the blowpipe. When excluded from the air, it may be heated to whiteness without undergoing fusion, but with the free access of air it burns at a temperature of 703° C, and is converted into carbonic acid. If mixed with nitre, the potassa retains the carbonic acid, and the carbon may be thus easily estimated. If a mineral containing carbonic acid is heated, the gas escapes with effervescence, or a strong mineral acid as the hydrochloric will expel the acid with the characteristic effervescence.

(4.) *Phosphorus, Phosphoric Acid* (PO^5).—This acid occurs in a variety of minerals, associated with yttria, copper, uranium, iron, lead, manganese, etc. Phosphoric acid may be detected in minerals by pursuing the following process: dip a small piece of the mineral in sulphuric acid, and place it in the platinum tongs: this is heated at the point of the blue flame, when the outer flame will become colored of a greenish-blue hue. This color will not be mistaken for those of boracic acid, copper, or baryta. Some of the phosphoric minerals, when heated in the inner flame, will color the outer flame green.

If alumina be present with the phosphoric acid, the following wet method should be adopted for the detection of the latter: the substance should be powdered in the agate mortar with a mixture of six parts of soda, and one and a half parts of silica. The entire mass should now be placed on charcoal, and melted in the flame of oxidation. The residue should be treated with boiling water, which dissolves the phosphate and the excess of carbonate of soda, while the silicate of alumina, with some of the soda, is left. The clear liquor is now treated with acetic acid, and heated over the spirit-lamp, and a small portion of crystallized nitrate of silver added; a lemon-yellow precipitate of phosphate of silver is quickly developed. Previous to the addition of the nitrate, the liquor should be well heated; otherwise, a white precipitate of dipyrophosphate of silver will be produced.

If the examination be of any of the metallic phosphides, the substances should be powdered in the agate mortar, and fused with nitrate of potassa on the platinum wire; the fused mass should be treated with soda in the same manner as any substance containing phosphoric acid. The metal and the phosphorus are oxidized, while the phosphate of potassa is fused, and the metallic oxide separates.

(5.) *Sulphur* (S).—Sulphur is found native in crystals It is frequently found associated with lime, iron, silica, carbon, etc., and combined extensively with metals.

The principal acid of sulphur (the sulphuric, SO^3) occurs combined with the earths, the alkalies, and the metallic oxides. Native sulphur is recognized, when heated upon charcoal, by its odor (sulphurous acid) and the blue color of its flame. The compounds of sulphur may be detected by several methods. If the substance is heated in a glass tube, closed at one end, the yellow sublimate of sulphur will subside upon the cool portions of the tube; if the substance should also contain arsenic, the sublimate will present itself as a light brown incrustation, consisting of the sulphide of arsenic.

If the assay is heated in the open glass tube, sulphurous acid will thus be generated; but, if the gas is too little to be detected by the smell, a strip of moistened litmus paper will indicate the presence of the acid.

The assay will give off sulphurous fumes if heated in the flame of oxidation.

If the powdered substance is fused with two parts of soda, and one part of borax, upon charcoal, the sulphide of sodium is formed. This salt, if moistened and applied to a polished silver surface, will blacken it. The borax serves no other purpose than to prevent the absorption of the formed sulphide of sodium by the charcoal. As selenium will blacken silver in the manner above indicated, the presence of this substance should be first ascertained, by heating the assay; when, if it be present, the characteristic horse-radish odor will reveal the fact.

Sulphuric acid may be detected by fusing the substance with two parts of soda, and one part of borax, on charcoal, in the flame of reduction; the mass must now be wetted with water, and placed in contact with a surface of bright silver; when, if sulphuric acid be present, the silver will become blackened.

Or the substance may be fused with silicate of soda in the flame of reduction. In this case, the soda combines with a portion of the sulphuric acid, which is then reduced to the sulphide, while the bead becomes of an orange or red color, depending upon the amount of the sulphuric acid present. If the assay should, however, be colored, then the previous treatment should be resorted to.

(6.) *Boron, Boracic Acid* (BO^3).—This acid occurs in nature in several minerals combined with various bases, such as magnesia, lime, soda, alumina, etc. Combined with water, this acid exists in nature as the native boracic acid; this acid gives with test paper prepared from Brazil wood, when moistened with water, a characteristic reaction, for the paper becomes completely bleached. An alcohol solution turns curcuma test paper brown. Heated on charcoal, it fuses to a clear bead; but, if the sulphate of lime be present, the bead becomes opaque upon cooling.

The following reaction is a certain one: the substance is pulverized and mixed with a flux of four and a half parts of bisulphate of potassa, and one part of pulverized fluoride of calcium. The whole is made into a paste with water, and the assay is placed on the platinum wire, and submitted to the point of the blue flame. While the assay is melting, fluoboric gas is disengaged, which tinges the outer flame green. If but a small portion of boracic acid is present, the color will be quite evanescent.

(7.) *Silica, Silicic Acid* (SiO^3).—This acid exists in the greatest plenty, forming no inconsiderable portion of the solid part of this earth. It exists nearly pure in crystallized quartz, chalcedony, cornelian, flint, etc., the coloring ingredients of these minerals being generally iron or manganese.

With *microcosmic salt*, silica forms a bead in the flame of oxidation which, while hot, is clear, while the separated silica floats in it. A platinum wire is generally used for the purpose, the end of it being first dipped in the salt which is fused into a bead, after which the silica must be added, and then the bead submitted to the flame of oxidation.

The silicates dissolve in soda but partially, and then with effervescence. If the oxygen of the acid be twice that of the base, a clear bead will be obtained that will retain its transparency when cold. If the soda be added in small quantity, the bead will then be opaque. In the first instance, a part of the base which separates is re-dissolved, and, therefore, the transparency of the glass; but, if too large a quantity of the soda is added, the separation of the base is sufficient to render the assay infusible.

(8.) *Chlorine* (Cl).—Chlorine exists in nature always in combination, as the chlorides of sodium, potassium, calcium, ammonium, magnesia, silver, mercury, lead, copper, etc.

The chlorine existing in metallic chlorides may be detected as follows: the wet way may be accomplished in the following manner. If the substance is insoluble, it must be melted with soda to render it soluble; if it be already soluble it must be dissolved in pure water, and nitrate of silver added, when the one ten-thousandth part of chlorine will manifest its presence by imparting a milky hue to the fluid.

By the blowpipe, chlorine may be detected in the following manner: Oxide of copper is dissolved in microcosmic salt on the platinum wire in the flame of oxidation, and a clear bead is obtained. The substance containing the chlorine is now added, and heat is applied. The assay will soon be enveloped by a blue or purplish flame. As none of the acids that occur in the mineral kingdom give this reaction, chlorine cannot be confounded with them, for those which impart a color to the flame, when mixed with a copper salt, will not do so when tested in the microcosmic salt bead as above indicated.

If the assay is soluble in water, the following method may be followed: a small quantity of sulphate of copper or iron is dissolved; a few drops of the solution is placed upon a bright surface of silver, and the metallic chloride added; when, if chlorine is present, the silver is blackened. If the chloride is insoluble in water, it must be rendered soluble by fusion upon a platinum wire with soda, and then treated as above.*

* Plattner.

(9.) *Bromine* (Br).—The bromide of magnesium and sodium exists in many salt springs, and it is from these that the bromine of commerce is obtained. The metallic bromides give the same reactions on silver with the microcosmic bead and copper salt as the metallic chlorides. The purplish color which, however, characterizes the chlorides, is more inclined to greenish with the bromides. If the substance be placed in a flask or glass tube, and fused with bisulphate of potassa, over the spirit-lamp, sulphurous gas and bromine will be eliminated. Bromine will be readily detected by its yellow color and its smell. Bromine may be readily detected by passing a current of chlorine through the fluid, after which ether is added and the whole is agitated. The ether rises to the top, carrying with it the bromine in solution; after being withdrawn, this ether is mixed with potassa, by which the bromide and bromate of potassa are formed. The solution is evaporated to dryness, the residue is fused in a platinum vessel, the bromate is decomposed, while the bromide remains; this must be distilled with sulphuric acid and the binoxide of manganese. A red or brown vapor will then appear, indicating the presence of bromine; this vapor will color starch paste—which may be put in the receiver on purpose—of a deep orange color.

If, to a solution containing a bromide, concentrated sulphuric or nitric acid be added, the bromine is liberated and colors the solution yellow or red. The hypochlorites act in the same manner. The bromine salts are coming into use extensively in photography, in consequence of their greater sensitiveness to the action of light than the chlorides alone.

(10.) *Iodine* (I).—This element occurs in salt-springs, generally combined with sodium; it also exists in rock-salt; it has likewise been found in sea-water, also in a mineral from Mexico, in combination with silver, and in one from Silesia, in combination with zinc. As sea-water contains iodine, we would consequently expect to find it existing in the sea-weeds, and it is generally from the ashes of these that it is obtained in commerce.

When the metallic iodides are fused with the microcosmic salt and copper, as previously indicated, they impart a green color to the flame. This color cannot be mistaken for the color imparted to the flame by copper alone. When the metallic iodides are fused in a glass tube, closed at one end, with the bisulphate of potassa, the vapor of iodine is liberated, and may be recognized by its characteristic color. Those mineral waters containing iodine can be treated the same as for bromine, as previously indicated, while the violet-colored vapor of the iodine can be easily discerned. The nitrate of silver is the best test for iodine, the yellow color of the iodide of silver being not easily mistaken, while its almost insolubility in ammonia will confirm its identity. The chloride of silver, on the contrary, dissolves in ammonia with the greatest facility.

The reactions of iodine are similar to those of bromine with concentrated sulphuric acid and binoxide of manganese, and with nitric acid: The iodine is released and, if the quantity be not too great, colors the liquid brown. If there be a considerable quantity of iodine present, it is precipitated as a dark colored powder. Either of these, when heated, gives out the violet-color of the iodine.

With starch paste free iodine combines, producing a deep blue compound. If, however, the iodine be in very minute quantity, the color, instead of being blue, will be light violet or rose color.

If to a solution of the sulphate of copper, to which a small portion of sulphurous acid has been added, a liquid containing iodine and bromine is poured in, a dirty, white precipitate of the subiodide of copper is produced, and the bromine remains in the solution. The latter may then be tested for the bromine by strong sulphuric acid.

(11.) *Fluorine* (Fl).—This element exists combined with sodium, calcium, lithium, aluminium, magnesium, yttrium, and cerium. Fluorine also exists in the enamel of the teeth, and in the bones of some animals. This element has a strong affinity for hydrogen, and, therefore, we find it frequently in the form of hydrofluoric acid. Brazil-wood paper is the most delicate test for hydrofluoric acid, which it tinges of a light yellow color. Phosphoric acid likewise colors Brazil paper yellow, but as this acid is not volatile at a heat sufficient to examine hydrofluoric acid, there can be no mistake. If the substance is supposed to contain this acid, it should be placed on a slip of glass, and moistened with hydrochloric acid, when the test paper may be applied, and the characteristic yellow color will indicate the presence of the fluorine.

As hydrofluoric acid acts upon glass, this property may be used for its detection. The substance may be put into a glass tube, and sulphuric acid poured upon it in sufficient quantity to moisten it; a slight heat applied to the tube will develop the acid, which will act upon the glass of the tube. If the acid is retained in the mineral by a feeble affinity, and water be present, a piece of it may be put in the tube and heated, when the acid gas will be eliminated. The test paper will indicate its presence, even before it has time to act upon the glass. If the temperature be too high, fluosilicic acid is generated, and will form a silicious incrustation upon the cool portion of the tube.

If the fluorine is too minute to produce either of the above reactions, then the following process, recommended by Plattner, should be followed: the assay should be mixed with metaphosphate of soda, formed by heating the microcosmic salt to dull redness. The mass must then be placed in an open glass tube, in such a position that there will be an access of hot air from the flame. Thus aqueous hydrofluoric acid is formed, which can be recognized by its smell being more suffocating than chlorine, and also by the etching produced by the condensation of vapor in the tube. Moist Brazil paper, applied to the extremity of the tube, will be instantly colored yellow.

Merlet's method for the detection of this acid is the following: * Pulverize the substance for examination, then triturate

* Quoted by Plattner.

it to an impalpable powder, and mix it with an equal part of bisulphate of potassa. Heat the mass gradually in a moderately wide test-tube. The judicious application of heat must be strictly observed, for if the operator first heats the part of the tube where the assay rests, the whole may be lost on account of the glass being shattered. The spirit-flame must be first applied to the fore part of the tube, and then made to recede slowly until it fuses the assay. After the mixture has been for some time kept in a molten state, the lamp must be withdrawn, and the part containing the assay severed with a file. The fore part of the tube must then be well washed, and afterwards dried with bibulous paper. Should the fluorine contained in the substance be appreciable, the glass tube, when held up to the light, will be found to have lost its transparency, and to be very rough to the touch.

Great care should be observed not to allow this very corrosive acid to come into contact with the skin, as an ulcer will be the consequence that will be extremely difficult to heal.

When hydrofluoric acid comes in contact with any silicious substance, hydrofluosilicic acid gas is always formed.

(12.) *Selenium* (Se).—This element occurs in combination with lead as the selenide, and with copper as the selenide of copper. It exists also combined with cobalt and lead, as the selenide of these metals; also as the selenide of lead and mercury.

The smallest trace of selenium may be detected by igniting a small piece of charcoal in the flame of oxidation, when the peculiar and unmistakable odor of decayed horse-radish will indicate the presence of that element. An orange vapor is eliminated if the selenium be present in any quantity, while there is an incrustation around the assay of a grey color, with a metallic lustre. This incrustation frequently presents a reddish-violet color at its exterior edges, often running into a deep blue. If a substance containing selenium be placed in a glass tube, closed at one end, and submitted to heat, the selenium is sublimed, with an orange-colored vapor, and with the characteristic odor of that substance. Upon the cool portions of the tube a steel-grey sublimate is deposited, and, beyond that, can be discerned small crystals of selenic acid. If the mineral be the seleniferous lead glance, sulphurous acid gas will be given off, and may be detected by the smell, or by a strip of moistened litmus paper.

If arsenic is present, heating upon charcoal will quickly lead to the determination of the one from the other.

TABULAR STATEMENT OF THE REACTIONS OF MINERALS BEFORE THE BLOWPIPE.

In PART THIRD of this work, commencing at page 109, the student will find a sufficiently explicit description of the blowpipe reactions of those principal substances that would be likely to come beneath his attention. The following tabular statement of those reactions—which we take from Scheerer and Blanford's excellent little work upon the blowpipe—will be of great benefit, as a vehicle for consultation, when the want of time—or during the hurry of an examination—precludes the attentive perusal of the more lengthy descriptions in the text.

In the examination of minerals, before the student avails himself of the aid of the blowpipe, he should not neglect to examine the specimen rigidly in relation to its physical characters, such as its hardness, lustre, color, and peculiar crystallization. It is where the difference of two minerals cannot be distinguished by their physical appearance, that the aid of the blowpipe comes in most significantly as an auxiliary. For instance, the two minerals molybdenite and graphite resemble each other very closely, when examined in regard to their physical appearance, but the blowpipe will quickly discriminate them, for if a small piece of the former mineral be placed in the flame of oxidation, a bright green color will be communicated to the flame beyond it, while in the latter there will be no color. Thus, in a very short time, these two minerals can be distinguished from each other by aid of the blowpipe, while no amount of physical examination could determine that point. The blowpipe is equally an indispensable instrument in the determination of certain minerals which may exist in others as essential or non-essential constituents of them. For instance, should a minute quantity of manganese be present in a mineral, it must be fused with twice its bulk of a mixture of two parts of carbonate of soda, and one part of the nitrate of potassa, in the flame of oxidation upon platinum foil. The manganate of soda thus formed will color the fused mass of a bluish-green tint.

Or a slight quantity of arsenic may be discerned by the following process récommended by Plattner:* one grain of the finely pulverized metal is mixed with six grains of nitrate of potassa, and slowly heated on the platinum spoon. By this means the metals are oxidized, while the arseniate of potassa is obtained. Then boil the fused mass in a small quantity of water in a porcelain vessel till all the arseniate is dissolved. The metallic oxides are allowed to subside, and the above solution decanted off into another porcelain vessel. A few drops of sulphuric acid are added, and the solution boiled to expel the nitric acid, after which it is evaporated to dryness. In this operation, the sulphuric acid should be added only in sufficient quantity to drive off the nitric acid, or, at the utmost, to form a bisulphate with the excess of potassa. When dry, the salt thus obtained is pulverized in an agate mortar, and mixed with about three times its volume of oxalate of potassa, and a little charcoal powder. The mixture is introduced into a glass bulb having a narrow neck, and gently warmed over a spirit-lamp in order to drive off the moisture, which must be absorbed by a piece of blotting-paper in the neck of the bulb. After a short time, the temperature is increased to a low red heat, at which the arsenious acid is reduced and the metallic arsenic sublimed, and which re-condenses in the neck of the

* Quoted by Scheerer.

bulb. If there the arsenic be so small in quantity as to exhibit no metallic lustre, the neck of the bulb may be cut off with a file immediately above the sublimate, and the latter exposed to the flame of the blowpipe, when the arsenic is volatilized, and may be recognized by its garlic odor.

If the presence of cadmium is suspected in zinc-blende, it may be detected by fusing a small piece of the blende upon charcoal in carbonate of soda. The peculiar bright yellow sublimate of the oxide of cadmium, if it be present, will not fail to indicate it. This incrustation can be easily distinguished from that of zinc. Thus, with the three illustrations we have given, the student will readily comprehend the great utility of the blowpipe in the examination of minerals.

Although the following tables were not arranged especially for the last part of this work, still this arrangement is so good that by their consultation the student will readily comprehend at a glance what requires some detail to explain, and we feel no hesitation in saying that, although they are not very copious, they will not fail to impart a vast amount of information, if consulted with any degree of carefulness.

The minerals given are such as are best known to English and American mineralogists under the names specified. For more detailed reactions than could be crowded into a table, the student will have to consult the particular substance as treated in Part Third. If this part is perused carefully previous to consulting the tables, these will be found eminently serviceable as a refresher of the memory, and may thus save much time and trouble.

And, finally, we would certainly recommend the student, after he shall have gone through our little volume (if he is ambitious of making himself a thorough blowpipe analyst), to then take up the larger works of Berzelius and Plattner, for our treatise pretends to nothing more than a humble introduction to these more copious and scientific works.

Mineral.	Formula.	Behavior in glass-bulb.	Behavior on platinum foil.
Diamond....	C		In fine powder is slowly consumed without residue in a strong oxidizing flame.
Graphite.....	C with some iron, silica, etc.	Generally gives off water.	Is slowly consumed leaving more or less ash, principally Fe^2O^3.
Anthracite...	$C+x\dot{H}$ and some ash.	Evolves water.	Is slowly consumed with the exception of a small quantity of ash.
Wallsend-coal	C,H,N,O,S and ash.	Intumesces and gives off water and tarry matters which partly condense in bulb, and leave a porous coke.	Takes fire under blowpipe flame, and burns with a smoky flame, depositing much soot and leaving a porous cinder which burns slowly and leaves a small ash.
Cannel-coal..	C,H,N,O,S and ash.	As the preceding, but gives off more tar.	Similar to the preceding. If held to the lamp-flame, takes fire and burns for some seconds.
Brown-coal..	C,H,N,O,S and ash.	Gives off much water and tar, and leaves a porous cinder retaining the form of the original fragment.	Burns slowly and without flame, leaving some ash.
Asphaltum...	C+H+O.	Fuses with ease affording an	Takes fire and burns with a bright

Continuation of page 181.

Mineral.	Formula.	Behavior	
		in glass-bulb.	on platinum foil.
Asphaltum...	C+H+O.	empyreumatic oil having an alkaline reaction, and combustible gases, and leaves a carbonaceous residue, which is entirely consumed under the blowpipe flame, except a little ash.	flame and a thick smoke.
Elaterite	C+H.	Fuses and gives off water having an acid reaction, naphtha and a tarry fluid, which chiefly condense in the neck of the bulb, and leave a light, pulverulent, carbonaceous residue.	Fuses, takes fire, and burns with a smoky flame, leaving a carbonaceous residue, which under the blowpipe flame, is quickly consumed, with the exception of the ashes.
Hachettine ..	C+H.	Fuses to a clear colorless liquid, which solidifies on cooling and has a tallow-like smell.	Fuses, takes fire, and burns with a bright flame until entirely consumed.
Ozokerite....	C+H.	Fuses readily to a clear brown oily fluid, which solidifies on cooling.	As the preceding.
Amber......	C+H+O.	Fuses with difficulty, and affords water, an empyreumatic oil, and succinic acid which condense in the	Takes fire and burns with a yellow flame and a peculiar aromatic odor.

Continuation of page 182.

Mineral.	Formula.	Behavior	
		in glass-bulb.	on platinum foil.
Amber......	$C + H + O$.	neck of the bulb, leaving a shining black residue.	
Mellite	$\ddot{\text{A}}\text{l}\,\overline{\text{M}}^{3} + 15\,\dot{\text{H}}$.	Gives off water. If heated to redness, is carbonized, and gives a slight empyreumatic odor.	On charcoal burns to a white ash, which moistened with nitrate of cobalt and heated shows the alumina reaction.

POTASH.

Mineral.	Formula.	Behavior		
		(1) in glass-bulb.	(2) in open tube.	(3) on charcoal.
Nitre.........	$\dot{K}\overset{\cdot\cdot\cdot\cdot\cdot}{N}$	Fuses readily to a clear liquid and with a strong heat boils with the evolution of oxygen.	—	Deflagrates leaving a saline mass, which is absorbed into charcoal and gives a sulphur reaction on silver.
Polyhalite	$\dot{K}\dddot{S}+\dot{M}g\dddot{S}+2\dot{C}a\dddot{S}+2\dot{H}$.	Gives off water.	—	Fuses to a reddish bead, which in the reducing flame solidifies and shrinks to a hollow crust.

Continuation of page 184.

Behavior				(8) Special reactions.
(4) in forceps.	(5) in borax.	(6) in mic. salt.	(7) with carb. soda.	
On platinum wire fuses and colors the flame violet more or less modified by lime and soda.	—	—	—	With bisulphate of potassa in the glass-bulb evolves nitrous fumes.
On platinum wire fuses and colors the flame yellow from a small quantity of soda.	Dissolves with ebullition to a clear glass, which is slightly colored by iron, and when saturated becomes opaque on cooling.	As in borax.	Fuses. The alkalies are absorbed by the charcoal leaving the lime and magnesia infusible on the surface.	The alkaline mass when laid on silver gives a sulphur reaction.

SODA.

Mineral.	Formula.	Behavior (1) in glass-bulb.	(2) in open tube.	(3) on charcoal.
Rock-salt.....	NaCl.	Fuses to a clear liquid.	—	Fuses, is absorbed by the charcoal and partially volatilized incrusting the charcoal around.
Natron.......	$\dot{N}a\ddot{C}+10\dot{H}$	Fuses with the evolution of water.	—	Fuses, and is absorbed into the pores of the charcoal.
Soda-nitre....	$\dot{N}a\ddot{\ddot{N}}$	Fuses, and if strongly heated evolves nitrous fumes.	—	Deflagrates and is absorbed into the charcoal.
Glauber-salt...	$\dot{N}a\dddot{S}+10\dot{H}$	Fuses and gives off water having a neutral reaction.	—	Fuses, and is absorbed by the charcoal. The saturated charcoal laid upon silver gives the sulphur reaction.
Glauberite....	$\dot{N}a\dddot{S}+\dot{C}a\dddot{S}$.	Decrepitates with the evolution of more or less water, and when strongly heated fuses to a clear liquid.	—	Fuses to a clear bead, then spreads out; the soda is absorbed and the lime left on the surface. Laid on silver, the fused mass gives a sulphur reaction.

SODA. (Continuation of page 186.)

Behavior				(8) Special reactions.
(4) in forceps.	(5) in borax.	(6) in mic. salt.	(7) with carb. soda.	
Fuses with great ease and colors the flame yellow.	—	—	—	Gives the chlorine reactions.
Fuses and behaves as the preceding.	—	—	—	Dissolves in acids with violent effervescence.
Deflagrates on platinum wire, coloring the flame yellow.	—	—	—	In a glass-bulb with bisulphate of potassa, gives the NO^5-reaction.
Fuses and colors the flame yellow.	—	—	—	Gives the SO^3-reaction.
Fuses easily to a clear glass, coloring the flame yellow.	Fuses easily and gives the lime reaction.	As in borax.	As alone on charcoal.	As in the preceding.

SODA. (Continuation of page 187.)

Mineral.	Formula.	Behavior		
		(1) in glass-bulb.	(2) in open tube.	(3) on charcoal.
Borax........	$\dot{N}a\ddot{B}^2 + 10\dot{H}$.	Intumesces with the evolution of water, and under a strong heat fuses.		Intumesces and fuses to a clear bead more or less colored by impurities.
Cryolite......	$3NaFl + Al^2Fl^3$.	Decrepitates slightly and gives a trace of water.	If heated so that the flame be allowed to play up the tube upon the mineral, fluorine is evolved, which corrodes the interior of the tube.	Fuses to a limpid bead, which on cooling becomes a white enamel. If heated for some time, it bubbles, gives off fluorine and becomes infusible.

SODA. (Continuation of page 188.)

Behavior				(8) Special reactions.
(4) in forceps.	(5) in borax.	(6) in mic. salt.	(7) with carb. soda.	
As on charcoal.			Fuses to a clear bead, which becomes crystalline on cooling.	Gives the boracic-acid-reaction.
Fuses, coloring the flame yellow.	Dissolves to a clear bead, which is rendered opaque by a large addition.	As in borax.	Fuses to a clear bead, then spreads out on the charcoal, the soda is absorbed, and an infusible mass of alumina remains.	If the alumina residue obtained be moistened with cobalt solution and heated strongly, it assumes a beautiful blue color.

BARYTA AND STRONTIA.

Mineral.	Formula.	Behavior		
		(1) in glass-bulb.	(2) in open tube.	(3) on charcoal.
Heavy-spar ...	$\dot{Ba}\dddot{S}$.	Sometimes decrepitates and gives off more or less water.	—	Fuses in the reducing flame.
Celestine	$\dot{Sr}\dddot{S}$.	—	—	Fuses to a milk-white bead.
Witherite	$\dot{Ba}\ddot{C}$.	Decrepitates more or less and evolves water.	—	Fuses, effervesces, and is partially absorbed by the charcoal.
Strontianite ...	$\dot{Sr}\ddot{C}$.	Becomes opaque.	—	As in the forceps.
Barytocalcite..	$\dot{Ba}\ddot{C} + \dot{Ca}\ddot{C}$.	As the preceding.	—	In powder frits together, but does not fuse.

BARYTA AND STRONTIA. (Continuation of page 190.)

Behavior				(8) Special reactions.
(4) in forceps.	(5) in borax.	(6) in mic. salt.	(7) with carb. soda.	
Fuses with difficulty on edges. Colors the outer flame green. In the reducing flame forms BaS, which fuses readily.	Gives the baryta-reaction.	As in borax.	Fuses to a clear bead; then spreads out and is absorbed into the charcoal. The fused mass laid on silver, gives the S-reaction.	If fused with potassa on platinum, gives the SO^3-reaction.
Colors the flame crimson.	Gives the strontia-reaction.	As in borax.	Similar to the preceding.	Similar to the preceding.
Colors the outer flame intensely green.	Dissolves with effervescence and gives the baryta-reaction.	As in borax.	Fuses to a clear bead; then spreads out and passes into the charcoal.	In dilute HCl dissolves with much effervescence.
Exfoliates and becomes arborescent. The filaments glow brilliantly and fuse on the point. Colors the flame brilliantly crimson.	Resembles the preceding.	As in borax.	As the preceding.	As the preceding.
Colors the flame green in the centre and red towards the point.	Dissolves with effervescence. In large quantity gives a semi-crystalline bead.	As in borax, but the saturated bead is milk-white.	Fuses, and is partially absorbed leaving the lime on the surface.	As witherite.

LIME.

Mineral.	Formula.	Behavior (1) in glass-bulb.	Behavior (2) in open tube.	Behavior (3) on charcoal.
Gypsum......	$\dot{\mathrm{C}}\mathrm{a}\dddot{\mathrm{S}} + 2\dot{\mathrm{H}}$.	Turns white, giving off water and being converted into plaster of Paris.	—	In the reducing flame forms CaS, which has an alkaline reaction on test paper, and gives a sulphur-reaction when laid on silver and moistened.
Apatite......	$\mathrm{Ca}\left\{\frac{\mathrm{Cl}}{\mathrm{Fl}}\right. + 3\dot{\mathrm{C}}\mathrm{a}^{3}\dddot{\mathrm{P}}$	Occasionally decrepitates and gives off some water.	—	—
Pharmacolite..	$\dot{\mathrm{C}}\mathrm{a}^{2}\,\ddot{\mathrm{A}}\mathrm{s} + 6\dot{\mathrm{H}}$.	Gives off water, and emits an arsenical odor.	—	Fuses to an opaque bead and emits a strong smell of arsenic.
Calcspar......	$\dot{\mathrm{C}}\mathrm{a}\ddot{\mathrm{C}}$.	Turns white and sometimes decrepitates. Strongly heated loses CO^{2} and becomes caustic.	—	Turns white, or brown if containing much iron or manganese, and glows brilliantly.

LIME. (Continuation of page 192.)

Behavior				(8) Special reactions.
(4) in forceps.	(5) in borax.	(6) in mic. salt.	(7) with carb. soda.	
Fuses with difficulty to a bead, coloring the flame red.	Dissolves to a clear bead, which gives the lime-reaction.	As in borax.	Behaves as lime. The alkaline mass laid on silver and moistened gives the sulphur-reaction.	Gives the sulphuric-acid-reaction.
IV. Previously dipped in SO^3 colors the flame green, afterwards red.	Dissolves easily and when in some quantity gives an opaline bead.	Gives the lime-reaction.	Is infusible. The alkali is absorbed, leaving the lime on the surface of the charcoal.	With microcosmic salt and oxide of copper, gives the chlorine-reaction. With microcosmic salt in the open tube evolves fluorine.
Fuses to a translucent violet colored bead, the color being due to cobalt Colors the flame blue at first, then faintly red.	Dissolves readily to a bead strongly colored by cobalt, which obscures the lime-reaction.	As in borax.	Fuses, and emits As. The alkali is then absorbed by the charcoal, as in the preceding.	—
Glows brilliantly, coloring the flame red. Becomes caustic and shows a strong alkaline reaction.	Dissolves with evolution of CO^2 and when pure gives the lime-reaction. The bead is generally more or less colored by iron and manganese.	As in borax.	Fuses, and behaves as other lime-salts.	Dissolves with effervescence in cold HCl.

LIME. (Continuation of page 193.)

Mineral.	Formula.	Behavior (1) in glass-bulb.	Behavior (2) in open tube.	Behavior (3) on charcoal.
Fluorspar.....	CaFl.	Phosphoresces with various colors, when heated in the dark. Sometimes decrepitates and gives a trace of water. Becomes opalescent.	—	Fuses easily to a clear bead, which becomes opaque on cooling, then loses fluorine, glows brilliantly and becomes infusible.

LIME. (Continuation of page 194.)

Behavior				(8) Special reactions.
(4) in forceps.	(5) in borax.	(6) in mic. salt.	(7) with carb. soda.	
As on charcoal. Colors the flame red.	Gives the lime-reaction.	As in borax.	Fuses to a clear bead, opaque on cooling. With an addition of the alkali behaves as lime.	With microcosmic salt in open tube gives the fluorine-reaction.

MAGNESIA.

Mineral.	Formula.	Behavior (1) in glass-bulb.	(2) in open tube.	(3) on charcoal.
Brucite	$\dot{M}g\dot{H}$.	Evolves water.	—	—
Epsomite......	$\dot{M}g\dddot{S} + 7\dot{H}$.	Evolves water having an acid reaction on test paper.	—	Gives off HO and SO^3, shines brilliantly, and becomes alkaline and caustic.
Boracite	$\dot{M}g\dddot{B}^2 + 2\dot{M}g\dddot{B}$	Occasionally gives off a trace of water.	—	Fuses with intumescence to a white crystalline bead.
Magnesite	$\dot{M}g\ddot{C}$.	Sometimes gives off a small quantity of water.	—	Is infusible. With cobalt-solution, assumes a dusky flesh tint.

MAGNESIA. (Continuation of page 196.)

Behavior				(8) Special reactions.
(4) in forceps.	(5) in borax.	(6) in mic. salt.	(7) with carb. soda.	
V.	Behaves as magnesia. Sometimes gives a faint iron-reaction.	As in borax.	Behaves as magnesia.	With nitrate of cobalt, gives the magnesia-reaction.
V. As on charcoal.	Behaves as magnesia.	As in borax.	The alkali is absorbed leaving the magnesia on the surface of the charcoal. Gives the sulphur-reaction on silver.	The magnesian residue obtained on treating with carbonate of soda (7), assumes a flesh-tint, when treated with cobalt.
I. As on charcoal. Colors the flame green.	Fuses easily to a clear bead, which is crystalline, when containing much of the mineral, and is usually slightly tinted by iron.	As in borax.	With a small quantity of alkali fuses to a clear bead crystalline on cooling. With a larger quantity gives a clear uncrystallizable bead.	—
—	Behaves as magnesia. Sometimes gives a slight iron-reaction.	As in borax.	Fuses to a bead, the soda is then absorbed, leaving an infusible mass of magnesia.	The magnesian residue obtained by fusing with carbonate of soda gives the magnesian-reaction with nitrate of cobalt. Dissolves with effervescence in warm HCl.

MAGNESIA. (Continuation of page 197.)

Mineral.	Formula.	Behavior		
		(1) in glass-bulb.	(2) in open tube.	(3) on charcoal.
Mesitine spar..	$(\dot{M}g\dot{F}e\dot{M}n)\ddot{C}$.	As magnesite.	—	Is infusible. Assumes a deep brown color.

MAGNESIA. (Continuation of page 198.)

Behavior				(8) Special reactions.
(4) in forceps.	(5) in borax.	(6) in mic. salt.	(7) with carb. soda.	
V.	Gives the iron and manganese-reaction.	As in borax.	As magnesite, but the residual mass has a dark color from iron and manganese.	Dissolves with effervescence in warm HCl. With carbonate of soda and nitre gives a manganese-reaction.

ALUMINA.

Mineral.	Formula.	Behavior (1) in glass-bulb.	Behavior (2) in open tube.	Behavior (3) on charcoal.
Sapphire, Corundum, Emery ..	$\dddot{\overline{Al}}$.	—	—	—
Websterite ...	$\dddot{\overline{Al}}\dddot{S} + 9\dot{\overline{H}}$.	Gives off water, and, when heated to incipient redness, sulphurous acid.	—	Gives off water and SO^3, leaving an infusible mass.
Native Alum..	$\dot{R}\dddot{S} + \dddot{\overline{Al}}\dddot{S}^3 + 24\dot{\overline{H}}$.	Intumesces greatly and gives off much water. Strongly heated, evolves SO^3, which reddens litmus.	—	Intumesces and becomes infusible.
Turquoise	$\dddot{\overline{Al}}^2\dddot{\dot{\dot{P}}} + 5\dot{\overline{H}}$.	Evolves water, occasionally decrepitates and turns black.	—	Turns brown, but remains infusible.

ALUMINA. (Continuation of page 200.)

Behavior				(8) Special reactions.
(4) in forceps.	(5) in borax.	(6) in mic. salt.	(7) with carb. soda.	
V.	In fine powder dissolves slowly to a colorless glass.	As in borax.	—	In fine powder moistened with cobalt-solution and heated assumes a blue color.
V.	Behaves as alumina.	As in borax.	Yields an infusible mass, which laid on silver and moistened, produces a black stain.	Fused with potassa in platinum has no action on silver. Cobalt-solution produces the alumina reaction.
V. Colors the flame violet if a potassa alum—yellow if soda—be present.	Dissolves and gives the iron and manganese reaction, if these oxides be present. Otherwise the bead is colorless.	As in borax.	The alkali is absorbed into the charcoal, leaving an infusible mass, which gives the sulphur reaction on silver.	If not containing much iron or manganese, gives an allumina reaction with nitrate of cobalt. In other respects as the preceding.
V. As on charcoal. Colors the outer flame green.	In the oxidizing flame, gives a green bead, due to copper and iron. In reducing flame, opaque red.	As in borax.	Intumesces, then fuses to a semi-clear glass colored by iron. With more alkali, yields an infusible mass.	Gives the phosphoric-acid reaction.

ALUMINA. (Continuation of page 201.)

Mineral.	Formula.	Behavior (1) in glass-bulb.	Behavior (2) in open tube.	Behavior (3) on charcoal.
Wavellite	$\bar{A}lF^3+3(\ddot{\bar{A}}l^4\dot{\bar{P}}^3+18\dot{\bar{H}}.)$	Evolves water and some fluorine, which attacks the glass.	—	Exfoliates and turns white.
Spinel........	$\dot{R}\ddot{\bar{A}}l.$	—		

ALUMINA. (Continuation of page 202.)

Behavior				(8) Special reactions.
(4) in forceps.	(5) in borax.	(6) in mic. salt.	(7) with carb. soda.	
V. As on charcoal. Colors the outer flame green, especially if moistened with SO^3.	As alumina. Generally gives also a slight iron reaction.	As in borax.	Forms an infusible white mass.	With cobalt-solution on charcoal gives the alumina reaction.
V.	Gives a slight iron reaction.	As in borax.	Fuses partially and forms a porous mass.	With nitrate of cobalt gives the alumina reaction. With nitre and carbonate of soda a slight manganese reaction.

SILICATES.

The presence of silica in a mineral can easily be ascertained by treating a small fragment in a bead of microcosmic salt. The bases will dissolve out with more or less difficulty in the salt, and the silica being insoluble will remain suspended in the bead, retaining the original form of the fragment. In borax, the silicates of lime and magnesia generally dissolve with considerable ease, but those of alumina slowly and with difficulty. The silicates of lime are moreover frequently characterized by intumescence or ebullition, when heated in the forceps in the blowpipe flame. The minerals presenting this character are marked in the table. As the most convenient mode of classifying the silicates for blowpipe examination, the following arrangement will be adopted :

TABLE I.—ANHYDROUS SILICATES.
TABLE II.—HYDROUS SILICATES.

FUSIBILITY.

I. Readily fusible to a bead.
II. With difficulty fusible to a bead.
III. Readily fusible on the edges.
IV. With difficulty fusible on the edges.
V. Infusible.

a. Afford a fluid bead with carbonate of soda.
b. Afford a fluid bead with but little of that salt, but with a larger quantity a slaggy mass.
c. Afford a slaggy mass only.

This classification of minerals, according to their fusibility and their behavior with carbonate of soda, was originally proposed by *Berzelius*, and a table of the principal oxidized minerals arranged according to these characters is given in his handbook of the blowpipe, and thence adopted, with some alterations by *Plattner*, in the very excellent and detailed work already many times cited. In the following general table I., the more important silicates only are included, and in table II. are enumerated in alphabetical order those which afford characteristic reactions.

TABLE I.

Anhydrous Silicates.

Fus. alone and with $\dot{Na}\ddot{C}$.	Mineral.	Formula.	
I. a.	Axinite...........	$(\dot{Ca}\dot{Mg})^3(\dddot{B}\dddot{Si})^3+(\dddot{\bar{Al}}\dddot{\bar{Fe}}\dddot{\bar{Mn}})^2$ $(\dddot{Si}\dddot{B})$	Int.
	Elaolite	$(\dot{K}\dot{Na})^3\,\dddot{Si}+3\dddot{\bar{Al}}\dddot{Si}$	Int.
	Garnet.............	$\dot{R}^3\dddot{Si}+\dddot{\bar{R}}\dddot{Si}$	
	Oligoclase..........	$\dot{Na}\dddot{Si}+\dddot{\bar{Al}}\dddot{Si}^2$	
	Scapolite...........	$(\dot{Ca}\dot{Na})^3\,\dddot{Si}^2+2\dddot{\bar{Al}}\dddot{Si}$	Int.
	Spodumene.........	$(\dot{Li}\dot{Na})^3\,\dddot{Si}^2+4\dddot{\bar{Al}}\dddot{Si}^2$	Int.
b.	Asbestos to II.......	As Hornblende	
	Augite some var.....	$(\dot{Ca}\dot{Mg}\dot{Fe}\dot{Mn})^3\,\dddot{Si}^2$	Int.
	Epidote to III.......	$(\dot{Ca}\dot{Fe})^3\,\dddot{Si}+2(\dddot{\bar{Al}}\dddot{\bar{Fe}}\dddot{\bar{Mn}})\dddot{Si}$	Int.
	Hornblende some var.	$(\dot{Ca}\dot{Mg}\dot{Fe})^4+(\dddot{Si}\dddot{\bar{Al}})^3$	Int.
	Sodalite to III.	$\dot{Na}^3\,\dddot{Si}+3\dddot{\bar{Al}}\dddot{Si}+NaCl$	Int.
	Vesuvian	$3(\dot{Ca}\dot{Mg})^3\,\dddot{Si}+2(\dddot{\bar{Al}}\dddot{\bar{Fe}})\dddot{Si}$	Int.
c.	Biaxial Mica to III...	$\dot{K}\dddot{Si}+4(\dddot{\bar{Al}}\dddot{\bar{Fe}})\dddot{Si}$	
	Hauyne............	$(\dot{K}\dot{Na})^3\,\dddot{Si}+3\dddot{\bar{Al}}\dddot{Si}+\dot{Na}\dddot{Si}$	
	Tourmaline to V.....	$(\dot{R}\dddot{\bar{R}}\dddot{B})^4\,\dddot{Si}^3$	Int.
II. a.	Labradorite	$(\dot{Ca}\dot{Na}\dot{K})\dddot{Si}+(\dddot{\bar{Al}}\dddot{\bar{Fe}})\dddot{Si}$	
	Lepidolite..........	$(KNaL)F+(\dddot{\bar{Al}}\dddot{\bar{Fe}})\dddot{Si}^2$?	
	Ryacolite	$\dot{K}\dddot{Si}+\dddot{\bar{Al}}\dddot{Si}^3$	
	Albite	$\dot{Na}\dddot{Si}+\dddot{\bar{Al}}\dddot{Si}^3$	
b.	Augite some var. ...	$\dot{R}^3\,\dddot{Si}^2$	
	Actinolite..........	$(\dot{Ca}\dot{Mg}\dot{Fe})^4\,\dddot{Si}^3$	Int.
	Diopside	$(\dot{Ca}\dot{Mg})^3\,\dddot{Si}^2$	
	Humboltilite........	$2(\dot{Ca}\dot{Mg}\dot{Na}\dot{K})\dddot{Si}+(\dddot{\bar{Al}}\dddot{\bar{Fe}})\dddot{Si}$	
	Sahlite....	As Augite	
	Tremolite	$(\dot{Ca}\dot{Mg})^4\,\dddot{Si}^3$	
c.	Pyrope............	$(\dot{Ca}\dot{Mg}\dot{Fe})^3\,\dddot{Si}+\dddot{\bar{Al}}\dddot{Si}+m\ddot{Cr}$?	

Fus. alone and with $\dot{Na}\ddot{C}$.	Mineral.	Formula.	
III. a.	Anorthite	$(\dot{Ca}\dot{Mg}\dot{Na}\dot{K})^3 \dddot{Si} + 3(\dddot{\bar{Al}}\dddot{\bar{Fe}})\dddot{Si}$	
	Nepheline..........	$(\dot{Na}\dot{K}\dot{Ca})^2 \dddot{Si} + 2\dddot{\bar{Al}}\dddot{Si}$	
	Obsidian	$\dddot{Si}, \dddot{\bar{Al}}, \dddot{\bar{Fe}}, \dot{Fe}, \dot{Ca}\dot{Na}\dot{K}$	Int.
	Orthoclase	$(\dot{K}\dot{Na})\dddot{Si} + \dddot{\bar{Al}}\dddot{Si}^3$	
	Petalite............	$(\dot{\bar{Li}}\dot{Na})^3 \dddot{Si}^4 + 4\dddot{\bar{Al}}\dddot{Si}^4$	
	Pumice............	$\dddot{Si}, \dddot{\bar{Al}}, \dot{Ca}, \dot{K}, \dot{Na}, \dot{\bar{H}}$	Int.
b.	Gadolinite to V......	$(\dot{Y}\dot{Ce}\dot{\bar{La}}\dot{Fe}\dot{Ca})^3 \dddot{Si}$	
	Nephrite	$(\dot{Ca}\dot{Mg}\dot{Fe})^4 \dddot{Si}^3$?	Int.
	Wollastonite	$\dot{Ca}^3 \dddot{Si}^2$	
c.	Iolite..............	$(\dot{Mg}\dot{Fe})^3 \dddot{Si}^2 + 3\dddot{\bar{Al}}\dddot{Si}$	
IV. a.	Beryl..............	$\dddot{Be}\dddot{Si}^2 + \dddot{\bar{Al}}\dddot{Si}^2$	
b.	Diallage	$(\dot{Ca}\dot{Mg}\dot{Fe})^3 (\dddot{Si}\dddot{\bar{Al}})^2$	
	Hypersthene	$(\dot{Mg}\dot{Fe})^3 \dddot{Si}^2$	
c.	Fuchsite	$(\dot{K}^5\dddot{Si})^2 + 9(\dddot{\bar{Al}}\dddot{\bar{Cr}})^5 \dddot{Si}^6$	
V. a.	Leucite	$\dot{K}^3\dddot{Si}^2 + \dddot{\bar{Al}}\dddot{Si}^2$	
b.	Chondrodite........	$(\dot{Mg}, MgF)^4 (\dddot{Si}SiF^3)$	
	Olivine	$(\dot{Mg}\dot{Fe}\dot{Ca})^3 \dddot{Si}$	
c.	Andalusite	$(\dddot{\bar{Al}}\dddot{\bar{Fe}})^3 \dddot{Si}^2$	
	Chrysoberyl	$\dddot{Be} + \dddot{\bar{Al}}$	
	Kaynite............	$\dddot{\bar{Al}}^3 \dddot{Si}^2$	
	Pycnite .... } Topaz .... }	$6\dddot{\bar{Al}}^3 \dddot{Si}^2 + (3\dddot{\bar{Al}}F^3 + 2SiF^3)$	
	Zircon	$\dddot{\bar{Zr}}\dddot{Si}$	
	Staurolite	$(\dddot{\bar{Al}}\dddot{\bar{Fe}})^2 \dddot{Si}$	

Hydrous Silicates.

Fus. alone and with $\dot{N}a\ddot{C}$.	Mineral.	Formula.	
I. a.	Analcime...........	$\dot{N}a^3\dddot{Si}^2 + 3\dddot{Al}\dddot{Si}^2 + 6\dot{H}$	Int.
	Apophyllite	$(\dot{K},KF)(\dddot{Si},SiF^3) + 6\dot{C}a\dddot{Si} + 15\dot{H}$	Int.
	Brewsterite	$(\dot{S}r\dot{B}a)\dddot{Si} + \dddot{Al}\dddot{Si}^3 + 5\dot{H}$	Int.
	Chabasite...... ...	$(\dot{C}a,\dot{N}a,\dot{K})^3\dddot{Si}^2 + 3\dddot{Al}\dddot{Si}^2 + 18\dot{H}$	Int.
	Lapis Lazuli........	$\dddot{Si},\ddot{S},\dddot{Al},\dddot{Fe},\dot{C}a,\dot{N}a,\dot{H}$	
	Laumonite..........	$\dot{C}a^3\dddot{Si}^2 + 3\dddot{Al}\dddot{Si}^2 + 12\dot{H}$	Int.
	Mesotype	$(\dot{N}a\dot{C}a)\dddot{Si} + \dddot{Al}\dddot{Si} + 3\dot{H}$	Int.
	Natrolite...........	$\dot{N}a\dddot{Si} + \dddot{Al}\dddot{Si} + 2\dot{H}$	Int.
	Prehnite...........	$\dot{C}a^2\dddot{Si} + \dddot{Al}\dddot{Si} + \dot{H}$	Int.
	Scolezite...........	$\dot{C}a\dddot{Si} + \dddot{Al}\dddot{Si} + 3\dot{H}$	Int.
	Thomsonite	$(\dot{C}a\dot{N}a)^3\dddot{Si} + 3\dddot{Al}\dddot{Si} + 7\dot{H}$	Int.
	Datholite	$2\dot{C}a^3\dddot{Si} + \dddot{B}^3\dddot{Si}^2 + 3\dot{H}$	Int.
	Heulandite.........	$\dot{C}a\dddot{Si} + \dddot{Al}\dddot{Si}^3 + 5\dot{H}$	Int.
	Stilbite	$\dot{C}a\dddot{Si} + \dddot{Al}\dddot{Si}^3 + 6\dot{H}$	Int.
b.	Okenite............	$\dot{C}a^3\dddot{Si}^4 + 6\dot{H}$	Int.
	Pectolite...........	$(\dot{C}a\dot{N}a)^4\dddot{Si}^3 + \dot{H}$	
c.	Saponite....... ...	$2\dot{M}g^3\dddot{Si}^2 + \dddot{Al}\dddot{Si} + 10$ or $6\dot{H}$	
II. a.	Antrimolite	$3(\dot{C}a\dot{K})\dddot{Si} + 5\dddot{Al}\dddot{Si} + 15\dot{H}$	
	Harmatome	$\dot{B}a\dddot{Si} + \dddot{Al}\dddot{S}^2 + 5\dot{H}$	
b.	Brevicite...........	$\dot{N}a\dddot{Si} + \dddot{Al}\dddot{Si} + 2\dot{H}$	
	Orthite	$\dot{R}^3\dddot{Si} + \dddot{R}\dddot{Si} + (\dot{H}\,?)$	Int.
III. c.	Pitchstone..........	$\dddot{Si},\dddot{Al},\dddot{Fe},\dot{M}g\dot{N}a,\dot{K}\dot{H}$	
	Talc to V...........	$\dot{M}g^6\dddot{Si}^5 + 2\dot{H}$	
	Chlorite	$3(\dot{M}g\dot{F}e)^3\dddot{Si} + (\dddot{Al}\dddot{Fe})^2\dddot{Si} + 9\dot{H}$	
	Pinite	$\dddot{Si},\dddot{Al},\dddot{Fe},\dot{K},\dot{M}g,\dot{H}$	

Fus. alone and with $\dot{Na}\ddot{C}$.	Mineral.	Formula.	
IV. a.	Steatite	$\dot{Mg}^6\dddot{Si}^5 + 4\dot{H}$	
c.	Gilbertite	$\dddot{Si}, \ddot{Al}, \dot{Fe}, \dot{Mg}, \dot{H}$	Int.
	Meerschaum........	$\dot{Mg}\dddot{Si} + \dot{H}$	
	Serpentine	$\dot{Mg}^9\dddot{Si}^4 + 6\dot{H}$	
V. a.	Gismondine	$(\dot{Ca}\dot{K})^2\dddot{Si} + 2\ddot{Al}\dddot{Si} + 9\dot{H}$	

TABLE II.

Analcime...	If transparent becomes white and opaque when heated, but on incipient fusion resumes its transparency and then fuses to a clear glass.
Andalusite..	When powdered and treated with cobalt solution on charcoal, assumes a blue color.
Apophyllite.	Fuses to a frothy white glass.
Axinite	Imparts a green color to the blowpipe flame, owing to the presence of boracic acid. This reaction is especially distinct, if the mineral be previously mixed with fluorspar and bisulphate of potassa.
Beryl	Sometimes gives a chromium reaction in borax and microcosmic salt.
Chabasite...	Fuses to a white enamel.
Chondrodite	Evolves fluorine in the glass tube, both when heated alone and with microcosmic salt. It sometimes also gives off a trace of water.
Chrysoberyl.	Is unattacked by carbonate of soda. With nitrate of cobalt on charcoal the finely powdered mineral assumes a blue color.
Datholite...	Fuses to a clear glass and colors the flame green.
Diallage....	Frequently gives off water in small quantity.
Fuchsite....	Gives the chromium reaction with borax and microcosmic salt.
Gadolinite ..	That from Hitteroe, if heated in a partially covered platinum spoon to low redness, glows suddenly and brilliantly.
Hauyne	Affords the sulphur reaction both on charcoal and when fused with potassa. It contains both sulphur and sulphuric acid.
Hypersthene	As Diallage.
Kyanite	As Andalusite.

Lapis Lazuli	Fuses to a white glass, and when treated with carbonate of soda on charcoal, gives the sulphur reaction on silver.
Laumonite..	When strongly heated, exfoliates and curls up.
Lepidolite...	Colors the blowpipe flame crimson, from lithia; also gives the fluorine reaction with microcosmic salt.
Leucite	Some varieties, when treated with cobalt solution, assume a blue color.
Meerschaum	In the glass bulb frequently blackens and evolves an empyreumatic odor due to organic matter. When this is burnt off, it again becomes white, and if moistened with nitrate of cobalt solution and heated, assumes a pink color.
Okenite.....	Behaves as Apophyllite.
Olivine	Some varieties give off fluorine, when fused with microcosmic salt.
Pectolite....	Similar to Apophyllite.
Petalite.....	Imparts a slight crimson color to the flame, like Lepidolite.
Prehnite ...	As Chabasite.
Pycnite.....	Assumes a blue color, when treated with nitrate of cobalt. Gives the fluorine reaction with microcosmic salt.
Pyrope.....	Gives the chromium reaction with borax and microcosmic salt.
Scolecite....	Similar to Laumonite, but more marked.
Scapolite ...	Occasionally contains a small quantity of lithia, and colors the flame red when fused with fluorspar and bisulphate of potassa.
Sodalite	If mixed with one-fifth its volume of oxide of copper, moistened to make the mixture cohere, and a small portion placed upon charcoal and heated with the blue oxidizing flame, the outer flame will be colored intensely blue from chloride of copper.

Spodumene	When not too strongly heated, colors the blowpipe flame red, when more strongly, yellow.
Stilbite.....	As Chabasite.
Topaz......	When heated, remains clear. Otherwise as Pycnite.
Tourmaline	Gives the boracic acid reaction with flourspar and bisulphate of potassa.
Wollastonite	Colors the blowpipe flame faintly red from lime.
Zircon	The colored varieties become white or colorless and transparent, when heated. Is only slightly attacked by carbonate of soda.

URANIUM.

Mineral.	Formula.	Behavior (1) in glass-bulb.	(2) in open tube.	(3) on charcoal.
Pitchblende...	$\dot{U}\dddot{\bar{U}}$ essentially.	Evolves some water and a small quantity of sulphur, sulphide of arsenic and metallic arsenic.	Evolves SO^2 and a white sublimate of arsenious acid.	Gives off arsenical fumes.
Uranium ochre	$\dddot{\bar{U}}\dot{H}^2$.	Evolves water and assumes a red color.	—	V. In reducing flame assumes a green color.
Uranite......	$(\dot{C}a+\dddot{\bar{U}}^2)\overset{\cdot\cdot\cdot\cdot\cdot}{\bar{P}}+8\dot{H}$.	Evolves water and becomes yellow and opaque.	—	Fuses with intumescence to a black bead having a semi-crystalline surface.
Chalcolite....	$(\dot{C}u+\dddot{\bar{U}}^2)\overset{\cdot\cdot\cdot\cdot\cdot}{\bar{P}}+8\dot{H}$.	As uranite.	—	As uranite.

URANIUM. (Continuation of p. 212.)

Behavior				(8) Special reactions.
(4) in forceps.	(5) in borax.	(6) in mic. salt.	(7) with carb. soda.	
III. Colors the flame blue beyond the assay, owing to the presence of Pb. Sometimes also green towards the point, due to Cu.	The roasted mineral affords the uranium reaction.	As borax. Also a small residue of silica.	Infusible. Affords the characteristic Pb incrustation, and sometimes yields minute particles of Cu.	—
—	Gives the uranium reaction.	As in borax.	—	—
—	Gives the uranium reaction.	As in borax.	Forms an infusible yellow slag.	Gives the PO^5 reaction.
As uranite.	In the oxidizing flame gives a green bead, which in the reducing flame becomes of an opaque red, from Cu.	As in borax.	In reducing flame yields a metallic bead of Cu.	As uranite.

IRON.

Mineral.	Formula.	Behavior (1) in glass-bulb.	Behavior (2) in open tube.	Behavior (3) on charcoal.
Iron pyrites...	FeS^2.	Gives a considerable yellow sublimate of sulphur, and sometimes sulphide of arsenic. Also HS.	Sulphurous acid and sometimes arsenious acid are evolved.	Gives off some sulphur, which burns with a blue flame. Residue fuses to a magnetic bead.
Magnetic pyrites...	$\overset{,}{Fe}{}^{5}\,\overset{,,,}{Fe}$.	—	Evolves sulphurous acid.	Fuses to a magnetic bead black on the surface, and with a yellow shining fracture.
Mispickel.....	$FeAs+FeS^2$.	A red sublimate of AsS^2 is first formed and then a black sublimate of metallic arsenic.	Sulphurous and arsenious acids are evolved, the latter forming a white sublimate.	Gives off much arsenic forming a white incrustation and fuses to a magnetic globule.
Magnetic iron ore...	Fe^3O^4.	—	—	—
Specular iron.. Red haematite.	Fe^2O^3.	—	—	—

IRON. (Continuation of page 214.)

Behavior				(8) Special reactions.
(4) in forceps.	(5) in borax.	(6) in mic. salt.	(7) with carb. soda.	
—	The roasted mineral gives a strong iron reaction.	As in borax.	Fuses to a black mass, which spreads out on charcoal and gives the sulphur reaction on silver.	—
—	As iron pyrites.	As in borax.	As iron pyrites.	—
—	As iron pyrites.	As in borax.	As iron pyrites.	—
In the blue flame, fuses on edges and remains magnetic.	Gives the iron reaction.	As in borax.	—	—
V. In the blue flame is converted into Fe^3O^4, and then behaves as the preceding.	As magnetic iron ore.	As in borax.	—	—

IRON. (Continuation of page 215.)

Mineral.	Formula.	Behavior (1) in glass-bulb.	Behavior (2) in open tube.	Behavior (3) on charcoal.
Göthite	$\overset{\cdots}{\bar{F}}e\dot{H}$.	Evolves water.	—	—
Franklinite ...	$(\dot{F}e\dot{Z}n\dot{M}n)$ $(\overset{\cdots}{\bar{F}}e\overset{\cdots}{\bar{M}}n)$.	—	—	Forms a white incrustation on the charcoal, which moistened with cobalt solution assumes a green color.
Ilmenite......	$\overset{\cdots}{\bar{T}}i$ and $\overset{\cdots}{\bar{F}}e$.	—	—	—
Chromic iron .	$\dot{F}e\overset{\cdots}{\bar{C}}r$.	—	—	—
Lievrite	$3(\dot{F}e\dot{C}a)^3\overset{\cdots}{S}i + 2\overset{\cdots}{\bar{F}}e\overset{\cdots}{S}i$.	Occasionally gives off some water and turns black.	—	Fuses to a black globule, which in the reducing flame becomes magnetic.
Chloropal	$\overset{\cdots}{\bar{F}}e\overset{\cdots}{S}i^2 + 3\dot{H}$.	Decrepitates more or less, gives off much water and turns black.	—	—

IRON. (Continuation of page 216.)

Behavior				(8) Special reactions.
(4) in forceps.	(5) in borax.	(6) in mic. salt.	(7) with carb. soda.	
As specular iron.	As specular iron.	As in borax.	—	—
V. In the blue flame fuses on edges and becomes magnetic.	Gives the iron and manganese reaction.	As in borax.	Affords a considerable white incrustation of ZnO.	Gives a strong manganese reaction with nitre and carbonate of soda.
V. In reducing flame fuses on edges and becomes magnetic.	Gives the iron reaction.	In oxidizing flame exhibits the iron reaction. In reducing flame assumes a deep brownish red color.	—	—
As the preceding.	Dissolves slowly and gives the chromium reaction.	As in borax.	On platinum foil with nitre and carbonate of soda affords a yellow mass of chromate of potassa.	—
I. In reducing flame is magnetic.	Gives the iron reaction.	Gives the iron and silica reactions.	Fuses to a black opaque bead.	Generally gives the manganese reaction with nitre and carbonate of soda.
V. Loses color and turns black.	Gives the iron reaction.	Gives the iron and silica reactions.	Fuses to a transparent green glass.	—

IRON. (Continuation of page 217.)

Mineral.	Formula.	Behavior (1) in glass-bulb.	Behavior (2) in open tube.	Behavior (3) on charcoal.
Green earth ..	$\dddot{Si}, \dot{Fe}, \dddot{Al}, \dot{Na}, \dot{K}, \dot{H}$, etc.	Gives off water and becomes darker in color.	—	—
Siderite	$\dot{Fe}\ddot{C}$.	Occasionally decrepitates. Gives off CO^2 and turns black and magnetic.	—	As in glass bulb.
Copperas	$\dot{Fe}\dddot{S} + 7\dot{H}$.	Gives off water, and, when strongly heated, SO^2 and SO^3, which redden litmus paper.	Evolves water and SO^2, which may be recognized by its odor.	Loses water and SO^3, and is converted into $\dddot{\overline{Fe}}$.
Vivianite	$\dot{Fe}^3\overline{\dddot{P}} + 8\dot{H}$.	Gives off water.	—	Froths up and then fuses to a grey metallic bead.

IRON. (Continuation of page 218.)

Behavior				(8) Special reactions.
(4) in forceps.	(5) in borax.	(6) in mic. salt.	(7) with carb. soda.	
V. In reducing flame fuses on edges and colors the outer flame yellow ($\dot{N}a$) or violet ($\dot{K}$).	As the preceding.	As the preceding.	Forms a slaggy mass.	—
Behaves similarly to the magnetic oxide.	Gives the iron and sometimes manganese reaction.	As in borax.	Behaves as an oxide. With nitre and carbonate of soda on platinum generally gives the manganese reaction.	In acid dissolves with effervescence.
Gives off H and SO^2, and then behaves as the magnetic oxide.	The roasted mineral affords an iron reaction.	As in borax.	Forms sulphide of sodium and oxide of iron. The former is absorbed into the charcoal, and if cut out and laid upon silver and moistened gives the S reaction.	If dissolved in water, and a strip of silver-foil be introduced into the solution, the metal remains untarnished.
As on charcoal. Singes flame green ($\dddot{P}$).	Gives the iron reaction.	As in borax.	In reducing flame becomes magnetic and fuses to a black slaggy mass.	—

IRON. (Continuation of page 219.)

Mineral.	Formula.	Behavior		
		(1) in glass-bulb.	(2) in open tube.	(3) on charcoal.
Triphyline.....	$(\dot{Fe}\dot{Mn}\dot{Li})^3\overset{\cdot\cdot\cdot\cdot\cdot}{\bar{P}}$.	Gives off water, having an alkaline reaction, and assumes a metallic lustre resembling graphite.	—	Fuses readily to a black magnetic bead with a metallic lustre.
Scorodite.....	$\overset{\cdot\cdot\cdot}{\bar{Fe}}\overset{\cdot\cdot\cdot\cdot\cdot}{As}+4\dot{H}$.	Evolves water.	Gives off water and AsO^3.	Emits arsenical fume and in the reducing flame fuses to a magnetic mass having a metallic lustre.
Cube ore	$\dot{Fe}^3\overset{\cdot\cdot\cdot\cdot\cdot}{As}+\overset{\cdot\cdot\cdot}{\bar{Fe}}^3\overset{\cdot\cdot\cdot\cdot\cdot}{As}^2+18\dot{H}$.	Evolves much water.	As the preceding.	As the preceding.

IRON. (Continuation of page 220.)

Behavior				(8) Special reactions.
(4) in forceps.	(5) in borax.	(6) in mic. salt.	(7) with carb. soda.	
I. On platinum wire colors the flame crimson ($\dot{L}i$) and green ($\ddot{\dot{P}}$), towards the point fuses to a black magnetic bead.	Gives the iron and manganese reactions.	Gives the iron reaction which overpowers that of the manganese.	Forms an infusible porous mass, which under the reducing flame becomes magnetic.	Gives the manganese reaction with nitre and carbonate of soda on platinum foil.
I. As on charcoal. Colors the outer flame blue.	The roasted mineral gives an iron reaction.	As in borax.	As alone on charcoal.	Gives the arsenic reactions.
As the preceding.	As the preceding.	As in borax.	As the preceding.	As the preceding.

MANGANESE.

Mineral.	Formula.	Behavior		
		(1) in glass-bulb.	(2) in open tube.	(3) on charcoal.
Manganblende	MnS.	—	Gives off SO^2 and becomes greyish green on surface.	Is slowly roasted and converted into oxide.
Pyrolusite....	$\ddot{Mn}$.	Frequently gives off a small quantity of water and, when strongly heated, oxygen.	—	—
Manganite....	$\dddot{\overline{Mn}}\dot{\overline{H}}$.	Gives off much water.	—	—
Psilomelane...	$(\dot{Ba},\dot{Ca},\dot{Mg},\dot{K})$ $\ddot{Mn}+\dot{\overline{H}}$.	Gives off water and, when strongly heated, oxygen.	—	—
Wad	$\ddot{Mn},\dot{Mn},\dot{\overline{H}}$, also $\dddot{\overline{Fe}},\dddot{\overline{Al}},\dot{Ba},\dot{Cu}$, $\ddot{Pb},\dddot{Si}$, etc.	Gives off water.	—	—

MANGANESE. (Continuation of page 222.)

Behavior				(8) Special reactions.
(4) in forceps.	(5) in borax.	(6) in mic. salt.	(7) with carb. soda.	
V.	The roasted mineral gives a strong manganese reaction.	In the unroasted state, dissolves with much ebullition and detonation due to the elimination of sulphide of phosphorus. The bead then exhibits the characteristic violet color of manganese.	Forms a slaggy mass, which laid on silver and moistened, gives the sulphur reaction.	—
V.	Gives the manganese reaction.	As in borax.	Forms a slaggy mass.	—
V. Exfoliates slightly.	As the preceding.	As in borax.	As the preceding.	—
V. Colors flame faintly green (Ḃa) and red towards the point (Ċa).	As pyrolusite.	As in borax.	As pyrolusite.	—
V. Colors flame variously according to its composition.	Gives the manganese reaction, more or less modified by the presence of other oxides.	As in borax.	As pyrolusite.	Various according to composition. When strongly heated and then moistened has an alkaline reaction on red litmus paper.

MANGANESE. (Continuation of page 223.)

Mineral.	Formula.	Behavior.		
		(1) in glass-bulb.	(2) in open tube.	(3) on charcoal.
Rhodonite....	$\dot{M}n^3\ddot{S}i^2$.	Gives off more or less water.	—	Under a strong flame fuses to a brown opaque bead.
Diallogite	$\dot{M}n\ddot{C}$.	Frequently decrepitates and gives off more or less water.	—	If strongly heated and moistened has an alkaline reaction on litmus paper due to the presence of $\dot{C}a$.
Triplite	$(\dot{M}n\dot{F}e)^4\dddot{P}$.	Generally gives off more or less water.	—	—

MANGANESE. (Continuation of page 224.)

Behavior				(8) Special reactions.
(4) in forceps.	(5) in borax.	(6) in mic. salt.	(7) with carb. soda.	
II. As on charcoal.	In the oxidizing flame gives the manganese reaction. In reducing flame the iron reaction more or less intense.	As in borax, but leaves an insoluble siliceous skeleton.	With a small quantity of the alkali fuses to a black bead. With a larger quantity forms a slag.	—
V. Frequently colors the flame slightly red.	Gives the manganese and iron reactions.	As in borax.	Forms an infusible slag.	In warm acid dissolves with much effervescence.
I. Colors the outer blowpipe flame green (P).	Gives the manganese and iron reactions.	As in borax.	Forms an infusible mass.	—

NICKEL AND COBALT.

Mineral.	Formula.	Behavior		
		(1) in glass-bulb.	(2) in open tube.	(3) on charcoal.
Millerite......	NiS.	—	Evolves SO^2.	Fuses with much ebullition to a magnetic bead.
Coppernickel...	Ni^2As.	Gives off a little AsO^3.	Gives off much AsO^3 and some SO^2 and falls to powder.	Fuses to a magnetic bead, with the evolution of arsenic, which colors the flame blue.
Smaltine	CoAs.	When strongly heated generally evolves metallic arsenic.	Gives a crystalline sublimate of AsO^3. Also some SO^2.	Gives off fumes of arsenic, and fuses to a dark grey magnetic bead, very brittle, colors flame blue.

NICKEL AND COBALT. (Continuation of page 226.)

Behavior				(8) Special reactions.
(4) in forceps.	(5) in borax.	(6) in mic. salt.	(7) with carb. soda.	
—	The roasted mineral gives a nickel reaction, slightly modified by small quantities of iron and copper.	As in borax.	Fuses to a slaggy mass, which on silver gives the sulphur reaction.	
—	The arsenical bead obtained by fusing the mineral on charcoal, if fused upon the same support with borax successively added and removed, gives firstly an iron reaction, then cobalt if present, and lastly nickel.	If the residual bead which has been treated with borax be further treated with microcosmic salt, the nickel reaction will be obtained and sometimes a slight copper reaction.	—	Affords a sublimate of metallic arsenic when treated with cyanide of potassium.
—	As the preceding, but the cobalt being in large excess requires some time for its perfect oxidation, before the nickel reaction is exhibited.	Gives the cobalt reaction, and after the cobalt has been removed, that of nickel.	—	As the preceding.

NICKEL AND COBALT. (Continuation of page 227.)

Mineral.	Formula.	Behavior		
		(1) in glass-bulb.	(2) in open tube.	(3) on charcoal.
Glance cobalt	$CoS^2 + CoAs$.	—	As the preceding, but gives off more SO^2.	Gives off S and As, and fuses to a magnetic bead. Colors flame blue.
Nickel glance	$NiS^2 + NiAs$.	Decrepitates and gives an orange colored sublimate of AsS^3.	As the preceding.	As the preceding.
Ulmannite....	$NiS^2 + Ni(AsSb)^2$.	Gives a slight white sublimate of SbO^3 and more or less AsS^3.	Gives off thick fumes of SbO^3 and SbO^5 with AsO^3 and SO^2.	As glance cobalt, but accompanied by dense fumes of SbO^3.
Cobalt pyrites	$(\overset{,}{Co}\overset{,}{Ni}\overset{,}{Fe})$ $(\overset{,,,}{\mathrm{Co}}\overset{,,,}{\mathrm{Ni}}\overset{,,,}{\mathrm{Fe}})$.	When strongly heated gives off sulphur and becomes brown.	Gives off much SO^2 and a small quantity of AsO^3.	In the reducing flame small fragments fuse with the evolution of sulphur to a magnetic bead having a bronze colored fracture.
Emerald nickel	$\dot{Ni}^3\ddot{C} + 6\dot{H}$.	Gives off much water and turns black.	—	—

NICKEL AND COBALT. (Continuation of p. 228.)

Behavior				(8) Special reactions.
(4) in forceps.	(5) in borax.	(6) in mic. salt.	(7) with carb. soda.	
—	Gives a cobalt and slight iron reaction when treated as the preceding minerals.	As in borax.	Gives a sulphur reaction of silver.	As the preceding.
—	As copper nickel.	Gives the nickel reaction, occasionally somewhat obscured by cobalt.	As the preceding.	As copper nickel.
—	As copper nickel.	As the preceding.	As the preceding.	As copper nickel generally, but arsenic is not always present.
—	In the oxidizing flame on charcoal gives a violet colored glass. In the reducing flame the nickel is reduced and may be collected in a gold bead. When the nickel is removed, the glass exhibits a slight iron reaction while warm.	As in borax, but the reduction of the nickel is more difficult than in the latter flux.	As glance cobalt.	As copper nickel, but the amount of arsenic is usually very small.
—	Dissolves with much effervescence and gives the nickel reaction.	As in borax.	Forms a slaggy mass.	In warm dilute HCl dissolves with much effervescence.

NICKEL AND COBALT. (Continuation of page 229.)

Mineral.	Formula.	Behavior		
		(1) in glass-bulb.	(2) in open tube.	(3) on charcoal.
Cobalt bloom..	$\dot{C}o^{3}\ddot{\bar{A}}s + 8\dot{\bar{H}}$.	Gives off water	—	Evolves arsenical fumes and in the reducing flame fuses to a dark grey bead of arsenide of cobalt.
Earthy cobalt..	$\ddot{M}n,\dot{C}o,\dot{C}u,$ $\ddot{F}e,\dot{\bar{H}}$, etc.	Gives off water.	—	Emits a slight smell of arsenic, but does not fuse.

NICKEL AND COBALT. (Continuation of page 230.)

Behavior				(8) Special reactions.
(4) in forceps.	(5) in borax.	(6) in mic. salt.	(7) with carb. soda.	
In the point of the blue flame fuses and colors the outer flame blue (As).	Gives the cobalt reaction.	As in borax.	—	Gives off arsenic with cyanide of potassium in glass tube.
Colors the flame blue.	In oxidizing flame gives the cobalt reaction which obscures those of $\dot{Mn}$,$\dot{Cu}$, etc. In reducing flame occasionally gives the $\dot{Cu}$ reaction.	As in borax. If a saturated bead be treated on charcoal with tin in the reducing flame for a few seconds, the $\dot{Cu}$ reaction is sometimes obtained.	Forms an infusible mass.	With carbonate of soda and nitre on platinum foil, gives a strong manganese reaction.

ZINC.

Mineral.	Formula.	Behavior		
		(1) in glass-bulb.	(2) in open tube.	(3) on charcoal.
Zincblende ...	ZnS.	Decrepitates strongly.	Evolves SO and becomes white or yellow if containing iron.	V. In the reducing flame incrusts the charcoal with ZnO; also with CdO, if that metal be present.
Red oxide of zinc........	$\dot{Zn}$.	—	—	In the reducing flame forms a thin incrustation of oxide of zinc on the charcoal.
Electric calamine.......	$2\dot{Zn}^3\ddot{Si} + 3\dot{H}$.	Gives off water and becomes white and opaque.	—	—
Calamine	$\dot{Zn}\ddot{C}$.	Gives off CO^2 and becomes opaque.	—	As the red oxide. Sometimes also gives a cadmium and lead incrustation.

ZINC. (Continuation of page 232.)

Behavior				(8) Special reactions.
(4) in forceps	(5) in borax.	(6) in mic. salt.	(7) with carb. soda.	
—	The roasted mineral gives a zinc reaction, and sometimes a slight iron-reaction.	As in borax.	As alone on charcoal. Moreover colors the flame blue. The fused alkali gives a S reaction on silver.	—
V.	Generally gives a manganese and slight iron reaction in addition to that of zinc.	As in borax.	On charcoal, forms a thick incrustation of ZnO.	With carbonate of soda and nitre on platinum foil gives a manganese reaction.
V.	Dissolves to a clear glass, which cannot be rendered opaque by the intermittent flame.	Dissolves to a clear glass, which becomes opaque on cooling. Silica remains insoluble.	With carbonate of soda alone is infusible. With 2 parts of alkali and 1 of borax fuses to a glass and sets free $\dot{Z}n$, which incrusts the charcoal.	—
V.	Gives a zinc reaction and frequently an iron and manganese reaction.	As in borax.	Forms a thick incrustation of zinc, sometimes also of $\dot{P}b$ and $\dot{C}o$.	Dissolves with much effervescence in cold acid.

BISMUTH.

Mineral.	Formula.	Behavior		
		(1) in glass-bulb.	(2) in open tube.	(3) on charcoal.
Native bismuth	Bi.	—	Fuses and is converted into a yellow oxide.	Fuses to a bead and incrusts the charcoal with oxide.
Bismuthine ...	BiS.	—	Fuses with ebullition and gives off S and SO^2.	Fuses with much spirting and in the reducing flame yields a metallic bead and incrusts the charcoal, with oxide.
Bismuthblende	$\dddot{B}i^2\ddot{S}i^3$.	Turns yellow and, when strongly heated, fuses.	—	Fuses with ebullition to a brown globule forming an incrustation of $\dddot{B}i$ on the charcoal.

BISMUTH. (Continuation of page 234.)

Behavior				(8) Special reactions.
(4) in forceps.	(5) in borax.	(6) in mic. salt.	(7) with carb. soda.	
—	The oxide formed upon charcoal gives the bismuth reactions.	As in borax.	—	—
—	The oxide obtained upon charcoal gives the bismuth reactions.	As in borax.	As alone on charcoal. The fused alkali gives the sulphur reaction on silver.	—
I. Fuses with ease to a yellow bead, coloring the outer flame bluish green, especially if moistened with HCl. This color is due to $\ddot{P}$.	Gives the bismuth and also an iron reaction.	As in borax, but leaves a silicious skeleton.	Fuses to a yellow mass. The bismuth is then reduced to the metallic state and partially volatilized, incrusting the charcoal beyond.	—

BISMUTH. (Continuation of page 235.)

Mineral.	Formula.	Behavior		
		(1) in glass-bulb.	(2) in open tube.	(3) on charcoal.
Tetradymite ..	Bi,Te,S.	Occasionally decrepitates and then fuses, forming a greyish white sublimate immediately above the mineral fragment.	Fuses and gives off white fumes, part of which pass up the tube and part deposit immediately above the mineral. This latter if heated fuses to clear drops (TeO^3). The mineral residue becomes surrounded by fused B̈i, characterized by its yellow color.	Fuses to a metallic bead, colors the outer flame bluish green (Te and Se) and incrusts the charcoal around with the orange B̈i, beyond which is a white incrustation partly consisting of Ṫe.

BISMUTH. (Continuation of page 236.)

Behavior				(8) Special reactions.
(4) in forceps.	(5) in borax.	(6) in mic. salt.	(7) with carb. soda.	
—	The yellow oxide obtained upon charcoal gives the bismuth reaction, and the white incrustation that of bismuth and telluric acid.	As in borax.	In the reducing flame yields a bead of metallic bismuth, part of which is with part of the tellurium volatilized and incrusts the charcoal around.	The fused alkaline mass gives the sulphur reaction on silver. Also gives the tellurium reaction with charcoal and carbonate of soda.

LEAD.

Mineral.	Formula.	Behavior (1) in glass-bulb.	Behavior (2) in open tube.	Behavior (3) on charcoal.
Galena.......	PbS.	Generally decrepitates and gives off a small quantity of sulphur.	Gives off SO^2, and when strongly heated, a white sublimate of $\dot{P}b,\dddot{S}$.	Fuses and is reduced affording a bead of metallic lead, and forming an incrustation of PbO on the charcoal. Colors the outer flame blue.
Clausthalite...	PbSe.	Decrepitates slightly.	Forms a sublimate of selenium, which is grey when thickly deposited, and red when thin.	Gives off fumes smelling strongly of selenium and coloring the flame blue. In the reducing flame fuses partially and incrusts the charcoal with Se and PbO. After some time a black infusible mass alone remains.
Jamesonite...	$\acute{P}b^3\,'''Sb^2$.	Fuses and gives off some sulphur, sulphide of antimony and antimony which condense in the neck of the bulb.	Fuses and emits dense white fumes of SbO^3, which pass off and redden blue litmus paper.	Fuses with great ease evolving much SbO^3 and PbO, which incrusts the charcoal around the mineral. When the fumes have ceased, a small bead of metallic lead remains.

LEAD. (Continuation of page 238.)

Behavior				(8) Special reactions.
(4) in forceps.	(5) in borax.	(6) in mic. salt.	(7) with carb. soda.	
—	The oxide formed upon charcoal gives the lead reaction.	As in borax.	As alone on charcoal. The fused alkali gives a sulphur reaction on silver.	—
—	The infusible residue obtained upon charcoal gives an iron and sometimes copper and cobalt reaction.	As in borax.	With carbonate of soda, or oxalate of potash yields a metallic bead, the fused alkali laid upon silver and moistened produces a stain similar to that produced by sulphur.	—
—	The yellow incrustation formed upon charcoal gives the reaction of lead, and the white those of antimony.	As in borax.	As alone on charcoal. The fused alkali gives the sulphur reaction on silver.	—

LEAD. (Continuation of page 239.)

Mineral.	Formula.	Behavior (1) in glass-bulb.	Behavior (2) in open tube.	Behavior (3) on charcoal.
Minium.......	Pb^3O^4.	—	—	Is reduced first to litharge (PbO) and then to metallic lead which forms the usual incrustation.
Mendipite	PbCl + 2PbO.	Decrepitates slightly and assumes a yellow color.	—	Fuses readily and is reduced to metallic lead with the evolution of acid fumes. Forms a white incrustation of PbCl, and a yellow one of PbO.
Cerusite......	$\dot{P}b\ddot{C}$.	Decrepitates, gives off CO^2, turns yellow, and fuses.	—	Is reduced to metallic lead, incrusting the charcoal around with PbO.
Anglesite.....	$\dot{P}b\dddot{S}$.	Decrepitates and gives off a small quantity of water.	—	In the oxidizing flame fuses to a clear bead, which becomes opaque on cooling. In reducing flame is reduced with much ebullition to a metallic bead and incrusts the charcoal around with PbO.

LEAD. (Continuation of page 240.)

Behavior				(8) Special reactions.
(4) in forceps.	(5) in borax.	(6) in mic. salt.	(7) with carb. soda.	
Colors the outer flame blue.	Gives the lead reactions.	As in borax.	As alone on charcoal.	—
As the preceding.	As the preceding.	As in borax.	As alone on charcoal.	Gives the chlorine reaction with CuO and microcosmic salt.
As the preceding.	Gives the lead reaction.	As in borax.	As alone on charcoal.	In nitric acid dissolves with much effervescence.
As the preceding.	Gives the lead reaction and occasionally a slight iron and manganese reaction.	As in borax.	Is reduced yielding a metallic lead bead. The fused alkaline mass gives a sulphur reaction on silver.	—

LEAD. (Continuation of page 241.)

Mineral.	Formula.	Behavior (1) in glass-bulb.	Behavior (2) in open tube.	Behavior (3) on charcoal.
Pyromorphite	$PbCl + 3\dot{P}b^{3}\dddot{P}$.	Decrepitates, and when strongly heated for some time, gives a slight white sublimate of PbCl.	—	In oxidizing flame fuses to a bead having a crystalline surface on cooling, and forms a thin film of PbCl on the charcoal. In reducing flame fuses without reduction and on cooling assumes a polyhedral form. Incrusts the charcoal slightly with PbO.
Mimetene	$PbCl+3\dot{P}b^{3}\dddot{As}$.	As the preceding.	—	Fuses, but less easily than the preceding, gives off AsO^3 and incrusts the charcoal with PbCl. Finally is reduced to a metallic bead and forms an incrustation of PbO.

LEAD. (Continuation of page 242.)

Behavior				(8) Special reactions.
(4) in forceps.	(5) in borax.	(6) in mic. salt.	(7) with carb. soda.	
Fuses and colors the flame blue.	—	—	Is reduced yielding a metallic bead and incrusting the charcoal with PbO.	Gives the chlorine reaction with microcosmic salt and CuO. Also the phosphoric acid reactions.
As the preceding.	The oxide formed on charcoal gives the lead reactions.	As in borax.	As the preceding.	Gives the chlorine reaction.

LEAD. (Continuation of page 243.)

Mineral.	Formula.	Behavior		
		(1) in glass-bulb.	(2) in open tube.	(3) on charcoal.
Vanadinite ...	$PbCl+3\dot{P}b^3\dddot{V}$?	As pyromorphite.	—	The powdered mineral fuses to a black shining mass, which in the reducing flame affords a metallic bead. Incrusts the charcoal first with a white film of PbCl and afterwards with PbO.
Crocoisite	$\dot{P}b\dddot{C}r$.	Decrepitates violently and assumes a dark color.	—	Fuses and detonates, yielding C^2O^3 and metallic lead, and forming an incrustation of PbO on the charcoal.
Molybdate of lead	$\dot{P}b\dddot{M}$.	As the preceding.	—	Fuses and is partly absorbed into the charcoal leaving a globule of metallic lead, which is partially oxidized and incrusts the charcoal.

LEAD. (Continuation of page 244.)

Behavior				(8) Special reactions.
(4) in forceps.	(5) in borax.	(6) in mic. salt.	(7) with carb. soda.	
As pyromorphite.	Dissolves readily to a clear glass, which, in the oxidizing flame, is yellow while hot, and colorless when cold. In reducing flame becomes opaque, and on cooling green.	In oxidizing flame is yellow while hot, becoming paler on cooling. In reducing flame brown while warm, and emerald green when cold.	On platinum wire fuses to a yellow bead, which is crystalline on cooling. On charcoal yields a button of metallic lead.	With microcosmic salt and CuO, gives the chlorine reaction. If fused in a platinum spoon with from 3 to 4 times its volume of $\dot{K},\dddot{S}^2$ it forms a fluid yellow mass having an orange color when cold.
As pyromorphite.	Dissolves readily and colors the glass yellow while warm, and green when cold. (See Chromium reaction.)	As in borax.	On platinum foil gives a dark yellow mass, which becomes paler on cooling. On charcoal yields a metallic button.	Treated as above with $\dot{K},\dddot{S}^2$ forms a violet colored mass, which on solidifying becomes reddish and on cooling pale grey.
As pyromorphite.	Dissolves readily and gives the molybdena reaction.	As in borax.	Yields metallic lead.	Fused as above with $\dot{K},\dddot{S}^2$ forms a yellow mass, which becomes white on cooling. If this be dissolved in water and a piece of zinc introduced into the solution, the latter becomes blue.

LEAD. (Continuation of page 245.)

Mineral.	Formula.	Behavior		
		(1) in glass-bulb.	(2) in open tube.	(3) on charcoal.
Scheeletine ...	$\dot{Pb}\dddot{W}$.	Decrepitates more or less.	—	Fuses to a bead incrusting the charcoal with PbO. The bead on cooling is crystalline and has a dark metallic surface.

LEAD. (Continuation of page 246.)

Behavior				(8) Special reactions.
(4) in forceps.	(5) in borax.	(6) in mic. salt.	(7) with carb. soda.	
As pyromorphite.	Dissolves to a clear colorless glass, which in the reducing flame becomes yellow, and on cooling grey and opaque.	Dissolves to a clear colorless glass, which in the reducing flame assumes a dusky blue color. After a time becomes opaque.	As the preceding.	With carbonate of soda and nitre gives the manganese reaction.

COPPER.

Mineral.	Formula.	Behavior (1) in glass-bulb.	Behavior (2) in open tube.	Behavior (3) on charcoal.
Native copper	Cu	—	—	Fuses to a brilliant metallic bead, which on cooling becomes covered with a coating of black oxide.
Vitreous copper........	Cu^2S.	—	Evolves SO^2 and, when pulverized and gently heated for some time is converted into CuO.	Fuses to a bead, which spirts considerably and gives off SO^2. When pulverized and gently roasted, is converted into CuO.
Copper pyrites	$\overset{,}{\text{Cu}}\overset{,,,}{\text{Fe}}$.	Decrepitates, sometimes gives a sublimate of sulphur and becomes bronze colored on the surface.	Evolves SO^2 and is finally converted into a dark red mixture of Fe^2O^3 and CuO.	Fuses readily with much ebullition and is magnetic on cooling.

COPPER. (Continuation of page 248.)

Behavior				(8) Special reactions.
(4) in forceps.	(5) in borax.	(6) in mic. salt.	(7) with carb. soda.	
Fuses and colors the outer flame blue.	In the oxidizing flame dissolves and then gives the copper reactions.	As in borax.	—	—
—	The roasted mineral gives the copper reaction, and sometimes also a slight iron-reaction.	As in borax.	In the reducing flame is decomposed, forming NaS and metallic copper. If the former be cut out and laid upon silver, it gives the sulphur reaction.	—
—	As the preceding; but when the copper has been removed by reducing on charcoal, the bead shows a strong iron color.	As the preceding, but the color in the oxidizing flame is green, owing to the presence of iron.	Yields a bead of metallic copper and some magnetic oxide of iron, which remains on the charcoal. The fused alkali gives a sulphur reaction on silver.	—

COPPER. (Continuation of page 249.)

Mineral.	Formula.	Behavior		
		(1) in glass-bulb.	(2) in open tube.	(3) on charcoal.
Fahlerz	$(\acute{Cu}\acute{Ag}\acute{Fe}\acute{Zn})^4$ $(\overset{'''}{Sb}\overset{'''}{As})$.	Sometimes decrepitates, fuses, and when very strongly heated, gives a red sublimate of $\overset{'''}{Sb}$ with $\ddot{Sb}$, also sometimes a black sublimate of $\acute{Hg}$ and occasionally $\overset{'''}{As}$.	Fuses and gives off thick fumes of SbO^3 and SO^2, also generally AsO^3, leaving a black infusible residue. If Hg be present, it is sublimed and condenses in the tube in small drops.	Fuses to a bead, which fumes strongly and incrusts the charcoal with SbO^3, and sometimes ZnO, which cannot be volatilized. Emits a strong smell of arsenic.
Tennantite ...	$(\acute{Cu}\acute{Fe})^4\overset{'''}{As}$.	Decrepitates occasionally and gives a red sublimate of $\overset{'''}{As}$.	Evolves $\ddot{S}$ and $\ddot{As}$, which condense and form a white sublimate.	Fuses to a magnetic bead giving off arsenical and sulphurous fumes.
Bournonite ...	$(\acute{Pb}^2\acute{Cu})\overset{'''}{Sb}$.	Decrepitates giving off sulphur and, when strongly heated, $\overset{'''}{Sb}$ and $\ddot{Sb}$.	Evolves thick white fumes of $\ddot{Sb}$, $\overset{\therefore}{Sb}$ and $\dot{Pb}\overset{\therefore}{Sb}$. Also $\ddot{S}$.	Fuses readily and incrusts the charcoal with $\ddot{Sb}$ and $\dot{Pb}$ leaving a dark colored bead.

COPPER. (Continuation of page 250.)

Behavior				(8) Special reactions.
(4) in forceps.	(5) in borax.	(6) in mic. salt.	(7) with carb. soda.	
—	The residue obtained on charcoal thoroughly roasted gives a copper reaction, and when the latter has been removed by reduction upon charcoal, an iron reaction.	As the preceding.	With this flux and a little borax yields a bead of metallic copper; on silver, the alkaline mass gives a sulphur reaction.	If the copper bead obtained by fusing upon carbonate of soda be cupelled with assay lead, a silver bead will be obtained. Or if dissolved in nitric acid and a drop or two of HCCl added, a white precipitate of AgCl will be formed, which may be collected and reduced with carbonate soda upon charcoal.
—	As the preceding.	As the preceding.	Yields a copper bead and metallic iron in the form of a dark grey powder. The fused alkali gives the sulphur reaction.	—
—	If the bead obtained on charcoal be fused on that support in the reducing flame with borax, a slight iron reaction is obtained, and after a time a copper reaction.	As with borax.	Yields a bead of metallic copper and lead and incrusts the charcoal with $\ddot{Sb}$ and $\dot{Pb}$. The alkaline mass laid on silver and moistened gives the sulphur reaction.	—

COPPER. (Continuation of page 251.)

Mineral.	Formula.	Behavior		
		(1) in glass-bulb.	(2) in open tube.	(3) on charcoal.
Red oxide of copper	Cu^2O.	—	Is converted into the black oxide CuO.	In the reducing flame is reduced, forming a bead of metallic copper.
Atacamite	$CuCl + 3\dot{Cu} + 6\dot{H}$.	Gives off much water, having an acid reaction, on test paper, and forms a light grey sublimate of CuCl.	—	Fuses, colors the flame blue, forms a brown and a pale grey incrustation on the charcoal, and is reduced to metallic copper, leaving a small quantity of slag.
Dioptase	$\dot{Cu}^3\dddot{Si}^2 + 3\dot{H}$.	Gives off water and turns black.	—	In the oxidizing flame becomes black. In the reducing flame red.
Malachite	$\dot{Cu}^2\ddot{C} + \dot{H}$.	Gives off water and turns black.	—	Fuses to a bead and with a strong flame is reduced to metallic copper.

COPPER. (Continuation of page 252.)

Behavior				(8) Special reactions.
(4) in forceps.	(5) in borax.	(6) in mic. salt.	(7) with carb. soda.	
Fuses and colors the flame emerald green, or if previously moistened with HCl, blue.	Gives the copper reaction.	As with borax.	Is reduced to a bead of metallic copper.	—
Fuses and colors the outer flame intensely blue and green towards the point.	Gives the copper reactions.	As with borax.	Is reduced, yielding a bead of metallic copper.	—
V. Colors the outer flame intensely green.	Gives the copper reactions.	As with borax. The silica remains undissolved.	With a small quantity of carbonate of soda fuses to a bead, which on cooling is opaque and has a red fracture. With more alkali forms a slag, containing little beads of reduced copper.	—
Fuses and colors the outer flame brilliantly green.	Gives the copper reaction.	As in borax.	Yields metallic copper.	Dissolves in HCl with much effervescence.

COPPER. (Continuation of page 253.)

Mineral.	Formula.	Behavior (1) in glass-bulb.	Behavior (2) in open tube.	Behavior (3) on charcoal.
Blue vitriol....	$\dot{C}u\dddot{S} + 5\dot{H}$.	Intumesces, gives off water and becomes white.	Strongly heated is decomposed, giving off SO^2 and being converted into CuO.	As in the glass-bulb. Then fuses, coloring the outer flame green, and is reduced to metallic copper and $\dot{C}u$.
Libethenite ...	$\dot{C}u^4\overset{.....}{P} + 2\dot{H}$.	Gives off water and turns black.	—	Gradually heated, turns black and fuses to a bead, having a core of metallic copper.
Olivenite	$\dot{C}u^4(\overset{.....}{As}\overset{.....}{P}) + \dot{H}$.	Gives off water.	—	Fuses with detonation and the evolution of arsenical fumes to a brittle regulus, brown externally and having a white fracture.

COPPER. (Continuation of page 254.)

Behavior				(8) Special reactions.
(4) in forceps.	(5) in borax.	(6) in mic. salt.	(7) with carb. soda.	
Fuses and colors the outer flame blue.	The roasted mineral gives the copper reaction.	As in borax.	Yields metallic copper. The alkaline mass laid on silver gives the S reaction.	Gives the sulphuric acid reaction.
Fuses, but does not color the flame distinctly. On cooling is black and crystalline.	Gives the copper reaction.	As in borax.	With much of the alkali is decomposed, yielding metallic copper. With small portions successively added first fuses and then intumesces, fuses with a strong flame, and is then absorbed into the charcoal, leaving metallic copper.	Gives the phosphoric acid reaction.
Fuses and colors the outer flame green. On cooling has a crystalline surface.	Gives a copper reaction.	As in borax.	Is reduced, yielding metallic copper.	Gives the arsenic reactions.

ANTIMONY.

Mineral.	Formula.	Behavior (1) in glass-bulb.	(2) in open tube.	(3) on charcoal.
Native antimony......	Sb.	Fuses and, when strongly heated, volatilizes being redeposited in the tube as a dark grey sublimate.	Fuses and gives off dense white fumes, which are partly redeposited on the tube. Sometimes also gives off arsenical fumes in small quantity.	Fuses and gives off dense white fumes, which thickly incrust the charcoal and color the blame blue immediately beyond the assay.
Grey antimony	SbS^3.	Fuses readily and occasionally gives off a small quantity of sulphur. Strongly heated forms a brown sublimate of SbS^3 and SbO^3.	Fuses and gives off SO^2, which passes off up the tube, and dense white fumes of SbO^3 and SbO^5, which are partly deposited in the tube.	Fuses and is partly absorbed by the charcoal and partly volatilized, incrusting the charcoal with the characteristic white oxides. Colors the flame blue.
Antimony blende.....	$\dddot{S}b^2 + \ddot{S}b$.	Fuses easily, gives off first SbO^3 and afterwards an orange colored sublimate. Strongly heated, is decomposed and gives a black sublimate, which becomes brown on cooling.	As the preceding.	As the preceding.

ANTIMONY. (Continuation of page 256.)

Behavior				(8) Special reactions.
(4) in forceps.	(5) in borax.	(6) in mic. salt.	(7) with carb. soda.	
—	The oxide formed upon charcoal gives the antimony reactions.	As in borax.	—	The incrustation on the charcoal, if treated with nitrate of cobalt assumes the characteristic green color.
—	As the preceding.	As in borax.	Fuses and is reduced, yielding metallic antimony, which behaves as the preceding mineral upon charcoal. The alkaline mass gives the sulphur reaction.	As the preceding.
—	As native antimony.	As in borax.	As the preceding.	As native antimony.

ANTIMONY. (Continuation of page 257.)

Mineral.	Formula.	Behavior		
		(1) in glass-bulb.	(2) in open tube.	(3) on charcoal.
White antimony	SbO^3.	Is sublimed and recondensed in the neck of the tube.	As in the glass-bulb.	Fuses with the evolution of dense white fumes, which incrust the surface of the charcoal. In the reducing flame is partly reduced, yielding metallic antimony. Colors flame blue.

ANTIMONY. (Continuation of page 258.)

Behavior				(8) Special reactions.
(4) in forceps.	(5) in borax.	(6) in mic. salt.	(7) with carb. soda.	
Fuses and is volatilized, coloring the outer flame blue.	Gives the antimony reaction.	As in borax.	In the reducing flame is reduced, yielding metallic antimony.	As native antimony.

ARSENIC.

Mineral.	Formula.	Behavior		
		(1) in glass-bulb.	(2) in open tube.	(3) on charcoal.
Native arsenic	As.	Sublimes without fusion and recondenses as a dark grey metallic sublimate, sometimes leaving a small residue.	If gently heated in a good current of air passes off as AsO^3, which is partly condensed as a white sublimate in the upper part of the tube.	Passes off as AsO^3, which thinly incrusts the charcoal beyond the assay.
Realgar......	AsS^2.	Fuses, enters into ebullition and is sublimed as a transparent red sublimate.	Gently heated passes off as SO^2 and AsO^3, the latter of which is redeposited in the upper part of the tube.	Fuses and passes off as arsenious and sulphurous acids.
Orpiment.....	AsS^3.	As the preceding, except that the sublimate is of a dark yellow color when cold.	As the preceding.	As the preceding.
White arsenic	AsO^3.	Sublimes without fusion and recondenses in white crystals.	—	Sublimes and is partly recondensed on charcoal forming a white incrustation.

ARSENIC. (Continuation of page 260.)

Behavior				(8) Special reactions.
(4) in forceps.	(5) in borax.	(6) in mic. salt.	(7) with carb. soda.	
Colors the flame blue.	—	—	—	—
Fuses and colors the flame blue.	—	—	As on charcoal, except that the S combines with the alkali forming NaS, which on silver gives the sulphur reaction.	—
As the preceding.	—	—	As the preceding.	—
Colors the flame blue.	—	—	—	Heated with charcoal in a glass-tube sealed at one end, is reduced and metallic arsenic sublimes

MERCURY.

Mineral.	Formula.	Behavior (1) in glass-bulb.	Behavior (2) in open tube.	Behavior (3) on charcoal.
Native mercury	Hg.	Volatilizes with little or no residue and recondenses in neck of bulb.	—	Is volatilized.
Cinnabar.....	HgS.	Volatilizes sometimes leaving a slight earthy residue, and recondenses as a black sulphide.	If gently heated is decomposed into metallic mercury, which volatilizes and recondenses in the upper part of the tube, and SO^2, which passes off and is easily recognized by its odor and bleaching properties.	Is volatilized, generally leaving a small earthy residue.
Native amalgam........	$AgHg^2$.	As native mercury, but leaves a residue of pure silver.	—	The mercury volatilizes leaving the silver, which fuses to a bead, and, in the oxidizing flame, incrusts the charcoal with its characteristic oxide.

MERCURY. (Continuation of page 262.)

Behavior				(8) Special reactions.
(4) in forceps.	(5) in borax.	(6) in mic. salt.	(7) with carb. soda.	
—	—	—	—	—
—	—	—	With carbonate of soda and cyanide of potassium is decomposed and metallic mercury volatilized.	When in the preceding experiment the mercury has been entirely dissipated, the alkaline residue laid on silver gives a sulphur reaction.
—	—	—	—	—

SILVER.

Mineral.	Formula.	Behavior (1) in glass-bulb.	Behavior (2) in open tube.	Behavior (3) on charcoal.
Native silver..	Ag.	—	—	Fuses and in a strong oxidizing flame forms an incrustation of dark brown oxide on the charcoal. If any antimony be present, it affords a crimson incrustation.
Antimonial silver......	Ag^2Sb.	—	Gives off dense white fumes, which are partly deposited in the tube.	Fuses, fumes strongly, forming a white incrustation, and when the antimony is nearly expelled a crimson one, a nearly pure silver bead remains.
Silver glance..	AgS.	—	Gives off sulphurous acid.	Gives off SO^2 and is reduced to metallic silver. If impure, a small quantity of slag also remains.

SILVER. (Continuation of page 264.)

Behavior				(8) Special reactions.
(4) in forceps.	(5) in borax.	(6) in mic. salt.	(7) with carb. soda.	
—	Gives the silver reactions.	As in borax.	—	—
—	The incrustation formed on charcoal gives an antimony reaction.	As in borax.	As alone on charcoal.	—
—	The residual slag (if any) obtained upon charcoal gives an iron reaction.	As in borax.	As alone on charcoal. The alkaline mass gives a sulphur reaction on polished silver.	—

SILVER. (Continuation of page 265.)

Mineral.	Formula.	Behavior (1) in glass-bulb.	Behavior (2) in open tube.	Behavior (3) on charcoal.
Stephanite....	$\dot{Ag}^{6}\overset{'''}{Sb}$.	Decrepitates, fuses and gives a slight sublimate of sulphide of antimony.	Fuses and gives off SO^2 and dense white antimonial fumes.	Fuses and incrusts the chacoal with antimonious acid, leaving Ag with some antimony. If the flame be continued, a red incrustation is formed and finally a bead of pure silver remains surrounded by a small slag.
Pyrargyrite...	$\dot{Ag}^{3}\overset{'''}{Sb}$.	Sometimes decrepitates, fuses readily, and, when strongly heated, gives a dark red sublimate of SbS^3.	As the preceding.	Fuses with much spirting and covers the charcoal with antimonial fumes. When the residual AgS is heated for some time in the oxidizing flame, a bead of pure silver is obtained.
Proustite.....	$\dot{Ag}^{3}\overset{'''}{As}$.	Fuses and at a low red heat affords a small sublimate of AsS^3.	Gradually heated it gives off AsO^3 and SO^2. Sometimes also antimony fumes.	As the preceding, except that a large quantity of AsO^3 and but little SbO^3 are given off.

SILVER. (Continuation of page 266.)

Behavior				(8) Special reactions.
(4) in forceps.	(5) in borax.	(6) in mic. salt.	(7) with carb. soda.	
—	The residual slag obtained on the charcoal gives an iron and copper reaction.	As in borax.	The silver is reduced and the antimony passes off in dense fumes. The fused alkali gives the sulphur-reaction on silver.	—
—	—	—	As the preceding.	—
—	—	—	As stephanite, except that much arsenic is given off and but little antimony.	—

SILVER. (Continuation of page 267.)

Mineral.	Formula.	Behavior		
		(1) in glass-bulb.	(2) in open tube.	(3) on charcoal.
Horn silver...	AgCl.	Fuses, but undergoes no further change.	—	Fuses readily in the oxidizing flame. In the reducing flame is slowly reduced yielding metallic silver.

SILVER. (Continuation of page 268.)

Behavior				(8) Special reactions.
(4) in forceps.	(5) in borax.	(6) in mic. salt.	(7) with carb. soda.	
—	—	—	Is rapidly reduced to metallic silver.	If cut up into small pieces mixed with oxide of copper and then heated before the oxidizing flame upon charcoal, it colors the flame blue.

THE END.

H. BAILLIERE'S

CATALOGUE OF

RECENT FOREIGN BOOKS

ON

CHEMISTRY, ELECTRICITY, PHYSICS,

METEOROLOGY, &c., &c.

Accum. Treatise on the Art of Brewing. 12mo. London 2 75

——— Treatise on Gas Lighting. Royal 8vo. London 3 60

Acken (A.) Arts and Manufactures, illustrated with historical and literary details. 8vo., half calf. London, 1831–45 . . . . 3 00

Aime, (Martin). Lettres a Sophie sur la Physique. 12mo. Paris, 1843 . . 87

Ajasson de Grandsagne. Nouveau Manuel complet de Chimie appliquee a la Medecine. 18mo. Paris, 1832 87

Ajasson de Grandsagne et Fouche. Nouveau Manuel complet de Physique et de Meteorologie. 2d edit. 18mo. Paris, 1835 87

An Explanatory Dictionary of the Apparatus and instruments employed in the various operations of Philosophical and Experimental Chemistry. 17 Plates. 8vo. London, 1824 . . . . 1 00

Annales de Chimie, ou Recueil de Memoires concernant la Chimie et les Arts qui en dependent. Paris, 1789 to 1815 inclusive. 8vo., et 3 vols. de Tables.
2e Serie, 1816 to 1840, incl. 75 vols., 8vo. et 3 vols. de Tables.
3e Serie, 1841 to ——. Cette serie est en cours de publication.
Prix par annee 11 25

Annuaire de Chimie, comprenant les applications de cette Science a la Medecine et a la Pharmacie, ou Repertoire des decouvertes et des nouveaux travaux en chimie faits dans les diverses parties de l'Europe. Par MM. E. Millon, J. Reiset. Avec la collaboration de MM. F. Hoefer et J. Nickles. 8vo. Paris, 1845–51. 7 vols. . . . 14 00

Arago. Œuvres completes.

——— Meteorological Essays. With an Introduction by Humboldt. Edited by Col. Sabine. 8vo. London, 1855 . . . . 5 50

Archambault. Precis Elementaire de Physique. Premiere partie, comprenant la Pesanteur, l'Hydrostatique et la Chaleur, avec 98 gravures intercalees dans le texte. 1854. 12mo. 1 00

——— Deuxieme partie, comprenant l'Electricite, le Magnetisme, le Galvanisme, l'Electro-dynamique, l'Acoustique et l'Optique, avec 142 gravures dans le texte. 1855. 12mo. 1 00

Arnott (A.) The Smokeless Fire-place, Chimney Valve, and other means, New and Old, of obtaining Healthful Warmth by Ventilation. 8vo. London, 1855 . . 1 80

Avogadro. Sui calori Speafico de Corpi Solidi e liquidi. 4to. 75

Barreswil et Davanne. Chimie Photographique, contenant les elements de Chimie expliques par les manipulations Photographiques. Les procedes de Photographie sur Plaques, sur Papier sec ou humide, sur Verres au Collodion et a l'Albumine. La maniere de preparer soi meme, d'employer tous les reactifs et d'utiliser les residus. Les Recettes les plus nouvelles les derniers perfectionnements. La Gravure et la Lithophotographie. 8vo. 1854 . . . . 1 50

Barreswil et Sobrino. Appendice a touts les traites d'Analyse Chimique, recueil des observations publiees depuis 10 ans sur l'Analyse qualit. et quant. 1 vol., 8vo. Paris, 1842 . . . . 1 75

Barruel (G.) Traite de Chimie Technique appliquee aux Arts et a l'Industrie, a la Pharmacie et a l'Agriculture. Tome 1er. 8vo. Paris, 1856 . . . . 1 75
L'ouvrage aura 6 vols.

Baudrimont (A.) Traite de Chimie Generale et Experimentale, avec les applications aux Arts, a la Medecine, a la Pharmacie, &c., accompagne de 200 planches intercalees dans le texte. 2 forts vol. in-8. Paris, 1844–46 . . . . . . 4 50

Baudrimont (A.) Du sucre et de sa fabrication, suivi d'un precis de la legislation qui regit cette industrie, par A. Trebuchet. 9vo., avec 21 fig. Paris, 1841 . . 0 75

Becquerel. Traite d'Electricite et de Magnetisme, et des Applications de ces Sciences a la Chimie, a la Physiologie et aux Arts. 3 vols. 8vo., plus planches. Paris, 1856 . 6 00
Ouvrage termine. Il est l'expose des lecons qui sont faites au Museum d'histoire naturelle et au Conservatoire des arts et metiers sur l'electricite, le magnetisme et toutes leurs applications. Chaque volume renferme les applications relatives au sujet principal qui s'y trouve traite. Les figures, dessinees et gravees avec soin, sont intercalees dans le texte.

——— Traite de l'Electricite et du Magnetisme. 7 vols., 8vo., avec atlas in-fol. Paris. 1834 . . . . 20 00

——— Traite complet du Magnetisme. 8vo. 2 50

——— Elements d'Electro-Chimie Appliques aux Sciences Naturelles et aux Arts. 8vo. Paris, 1843 . . . . 2 00

Becquerel (M. A.) Des Applications de l'Electricite a la Pathologie. 8vo. Paris, 1856

Bernay (A. J.) First Lines in Chemistry: a Manual for Students. 12mo. London, 1855 . . . . 2 12

——— Household Chemistry, or the Rudiments of the Science applied to every-day life. 12mo. London, 1852 . . . . 1 12

Berthier. Traite des Essais par la Voie Seche, ou des proprietes, de la composition et de l'essai des Substances Metalliques et des Combustibles. 2 vols., 8vo. 15 pl. Paris, 1848 8 00

Berthollet. Art of Dyeing and Bleaching by Ure. 8vo. London . . . 3 60

Berzelius. Traite complet de chimie minerale, vegetale et animale, seconde edition francaise, traduit, avec l'assentiment de l'auteur, par M. Esslinger et F. Hoefer. Paris, 1846–51. Vol. 1 to 6 . . . . 18 00
See **Gerhardt.**

——— Rapport annuel sur les progres de la chimie, presente le 30 mars de chaque annee, a l'Academie des Sciences de Stockholm, traduit du Suedois, par Plantamour, 8 vols. 8vo. Paris, 1841 to 1848 . . . . 9 00

——— View of Animal Chemistry. 8vo. London . . . . . .

——— Use of the Blowpipe, translated by Children. 8vo. London. (Very scarce.) .

——— Traite de Chimie. Nouv. edit., par B. Valerius. 4 vols., gr. 8vo., avec 8 planches. Half bound, cf. Bruxelles, 1841 to 1844 . . . . 18 00

——— Lehrbuch der Chemie. Funfte auflage. Bds. 1–5. Dresden, 1842–48 . .

Billard. Traite de la fabrication du Platine. 8vo., d'une feuille et quart. Paris, 1855 . 2 50

Biot. Instructions pratiques sur l'observations et la mesure des proprietes optiques appelees rotatoires, avec l'expose succinct de leur application a la chimie medicale scientifique et industrielle. Paris, 1845 . . . . 0 25

——— Precis elementaire de Physique. 2 vols., 8vo. Paris, 1825 . . . 5 00

——— Traite de Physique Experimentale. 4 vols., 8vo. Paris. (Very scarce.)

——— De la Polarisation de la Lumiere. 1 vol., 4to. Planches. (Scarce.)

Bird (G.) Elements of Natural Philosophy, being an Experimental Introduction to the study of the Physical Sciences. 12mo., cloth 3 75

Bischoff. Elements of Chemical and Physical Geology. Translated by Paul and Drummond. 2 vols., 8vo. London, 1854–56 . . . . 9 00

Blanchiment. Nouveau Manuel complet du Blanchiment, du Blanchissage, Nettoyage et Degraissage des fils et Etoffes de Coton, Chanvre, Lin, Laine, Soie, etc. 2 vols., 18mo. Paris, 1855 . . . . 1 50

Black (W.) Practical Treatise on Brewing. 4th edit. 8vo. London, 1849 . . 3 25

Blanquart (Evrard.) Traite de Photographie sur Papier. 8vo. Paris. 1851 . 1 25

Blowpipe. See SANDERS, Dr. J. M.

Bouchardat. Opuscules d'Economie Rurale. 8vo. Paris, 1851 . . . 1 00

Bouquet (J. P.) Histoire Chimique des Eaux Minerales et Thermales de Vichy. Cusset, Vaisse, Hauterive et Saint-Yorre; Analyses Chimiques des Eaux Minerales de Medague, Chateldon, Brugheas et Seuillet. 8vo., 3 cartes. Paris, 1855 . . . 1 75

Boussingault. Rural Economy; in its Relations with Chemistry, Physics, and Meteorology. 2d edition, with notes carefully revised and corrected. 1 vol., 8vo., cloth, bds. London, 1845 . . . . 4 50

Boutet de Monvel. Cours de Chimie, redige conformement aux derniers programmes de l'Enseignement Scientifique dans les Lycees, et a celui du Baccalaureat des Sciences, avec 118 gravures intercalees dans le texte. 12mo. Paris, 1856 . . . 1 25

Boutigny. Base d'une Nouvelle Physique, l'etat Spheroidal. 8vo. 1842 . . 1 25

Bowman (J. E.) Introduction to Practical Chemistry. 2d edit. 12mo. . , 2 00

Brande. Tables of Chemical Equivalents. 8vo. London 1 00

——— Dictionary of Science, Literature, and Art. 8vo. London . . . 7 50

——— Tables of Specific Gravity and Equivalents. 8vo. 2 50

——— Lectures on Organic Chemistry, as applied to Manufactures, Dyeing, Tanning, &c., &c., arranged by Scoffern. 12mo. London 2 25

Brande (W. T.) Manual of Chemistry. 2 vols., 8vo. London . . . 13 50

Brebisson (A. de). Nouvelle Methode Photographique sur collodion donnant des epreuves instantanees; traite complet des divers procedes. 8vo. Paris, 1852 . . 1 00

——— Traite Complet de Photographie sur Collodion; repertoire de la plupart des Procedes Connus. 8vo. Paris, 1855 . . . . 1 00

Brewster (Sir D.) A Treatise on Optics. 12mo. London, 1853 . . . 1 12

——— The Stereoscope; its History, Theory, and Construction, with its application to the fine and useful Arts and to Education. 12mo. London, 1856 . . . 1 62

Brown (A.) The Philosophy of Physics, or Process of Creative Development. 8vo. New York, 1854 . . . . 2 25

Cabart (C.) Leçons de Physique et de Chimie. 8vo., avec 28 planches. Paris, 1854 . 2 00

Cahours (A.) Leçons de Chimie Generale Elementaire, Professees a l'Ecole Centrale des Arts et Manufactures. Avec gravures sur bois intercalees dans le texte, et planches. 2 vols., 18mo. Paris, 1855 . . . . 3 00

Campbell. A practical Text-Book of Inorganic Chemistry, including the preparations of Substances, and their Qualitative and Quantitative Analyses, with Organic Analyses. 12mo. 1 50

Caoutchouc. Manuels-Roret. Nouveau Manuel complet du Fabricant d'Objets en Caoutchouc, en Gutta-Percha et en Gomme Factice; suivi de Documents Etendus sur la Fabrication des Tissus Impermeables, des Toiles Cirees et des Cuirs Vernis; par M. Paulin Desormeaux. 1 vol., 12mo., avec planches. Paris, 1855 . . . 1 00

Cavendish Society's publications already published:

GRAHAM'S Chemical Reports and Memoirs. Scarce.
GMELINS. Handbook of Chemistry. Vols. 1 to 10, 8vo.
LEHMAN'S Physiological Chemistry. 3 vols. and atlas.
Life and Works of CAVENDISH.
Life and Works of DALTON.
BISCHOFF. Chemical Geology. 2 vols.
Subscription, $7 per annum.

Chalmers (C.) Thoughts on Electricity, with notes of Experiments. 8vo., cloth. Edinburgh, 1851 . . . . 1 50

Chemical Technology; or Chemistry applied to the Arts and to Manufactures. By Professor Knapp and Drs. Ronolds and Richardson. 3 vols., 8vo. (vol. 1, 2nd edit.), illustrated with 776 woodcuts and 14 plates. London, 1848–55 . . . 18 00
The vols. can be had separately.
Vol. 1. Fuel and its Applications (Coal, Gas, Oil, Spermaceti, &c), and their application to purposes of illumination, Lighthouses, &c., Resin, Wax, Turpentine, Peat, Wood, Stoves, &c., &c., in 2 parts, 8vo., with 433 engravings and 4 plates. Price $9 00.
Vol. 2. Glass, Alum, Earthenware, Cements, &c., &c., Manufacture. 8vo., with 214 engravings and one plate. Price $4 00.
Vol. 3. On those branches of Chemical Industry, including the production of Food, and related to Agriculture. (Bread, Milk, Tea, Coffee, Sugar, Tobacco, &c.) With 9 engravings and 129 woodcuts. Price $5 00.

Chemical Society, Quarterly Journal and Transactions of. Vols. 1 to 8, cloth . 27 50
Vol. 9, in course of publication. Subscription price, $3 00 per vol.

Chemist (The), or Reporter of Chemical Discoveries and Improvements, and Protector of the Rights of the Chemist and Chemical Manufacturer. Edited by Charles and John Watt. 4 vols., 8vo., cloth. 1840–43 . . . . 10 00

——— A Monthly Journal of Chemical and Physical Science. Commencing October, 1853. Price, per year or volume 3 60

Chertier (F. M.) Nouvelles Recherches sur les Feux d'Artifice. 2me edit., 8vo., avec gravures. Paris, 1854 . . . . 2 25

Chevalier. Recueil de Memoires et de procedes nouveaux contenant la Photographie sur plaques metalliques et sur papier. 8vo., half bound, calf. Paris, 1847 . . 0 75

Chevalier (C.) Photographie sur Papier, Verre, et Metal. Galvanoplastie. Catalogue universel explicatif et illustre des appareils perfectionnes. 8vo., avec 3 planches. Paris, 1856 . . . . 0 62

Chevallier. Dictionnaire des Alterations et Falsifications des Substances Alimentaires, Medicamenteuses et Commerciales, avec l'Indication des Moyens de les Reconnaitre. 2me edition, 2 vols., 8vo. Paris, 1855 . . . . 8 25

Chevallier, Lamy, and Robiquet. Dictionnaire raisonne des denominations Chimiques et Pharmaceutiques, contenant tous les termes employes en Chimie, &c., &c. 2me edit., tome 1er. Paris, 1853 . . . . 2 25

Chevreul. De la Baguette divinatoire, du Pendule, dit Explorateur, et des Tables Tournantes, au point de vue d'Histoire, de la Critique et de la Methode Experimentale. 8vo. Paris, 1854 . . . . 1 25

——— The Principles of Harmony and Contrast of Colors, and their Application to the Arts. 12mo., 2nd edition. London, 1855 . . . . . . 3 75

——— De la loi du Contraste simultane des Couleurs et de ses Applications. 8vo., et 4to. Atlas. Paris, 1839 . . . . 12 50
Very scarce.

Claudet. Nouvelles Recherches sur la difference entre les Foyers Visuels et Photogeniques. 8vo. Paris, 1851 . . . . 0 50

Clegg (S.) Treatise on the Manufacture of Coal Gas. 4to. London . . . 8 37

Codex. Pharmacopee Francaise, redigee par ordre du gouvernement, avec appendice therapeutique, par Cazenave. 8vo. Paris, 1837 . . . . . . 2 50
In half calf 3 00

Coloriste. Nouveau Manuel Complet du Coloriste, ou Instructions Simplifiees et elementaires pour l'enluminure, le lavis et la retouche des gravures. Nouvelle edition. 18mo., avec 3 planches. Paris, 1856 . . . . 0 75

Colles. Nouveau Manuel de la Fabrication des Colles, comprenant la Fabrication des Colles de Matieres Vegetales, par M. Malpeyre. 12mo. Paris, 1856 . . . 0 50

Cooley (A. J.) Cyclopedia of Practical Receipts, and collateral information in the Arts. Manufactures, Professions, and Trades; including Medicine, Pharmacy, and Domestic Economy; designed as a comprehensive supplement to the Pharmacopœia, and general book of reference for the Manufacturer, Tradesman, Amateur, and heads of Families. 3rd edition. 8vo. London, 1856 . . . . 8 00

Cooper (C.) Identities of Light and Heat; of Caloric and Electricity. 8vo. Philadelphia, 1848 . . . . 0 75

Cotte. Observations Meteorologiques. 4to. 0 60

Coulomb. Methode de determiner l'Inclinaison d'une Aiguille Aimantee. 4to. . 0 25

Crabb (G. A.) Technical Dictionary; or a Dictionary explaining the terms used in all Arts and Sciences. 12mo. London, 1851 . . . . . . 3 75

Cumming, J. A Manual of Electro Dynamics. 8vo. London, 1827 . . 1 50

Cundall (J.) The Photographic Primer for the use of beginners in the Collodion process. Illustrated with a Photographic Picture. 2d edit. 12mo. London, 1856 . . 0 31

Cuvier. Analyse de ses Travaux sur la Physique et la Chimie. 4to. . . . 0 60

Daguin (P. A.) Traite Elementaire de Physique Theorique et Experimentale, avec les Applications a la Meteorologie et aux Arts Industriels. Tome 1er. Avec 300 gravures sur bois intercalees dans le texte. 8vo. Paris, 1856 . . . . . 3 00

Dalton (John), Life and Scientific Researches of. By W. C. Henry. 8vo. London, 1854 3 50
——— Chemical Philosophy. 2 vols., 8vo. London 9 50

Daniell (J. F.) An Introduction to the Study of Chemical Philosophy; being a preparatory view of the forces which concur to the production of Chemical Phenomena. 2nd edition. London, 1843 . . . . 3 00 7 21
Very scarce.

David (H.) Methode de Peinture appliquee uniquement a la Photographie de Portraits. 2nd edit., 8vo. Paris, 1856 . . . . 0 50

Davy (Sir H.) Chemical Philosophy. 8vo. London 5 50
——— Account of the Safety Lamp for Miners. 8vo. London . . . 1 50
See KNAPP's Technology.

Delamotte (P.) The Practice of Photography: a Manual for Students and Amateurs. With a Calotype Frontispiece. 3d edition revised. 12mo. London, 1856 . . 1 37
——— The Oxymel Process in Photography. 12mo. London, 1856 . . . 0 30

De la Rive (A.) A Treatise on Electricity in Theory and Practice. 2 vols., 8vo. London, 1853-6 . . . . 14 00
——— **(A.—A.)** Traite d'Electricite Theorique et applique. 2 vol., 8vo., avec 260 pl. intercalees dans le texte. Paris, 1853-1856 . . . . 4 50
Les nombreuses applications de l'electricite aux sciences et aux arts, les liens qui l'unissent a toutes les autres parties des sciences physiques, ont rendu son etude indispensable au chimiste aussi bien qu'au physicien, au geologue autant qu'au physiologiste, a l'ingenieur comme au medecin; tous sont appeles a rencontrer l'electricite sur leur route, tous ont besoin de se familiariser avec son etude. Personne mieux que M. de la Rive, dont le nom se rattache aux progres de cette belle science, ne pouvait presenter l'exposition des connaissances acquises en electricite et de ses nombreuses applications aux sciences et aux arts.

Desains (P.) Leçons de Physique, a l'Usage des Aspirants aux Baccalaureats et aux Ecoles du Gouvernement. 2 vols. 12mo. Figures intercalees dans le texte . . 2 50

Deschamps. Art (l') de Formuler, contenant: les Principes Elementaires de Pharmacie, etc. 1 vol., 18mo., avec 19 figures intercalees dans le texte. Paris . . 1 25

Descloizeaux. Memoire sur la Cristallisation et la Structure Interieure du Quartz. 8vo., plus 4 pl. Paris, 1856 . . . .

Desonge. Traite de Photographie sur Toile, dernier Perfectionnement. 8vo. Paris, 1855 0 75

Disderi. Manuel Operatoire de photographie sur collodion instantane. 8vo. Paris, 1854 0 75
——— Renseignements Photographiques Indispensables a tous. 8vo., de 3 feuilles. Paris, 1855 . . . . 1 25

Dodd (G.) The Curiosities of Industry and the Applied Sciences. 8vo. London, 1854 . 1 00

Dorure. Nouveau Manuel Complet de dorure et d'argenture par la methode electrochimique et par simple immersion par M. M. Selmi, de Valecourt, Malpeyre, etc. Nouv. edit, tres augmentee, ornee de figures. 12mo. Paris, 1856 . . . 0 50

Dove (H. W.) The Distribution of Heat over the Surface of the Globe, illustrated by Isothermal, Thermic Isabnormal, and other Curves of Temperature. 4to., with map. London, 1853 . . . . 5 00

Du Bois-Reymond on Animal Electricity, by Bence Jones. 8vo. London, 1852 . 1 75

Duhamel de Monceau. Traite de la Fabrique des Manœuvres pour les Vaisseaux ou l'art de la Corderie perfectionne. 4to. Paris, 1747 . . . . . 3 00

Dubrunfaut. Art of Distillation and Rectification. 12mo. London. (Very Scarce).

Dumas and Boussingault. The Chemical and Physiological Balance of Organic Nature: an Essay. 12mo. 1 00

Du Moncel (Th.) Projection des Principaux Phenomenes de l'Optique a l'aide des appareils de M. Duboscq. 8vo. Paris, 1855 50

——— Expose des Applications de l'Electricite. Tome 1er. Notions Technologiques 2me edit., 8vo., avec 8 pl. Paris, 1856. (Cette edition aura deux vols peut-etre meme trois) 1 25

Dumas (J.) Essai de Statique Chimique des Etres Organises. 2me edit. Paris, 1842 . 1 00

——— Memoires de Chimie. Avec 7 Planches. 8vo. Paris, 1843 . . . 1 50

——— Traite de Chimie appliquee aux Arts. 8 vols. and 4to atlas. 8vo. Paris, 1828–46. Very scarce 50 00

——— Edition de Bruxelles. 8 vols. and 4to atlas 30 00

Dunn (M.) History of the Steam Jet as applicable to the Ventilation of Coal Mines. 8vo. 0 75

Duplais (P.) Traite des Liqueurs et de la Distillation des Alcools, ou le Liquoriste et le Distillateur Modernes, contenant, etc. 2 vols., 8vo. Versailles, 1856 . . . 3 75

Durand (Faug.) Nouvelle Theorie Physique ou Etudes Analytiques sur la Physique et sur les actions Chimique fondamentales. 8vo. Paris, 1854 . . . 75

Encres. Nouveau Manuel complet de la Fabrication des Encres, telles que Encres a Ecrire, Chine, de Couleur a Marquer le Linge &c. 18mo. Paris, 1855 . . 1 00

Etoffes Imprimees. Nouveau Manuel Complet du fabricant d'Etoffes Imprimees et du Fabricant des papiers peints, par L. S. le Normand. 18mo. Paris, 1856 . 75

Exhibition of 1851 (Lectures on the Results of the Great,) delivered before the Society of Arts, Manufactures, and Commerce (Dr. Whewell, Professor Ansted, and others). 2 vols., post 8vo., each 2 25

Faraday (M.) Chemical Manipulations, being Instructions to Students in Chemistry. 8vo. London, 1827. (Very Scarce.) . . . . . . about 7 50

——— Experimental Researches in Electricity. 3 vols., 8vo. London, 1849–55. . 13 50

——— The Subject-matter of a Course of Six Lectures on the Non-metallic Elements. 12mo., cloth. London, 1853, ... 1 75

Fau (J.) Douze lecons de Photographie. Description de procedes simples et faciles, au moyen desquels on obtient, presque infailliblement, des epreuves sur verre et papier. 18mo. 0 75

Fau et Chevalier. Manuel du Physicien preparateur, ou description d'un cabinet de Physique. 2 vols., 18mo., with an atlas of 88 plates. Paris, 1853 . . . 3 75

Faucher (L.) Remarks on the Production of the Precious Metals, and on the Demonitization of Gold in Several Countries of Europe. 8vo. London, 1853, . . 0 75

Faure (J. J.) Analyse Chimique des Eaux du departement de la Gironde. 8vo. Bordeaux, 1853 . . . . 0 75

Figuier (L.) L'Alchimie et les Alchimistes ou Essai Historique et Critique sur la Philosophie Hermetique. 2d edit. 12mo. Paris, 1856 . . . . . . 1 00

Francœur (L. B.) Elements de Technologie ou Description des procedes des Arts. 8vo. 1 25

Francis (G. W.) The Dictionary of Practical Receipts; containing the Arcana of Trade and Manufacture, Domestic Economy, Pharmaceutical and Chemical Preparations, &c. 8vo. London, 1856 . . . . 2 50

Fresenius (Dr.) Instruction in Chemical Analysis. Quantitative. 2d edit. 8vo., cloth. 1855 . . . . 4 50

——— Instructions in Chemical Analysis. Qualitative. 4th edit. 8vo., cloth . . 2 75

Fresenius et Sacc. Precis d'Analyse Chimique quantitative. 18mo. Paris, 1845. (*Epuise.*)

——— Precis d'Analyse Chimique qualitative. 1 vol., 12mo., fig. Paris, 1847. (*Epuise.*)

Fyfe (A.) Elements of Chemistry. 8vo. London 7 25

——— Manual of Chemistry. 12mo. London 2 12

Galloway (R.) The First Step in Chemistry: a New Method for Teaching the Elements of the Science. 2d edit. 12mo. London, 1855 . . . . . . 1 50

——— Manual of Qualitative Analysis. 12mo., cloth 1 12

——— Chemical Diagrams, on four large sheets 1 75

Galvanoplastie. Nouveau Manuel complet de Galvanoplastie, ou Elements d'Electrometallurgie; contenant l'Art de reduire les metaux a l'aide du fluide galvanique, etc., par Smee. Augmente d'apres MM. Jacoby, Spencer, Elsner, etc. Ouvrage publie par E. de Valicourt. 2 vols., 18mo. 1 25

Ganot (A.) Traite Elementaire de Physique Experimentale et Appliquee, et de Meteorologie, avec un recueil nombreux de problemes, illustre de 500 gravures sur bois intercalees dans le texte. 6e edition, augmentee de 582 gravures nouvelles. 18mo. Paris, 1856 . . . . 1 75

Gas. Knapp's Chemical Technology, or Chemistry applied to the Arts: Fuel and its Application. 1 vol. In 2 Parts. 8vo. London, 1856 . . . . 9 00
This is the most recent and complete work on the manufacture of Gas, &c.

Gas Lighting (Journal of). Published in London on the 10th of every month. Price per year 8 75
5 Vols. are published.

Gaudin (M. A.) Traite Pratique de Photographie, expose complet des procedes relatifs au Daguerreotype. 8vo., hf. bd. cf. Paris, 1844 . . . . 1 50

Gauss (C. F.) Intensitas vis magnetica terrestris ad mensuram absolutum revocata. 4to. Gottingæ, 1833 . . . . 1 50

Gavarret (J.) De la Chaleur produite par les Etres Vivants. 12mo., avec 41 figures dans le texte. Paris, 1855 . . . . 1 50

Gerhardt. Introduction a l'Etude de la Chimie par le Systeme Unitaire. 12mo. Paris, 1848 . . . . 1 00

——— Precis de Chimie Organique. 2 vols., 8vo. Paris, 1844 . . . . 4 00
In half calf 5 00

——— Traite de Chimie Organique. 4 vols., 8vo. Paris, 1855–6 . . . 10 00

Ce Traite est une suite a Berzelius. Ce celebre chimiste etant mort avant d'avoir pu terminer son ouvrage, M. Gerhardt, ancien professeur de chimie a Montpellier, s'est charge de terminer son travail et de le mettre au courant de la science actuelle.

——— Aide-memoire pour l'Analyse Chimique. 12mo. Paris, 1852 . . . 0 75

Gerhardt et Chancel. Precis d'Analyse Chimique. 12mo., avec 48 gravures. Paris, 1855 . . . . 1 25

Glover (R. M.) A Manual of Elementary Chemistry: being a Class-book. Illustrated. 12mo. London, 1855 . . . . 2 50

Gmelin. Handbook of Chemistry. Vol. 1 to 6, Inorganic Chemistry . . . 14 00
" " Vol. 7 to 10, Organic Chemistry, each vol. . . 4 50

The work will be completed in 12 vols. (Cavendish Society Publications.)

Goebel. Pharmaceutische Waarenkunde, mit Illuminirten Kupfern. 2 vols., 4to. Eisenach, 1850 . . . . 10 00

Gore (G.) Theory and Practice of Electro-Deposition, including every known mode of depositing metals, etc. 8vo. London, 1856 . . . . . . 0 50

Gorham. Unfrequented Paths in Optics. Part 1. Light from a Pin-hole. Part 2. Light from a Fissure. 8vo. London, 1855 . . . . 1 25

Graham. Elements of Chemistry; including the application of the Science in the Arts. By T. Graham, F.R.S. L. & E., Professor of Chemistry at University College, London. 2d edition, entirely revised and greatly enlarged, copiously illustrated with Woodcuts. Vol. 1. 1850 . . . . 3 00

——— Vol. 2. London and New York, 1857 . . . . . . 4 00

This work, which ranks among the first on the subject, is now complete.

——— Chemical Catechism. 8vo. London 4 75

Gregory (Wm.) Elementary Treatise on Chemistry. 12mo. Edinburgh, 1855 . 1 50

——— Handbook of Inorganic Chemistry. For the use of Students. 3d edition. 12mo. London 1 75

——— Handbook of Organic Chemistry, for the use of Students. 4th edition, corrected and much extended. 12mo. London, 1856 . . . . . . 3 62

Griffin. Treatise on the Use of the Blowpipe. 18mo. London. (Scarce.)

Griffin (J. J.) Chemical Recreation. Div. 1, post 8vo. 0 60

Griffith (T.) Chemistry of the Four Seasons. 12mo. London, 1853 . . . 2 25

Grove (W. R.) On the Correlation of Physical Forces. 3d edit. 8vo. London, 1855 . 2 25

Gruyer (L. A.) Principes de Philosophie Physique pour servir de base a la Metaphysique de la Nature, et a la Physique Experimentale. 8vo. Paris, 1845 . . 1 75

Guibourt. Histoire naturelle des drogues simples, ou Cours d'histoire naturelle professe a l'Ecole de Pharmacie, quatrieme edition, augmentee. 4 vo., 8vo., avec 600 fig. intercalees dans le texte. Paris, 1849 . . . . 7 50
Half bound in Paris 9 50

[Cet ouvrage, que tous les pharmaciens considerent comme un *Vade-mecum* de premiere necessite, parce que la grande exactitude apportee par l'auteur dans la description des drogues leur permet de distinguer les diverses especes et varietes qui se rencontrent dans le commerce, ainsi que les falsifications qu'on leur fait subir. Cette quatrieme edition a ete soumise a une revision generale, et les augmentations ont ete tellement importantes, qu'on peut la considerer comme un ouvrage entierement neuf. C'est un *Cours complet d'histoire naturelle pharmaceutique et medicale*, que les medecins consulteront toujours avec fruit.]

Guitard. Histoire de l'Electricite. 12mo. Paris, 1854 . . . . . 1 00

Gurney. Lectures on Chemistry. 8vo. London 3 60

Hardy (R. W. H.) Incidental Remarks on some principles of Light; being Part 3 of an Essay on Vision. 8vo. London, 1856 . . . . . . 1 00

Hardwich (T. F.) A Manual of Photographic Chemistry, including the Practice of the Collodion Process. 2d edition. 12mo, cloth. London . . . 2 00

Harris (Sir W. S.) Rudimentary Treatise on Galvanism, and the general principles of Animal and Voltaic Electricity. 12mo., illustrated, cloth . . . 0 50

Hassal (A. H.) Food and its Adulterations. With 159 illustrations. 8vo. London, 1855 . . . . 3 50

Heath. Photography. A New Treatise, theoretical and practical, of the Processes and Manipulations on Paper and Glass. 8vo. New York, 1855 . . . . 1 00

Hedley (John). Practical Treatise on the Working and Ventilation of Coal Mines; with suggestions for Improvements in Mining. 8vo., cloth 3 75

Hennah (T. H.) The Collodion Process. 4th edition. 12mo. London, 1855 . 0 30

Henry (W.) Elements of Experimental Chemistry. 2 vols., 8vo. London . . 10 00

Herling (A.) Traite de Photographie sur Collodion Sec. 2e edition. 12mo. Paris, 1856 0 50

Highton. Treatise on the Electric Telegraph. 12mo. London, 1852 . . 0 60

Hinds (Dr. W.) The Harmonies of Physical Science in relation to the Higher Sentiments, with Observations on the Study of the Medical Sciences, and the Moral and Scientific Relations of Medical Life. Fcap. 8vo. London, 1853 . . . . 0 50

Hoefer (F.) Nomenclature et classification chimiques, suivies d'un lexique historique et synonymique comprenant les noms anciens, les formules, les noms nouveaux, le nom et la date de la decouverte des principaux produits de la chimie. 12mo., avec tableaux. Paris, 1845 . . . . 0 75

Hoefer. Hist. de Chimie depuis les temps les plus recules jusqu'a nos jours. 2 vols., 8vo. Paris, 1842. (Very scarce.) . . . .

Hood (C.) A Practical Treatise on Warming Buildings by Hot Water, on Ventilation, &c. 3d edition. 8vo. London, 1855 . . . . 3 25

Hopkins (T.) On the Atmospheric Changes which produce Rain and Wind. 2d edit. 8vo. 1 50

Hopkinson (J.) The Working of the Steam Engine Explained by the Use of the Indicator. 8vo. London, 1854 . . . . 1 50

Horsley (J. A.) A Catechism of Chemical Philosophy; being a familiar exposition of the Principles of Chemistry and Physics. 12mo. London, 1856 . . . 2 00

Houzeau. Physique du Globe et Meteorologie. 18mo., with plates. Brussels, 1854 . 0 68

Howard (Luke.) Seven Lectures on Meteorology. 12mo. London, 1843 . . 1 00

Howlett (R.) On the various methods of Printing Photographic Pictures upon paper, with suggestions for their preservation. 12mo. London, 1856 . . . . 0 31

Hunt (Robert). Researches on Light. 8vo. London, 1844 . . . . 3 00

——— Photography: a Treatise on the Chemical Changes produced by Solar Radiation, and the production of Pictures from Nature. 12mo., clo. London . . 1 75

Hureaux. Histoire des Falsifications des Substances Alimentaires et Medicamenteuses, precedee d'une Instruction Elementaire sur l'Analyse, et suivie des Essais et Analyses Qualitatives pour Reconnaitre Instantanement les produits Chimiques usites en Pharmacie, dans les Arts et dans l'Industrie. 1 vol., 8vo. Paris, 1855 . . . . 1 75

Inorganic Chemistry (First Outlines of). 12mo. London 1 25

Isadore Geoffroy Saint-Hilaire. Lettres sur les Substances Alimentaires et particulierement sur la Viande de Cheval. 18mo. Paris, 1856 . . . . . 0 62

Illustrated Standard Scientific Works (Library of), beautifully printed and illustrated. Original London editions at the price of the Reprints:

Muller's Principles of Physics and Meteorology. With 530 woodcuts and 2 colored engravings. 8vo. 4 00

Weisbach's Mechanics of Machinery and Engineering. Vols. 1 and 2, with 900 woodcuts 7 50

Technology: or, Chemistry applied to the Arts and to Manufactures. By Drs. Knapp, Ronolds, & Richardson. Splendidly illustrated. 3 vols., 8vo. . . 18 00

Quekett's Practical Treatise on the use of the Microscope. With Steel and Wood Engravings. 8vo. 3d edition, with additions 5 00

Graham's Elements of Chemistry, with its applications in the Arts. 2d edition, with inumerable woodcuts. Vol. I 3 00

Fau's Anatomy of the External Forms of Man. For Artists. Edited by R. Knox, M.D. 8vo., and an atlas of 28 plates 4to. Plain, $6 00. Colored, . . 10 00

Nichol's Architecture of the Heavens. 9th edition. Entirely revised. Steel Plates and Woodcuts 3 00

Mitchell (J.) Manual of Practical Assaying. 2d edition, much enlarged. 8vo. London, 1855 . . . . 5 00

Johnson (J. F. W.) Instructions for the Analysis of Soils, Limestones, and Manures. 3d edit. 12mo. Edinburgh, 1855 . . . . 0 60

——— The Chemistry of Common Life. 2 vols. 12mo. Edinburgh, 1855 . . 3 00

Johnson (J. F. W.) Elements of Agricultural Chemistry and Geology. 12mo. 6th edit. London, 1852 . . . . 2 00

Jourdain. Pharmacopee Universelle, ou Conspectus de toutes les Pharmacopees. 2 vols. in-8. 2 edit. Paris, 1840 . . . . 6 25

Joyce (Rev. J.) Scientific Dialogues intended for the instruction and entertainment of young people. 12mo. London, 1852 . . . . 0 75

——— Dialogues on Chemistry. 2 vols. 12mo. 2 75

Julien. Quelques points de Science dans l'Antiquite. Physique, Metrique, Musique. 8vo. Paris, 1854 . . . . 2 00

Kæmtz. A Complete Course of Meteorology. With additions by C. V. Walker. 1 vol., post 8vo., pp. 624, with 15 plates., cloth boards. 1845 . . . . . 3 00

Kane (Sir Robert). Elements of Chemistry, theoretical and practical, including the most recent discoveries and applications of the Science to Medecine and Pharmacy, to Agriculture, and to Manufactures. Illustrated by 200 woodcuts. 8vo., cloth . . 8 00

Kemp (T. L.) The Phasis of Matter; being an Outline of the Discoveries and Applications of Modern Chemistry. 2 vols. 12mo. London, 1855 . . . . . 6 00

——— Agricultural Physiology Animal and Vegetable. For Practical Agriculturists. 12mo. Edinburgh, 1850 . . . . 2 00

Kerr (T.) A Practical Treatise on the cultivation of the Sugar Cane, and the Manufacturing of Sugar. 12mo., cloth 1 50

Knapp, Ronolds, and Richardson. Chemistry in its application to the Arts and Manufactures:

Vol. I.—Fuel and its Applications—Coal, Gas, Oil, Spermaceti, &c., and their application to purposes of Illumination, Lighthouses, &c.—Resin, Wax, Peat, Wood, Stoves, &c., &c., in 2 Parts, 8vo., with 433 Engravings and 4 Plates 9 00

Vol. II.—Glass, Alum, Earthenware, Cements, &c., &c., manufacture. 8vo., with 214 Engravings and one Plate 4 00

Vol. III.—On those branches of Chemical Industry, including the Production of Food, and Related to Agriculture. (Bread, Milk, Tea, Coffee, Sugar, Tobacco, &c.) With 9 Engravings and 129 Woodcuts 5 00

Kobell. Sketches from the Mineral Kingdom. Post 8vo. London, 1853 . . 1 50

Vol. III., embracing sugar, coffee, tea, &c., with 7 folio coloured plates, . . 5 00

Knight. Dictionary of Arts, Commerce, and Manufactures. 8vo. London, . . 2 50

Kyan (J. H.) On the Elements of Light, and their identity with those of Matter, Radiant and Fixed. 8vo. London, 1838 . . . . 2 00

Laboulaye. Dictionnaire des Arts et Manufactures, de l'Agriculture, des Mines, etc. Ouvrage formant 2 tres forts volumes in 4to., et illustre de 3,000 gravures. Now complete 15 00

Lacambre. Fabrication de la Biere et Distillation des Alcools. Vol. 1 8vo. (For the 2 vols.) 5 00

Lacan (E.) Esquisses Photographiques a propos de l'Exposition Universelle et de la Guerre d'Orient. 12mo. Paris, 1856 . . . . 0 75

Lambert. Sur la Meteorologie. 4to. 0 25

Lame (G.) Cours de Physique de l'Ecole Polytechnique. 2 vols., en 3 Parties. 8vo., avec 17 planches. Paris, 1836–37. (Very Scarce.) 5 00

Lardner (D.) Handbook of Natural Philosophy. Hydrostatics, Pneumatics, and Heat. 12mo. London, 1855 . . . . 1 50

——— The Museum of Science and Art. 10 vols., 12mo. Illustrated by engravings on wood 6 25

——— Handbook of Natural Philosophy and Astronomy. Third Course—Meteorology; Astronomy. 8vo., with 37 lithographic plates and upwards of 200 illustrations on wood, cloth. London, 1858 . . . . 5 00

——— A Treatise on Heat. 12mo. London, 1856 . . . . . . 1 00

Lassaigne. Dictionnaire des Reactifs Chimiques employes dans toutes le experiences. 8vo. fig. Paris, 1839 . . . . 2 50

Laurent (M.) Precis de Cristallographie suivi d'une Methode Simple d'Analyse au chalumeau. 12mo. Paris 0 37

Laurent (Aug.) Methode de Chimie. Precedee d'un Avis au Lecteur, par M. Biot. 1 vol., 8vo., avec figures dans le texte. Paris, 1854 . . . . . . 2 00

Laurent (A.) Chemical Method, Notation, Classification and Nomenclature. Translated by Odling. London, 1855 . . . . 3 50

(Cavendish Society Publication.)

Le Gray. Nouveau Traite de Photographie sur papier et sur verre. 8vo. Paris, 1851 . 0 75

Lehmann. Physiological Chemistry. With Illustrations. 2 vols. 8vo. Philadelphia, 1856, ... 6 00

——— Chemical Physiology. Translated by J. C. Morris. Philadelphia, 1856 . . 2 25

——— Precis de Chimie Physiologique Animale. Traduction du Professeur Drion. Paris, 1855. 1 vol., gr. 18mo., avec fig. 1 25

L'Heritier (S. D.) Traite de Chimie Pathologique ou Recherches chimiques sur les solides et les liquides du corps humain, dans leurs rapports avec la Physiologie et la Pathologie. 8vo. Paris, 1842 . . . . 2 25

Le Normand. L'art du distillateur des eaux-de-vie. 2 vols., 8vo. Paris, 1817 . 3 00

Lerebours. A Treatise on Photography, by J. Egerton. 8vo. London, 1843 . 2 50

Lerebours et Secretan. Traite de Photographie. 5e edit. 8vo. . . . 1 00

Levesque. Art of Brewing and Malting. 4th edit. 8vo. London, 1847 . . 7 00

Liebig (J. V.) Chemistry and Physics, in relation to Physiology and Pathology. 2d edition. 8vo. 0 75

——— Nouvelles Lettres sur la chimie, traduites par Charles Gerhardt. 12mo. Paris, 1852 . . . . 0 75

——— Letters on Chemistry. 12mo. London 2 00

——— Researches on the Chemistry of Food. 8vo. London. 1 62

——— Principles of Agricultural Chemistry, with special reference to the late researches made in England. 8vo. London, 1855 . . . . 1 12

——— Handbook of Organic Analysis, containing a detailed account of the various methods used in determining the elementary composition of Organic Substances. Edited by Hoffman. Post 8vo., woodcuts. London, 1853 . . . . . . 1 50

Liebig and Kopp's Annual Report of the Progress of Chemistry, &c. 4 vols., cloth. 1853. (To be continued.) 10 00

Light: It Nature, Sources, Effects, and Applications. Illustrated by a Photograph. 12mo. London, 1856 . . . . 1 25

Long (C. A.) Practical Photography on Glass and Paper. 2d edit. 12mo. Sewed. 1856. 0 31

Love (T.) The Art of Cleaning, Dyeing, and Scouring, &c. 12mo. London, 1854 . 2 25

Low (David). An Inquiry into the Nature of the Simple Bodies of Chemistry. 3d edit. 8vo. London, 1856 . . . . 2 75

Lowig. Principles of Organic and Physiological Chemistry, by D. Breed. 8vo. Philadelphia, 1853 . . . . 3 50

Mackenzie (C.) One Thousand Processes in Manufactures, and Experiments in Chemis- 8vo. London, 1825. Half bd. 3 50

——— Theory and Experiments in Chemistry. 8vo. London, ... 6 50

McGauley (Rev. J. W.) Lectures on Natural Philosophy. 2 vols. 8vo. London, 1850. Half bd. 5 00

Malaguti (F.) Lecons de Chimie Agricole, Professees in 1847. 18mo. Paris, 1856 . 1 00

——— (J.) Lecons Elementaires de Chimie. 2 vols. 12mo., avec 104 figures intercalees dans le texte. Paris, 1853 . . . . 2 50

Marcet (W.) On the Composition of Food, and how it is Adulterated; with practical directions for its analysis. 8vo. London, 1856 . . . . . . 2 00

Marters. Esquisse d'une nouvelle classification Chimique des Corps. 4to. . . 0 25

——— Combustion de la vapeur alcoolique et etheree, autour d'un fil de Platine. 4to. . 0 25

——— Sur la theorie Chimique de la Respiration et de la Chaleur Animal. 4to. . 0 50

Martins (A.) Handbuch der Photographie. Dritte auflage. 8vo. Wien, 1852 . 2 3[illegible]

Mather (James). Coal Mines, their Dangers and Means of Safety. 8vo., woodcuts. London, 1853 . . . . 1 12

Mattenci. Cours Special sur l'Induction, le Magnetisme et sur les relations entre la Force Magnetique et les Actions Moleculaires. 8vo. Paris, 1854 . . . . . 1 50

Matteucci et Savi. Traite des phenomenes Electro-Physiologiques des animaux. 8vo. Paris, 1844 . . . . 2 00

Matthews (W.) Compendium of Gas Lighting. 12mo. London . . . 1 25

——— Historical Sketch and Origin of Gas Lighting. 12mo. London . . . 2 25

Memoires d'Agriculture, d'Economie Rurale et Domestique, publies et par la Societe Imperiale et Centrale d'Agriculture. Annee 1854. 1ere partie, 8vo. Paris, 1855 . 1 50

Messier. Observations sur les grandes Chaleurs, la Secheresse, etc., de la Seine a Paris, 4to. Pendant 1793 . . . . 0 50

Metcalfe (S. T.) Caloric; its Mechanical, Chymical, and Vital Agencies in the Phenomena of Nature. 2 vols., 8vo. 10 50

Mialhe. Chimie appliquee a la Physiologie et a la Therapeutique. 8vo. Paris, 1855 . 2 50

Miller (W. A.) Elements of Chemistry, Theoretical and Practical, extensively illustrated. 3 vols. 8vo. London, 1855–57 . . . . . . 14 00
Just Completed.

Millar (James). Elements of Chemistry. 8vo. London 3 75

Miller (W.) (Cashier to the Bank of England.) Decimal Tables used at the Bank of England, for reducing Gross weight of Gold and Silver to Standard. 4to. London, 1854 1 25

Millon (M. E.) Etudes de Chimie Organique faites en vue des Applications Physiologiques et Medicales. 8vo. Lille, 1849 . . . . 0 75

Millon (M. E.) Des Phenomenes qui se produisent du contact de l'Eau et du Ble et de leur Consequences, Industrielles. 8vo. Paris, 1854 . . . . . 0 50

Mitchell (J.) Manual of Practical Assaying, intended for the use of Metallurgists, Captains of Mines, and Assayers in general. With a copious table, for the purpose of ascertaining in Assays of Gold and Silver the precise amount, in ounces, pennyweights, and grains, of noble metal contained in one ton of ore, from a given quantity. 1 vol., 8vo. 2nd edit. London, 1854 . . . . 5 00

——— Treatise on the Adulterations of Food, and the Chemical means employed to detect them. Containing Water, Flour, Bread, Milk, Cream, Beer, Cider, Wines, Spirituous Liquors, Coffee, Tea, Chocolate, Sugar, Honey, Lozenges, Cheese, Vinegar, Pickles, Anchovy Sauce and Pasta, Catsup, Olive (Salad) Oil, Pepper, Mustard. 12mo. London, 1848 . . . . 1 50

Moigno. Traite de Telegraphie Electrique. 8vo., and atlas. Paris, 1852 . . 3 75

——— Repertoire d'Optique. 4 vols., 8vo. Paris, 1849-50. (Very scarce.) . .

Morehead (S.) Essay on Inebriating Liquors and Distillation. 8vo. London . 4 75

Morfit (C.) A Treatise on Chemistry applied to the Manufacture of Soap and Candles. New edition. 8vo., woodcuts. Philadelphia, 1856 . . . . . 6 00

Mulder (G. J.) The Chemistry of Vegetable and Animal Physiology, with introduction and notes by J. E. W. Johnston, and twenty illustrations, colored and plain. 8vo., cloth 8 50

Muller. Principles of Physics and Meteorology. Illustrated with 500 Woodcuts, and 2 colored plates. 8vo. London, 1847 . . . . 4 00

Murphy (Rev. R.) Elementary Principles of the Theories of Electricity, Heat, and Molecular Actions. Part I. 8vo. Cambridge (England), 1832 . . . 2 25

Murphy (P.) Rudiments of the primary forces of Gravity, Magnetism, and Electricity in their Agency on the Heavenly Bodies. 8vo. London, 1830 . . . 4 00

Murray. System of Chemistry, 4 vols., 8vo. London 15 75

——— Sketch of Chemistry. 12mo. London 2 25

——— Manual of Chemical Experiments. 12mo. London 1 50

——— Chemical Tables and Diagrams. 8vo. London 1 00

——— Elements of Chemistry. 4 vols., 8vo. London 7 50

Muspratt (Dr. S.) The Use of the Blowpipe, in the Qualitative and Quantitative Examination of Minerals, Ores, Furnace products, and other metallic combinations. By Platner. 8vo., cloth 3 00

——— Chemistry Theoretical, Practical, and Analytical, as applied and relating to the Arts and Manufactures. Royal 8vo. Div. 1 and 2. London, 1856. Each . . 2 62
Each division of this fine work contains 4 portraits (engraved on steel) of the most celebrated chemists.
Will be completed in about 6 divisions.

Napier (J.) Manual of Electro-Metallurgy. Post 8vo. 1853 . . . 1 00

——— A Manual of the Art of Dyeing. 8vo, with illustrations. London, 1853 . 2 25

Nesbit (J. C.) On Agricultural Chemistry, and the Nature and Properties of Peruvian Guano. 3d edition. 8vo. London, 1856 . . . . . . 1 25

Nisbet (W.) Dictionary of Chemistry. 12mo. London 2 50

Nicollet (H.) Atlas de Physique et de Meteorologie Agricoles. Grand in-fol., de 13 pl. col., avec tableaux et texte. Paris, 1855 . . . . 13 50

Noad (H. M.) A Manual of Electricity, including Galvanism, Magnetism, Diamagnetism, Electro-Dynamics, Magneto-Electricity, and the Electric-Telegraph. 4th edition, entirely rewritten. Part I. Electricity and Galvanism. 8vo. London, 1856 . . 5 00

——— Chemical Manipulation and Analysis Qualitative and Quantitative. With an introduction explanatory of the general principles of Chemical Nomenclature, &c. 8vo. London, 1852 . . . . 3 00

——— Lectures on Chemistry. 8vo. London 3 75

Normandy. Commercial Handbook of Chemical Analysis. Post 8vo. London, 1850 . 3 75

——— A Practical Treatise on Chemical Analysis, Quantitative and Qualitative. By Rose. 2 vols., 8vo. London, 1848 . . . . 10 25

——— An Introduction to ditto, 8vo. London 2 75

Orfila (M. P.) Elements of Modern Chemistry. 8vo. London . . . 3 25

Ottley (W. C.) Dictionary of Chemistry and Mineralogy. 8vo. London . . 4 00

Paris (J. A.) Elements of Medical Chemistry. 8vo. London . . . 4 75

Parnell. Treatise on Dyeing and Calico Printing. 8vo. London . . . 2 12

——— Elements of Chemical Analysis, Qualitative and Quantitative. 8vo. London. 1845. Reduced to 2 75

——— Applied Chemistry in Manufactures. Vols. 1 and 2. 8vo. London. Each . 3 75

Payen. Cours de Chimie Appliquee, professe a l'Ecole Centrale des Arts et Manufactures, et au Conservatoire des Arts et Metiers. Redige par Dellisse et Poinsot. 1re partie: Chimie Organique. 8vo., avec atlas folio de 50 planches. Paris, 1847 . . . 9 00

Payen. Precis de Chimie Industrielle, a l'usage des Ecoles preparatoires aux Professions Industrielles des fabricants, et des agriculteurs. 3d edit. 8vo., avec atlas de planches in 8vo. Paris, 1855 . . . . 4 50

Payen et Richard. Precis d'Agriculture theorique et pratique. 2 vols., 8vo. Paris, 1851. . . . . 3 75

Peckston (T. S.) Treatise on the Manufacture of Gas. 8vo. London . . 7 75

Peclet (E.) Traite elementaire de Physique. 4me edition. 2 vols., 8vo., atlas, Paris, 1847 3 75

——— Traite de la Chaleur, consideree dans ses applications. Troisieme edition entierement refondue. Un atlas de 122 planches et un vol. de texte. Liege . . 12 50
Do., 2 vols., 4to., et atlas. Paris 17 50

——— Le supplement separement, 1853. 4to. 2 25

Pelouze. Traite de l'Eclairage au Gaz tire de la Houille, des Huiles, de Resines, etc. 1 vol., 8vo., et 24 pl. (Scarce.) . . . .

Pelouz et Fremy. Traite de Chimie generale, comprenant les applications de cette Science a l'Analyse Chimique, a l'Industrie, a l'Agriculture, et a l'Histoire Naturelle. 2nde edit. Tomes 1 a 5 et atlas. Paris, 1854–56 . . . . . 12 00
Il y aura un 6e vol., qui sera donne gratis.

——— Abrege de Chimie. Troisieme edition, conforme aux nouveax programmes de l'enseignement scientifique des Lycees. 3 vol., grand 18mo., avec 174 figures intercalees dans le texte. Paris, 1855 . . . .

——— Notions Generales de Chimie. Un beau volume imprime avec luxe, accompagne d'un Atlas de 24 planches en couleur, cartonne. Paris, 1853 . . . 5 50

Peltier (A.) Meteorologie. Observations et Recherches experimentales. 8vo. Paris, 1840 . . . . 2 00

Pereira. Lectures on Polarized Light. Second edition, greatly enlarged from materials left by the author. Edited by Prof. Powels, of Oxford. 12mo., woodcuts. London, 1854 2 25

Persoz. Traite theorique et pratique de l'impression des tissus. 4 beaux vol., 8vo., avec 165 figures et 429 echantillons d'etoffes, intercales dans le texte, et accompagnes d'un atlas de 10 pl. 4to., gravees en taille-douce, dont 4 sont coloriees. Ouvrage auquel la societe d'encouragement a accorde une medaille de 3,000 fr. Paris, 1846 . . 17 00

Pharmaceutical Journal and Transactions. Vols. 1 to 15. Half bound. London, 1841 to 1856 . . . . 50 00
Annual Subscription (published monthly) 3 75

Pharmacopœia. The New London, including also the Dublin and Edinburgh Pharmacopœias by J. B. Nevins, M.D. 8vo. London, 1851. . . . . 5 00

Phillips (J. A.) Gold Mining and Assaying; a Scientific Guide for Australian Emigrants. 12mo. With woodcuts, London, 1852. . . . . . 1 00

——— Manual of Metallurgy. Post 8vo. New edit. London, 1854. . . . 3 75

Phillips (R.) A Million of Facts of correct data and elementary constants in the entire circle of the Sciences, and on all subjects of speculation and practice. New edit. 12mo. 1856. . . . . 3 62

Philosophical Transactions of the Royal Society of London, from 1825 to 1851, inclusive, forming 25 vols. 4to. Half bound in Russia . . . 180 00
(Published price, £70 unbound.)

Piesse (S.) The Art of Perfumery, and the Method of obtaining Odors of Plants; with instructions for the Manufacture of Perfumes for the Handkerchief, Scented Powders, Odorous Vinegars, Dentifrices, Pomatums, Cosmetiques, Perfumed Soap, &c. With appendix, &c. Crown 8vo., cloth. London, 1856. . . . . . 2 25

Plattner (C. F.) Tableau de Caracteres que presentent au Chalumeau les alcalis, les terres et les oxydes metalliques, soit seuls, soit avec les reactifs. Traduit de l'Allemand par Sobrero, 4to. Paris, 1843 . . . . 0 50

——— The Use of the Blowpipe in the Qualitative and Quantitative Examination of Minerals, Ores, furnace products, &c. 8vo. London, 1850 . . . 3 00

Poisson (S. D.) Theorie Mathematique de la chaleur. 8vo. 1835 . . 0 50

Pouillet. Elements de Physique Experimentale et de meteorologie. 7me edition. 2 volumes, 8vo. de texte et un volume de 40 pl. 8vo., 4to. Paris, 1856 . . 4 50

Prechtl (J. J.) Technologische Encyclopædie oder alphabetisches handbuch der Technologie der Technischen Chemie und des Maschinenwesens. Vols. 1 to 18. 8vo., und plates fol. . . . .

Prideaux (T. S.) On Economy of Fuel, particularly with reference to Reverberatory Furnaces for the Manufacture of Iron, and to Steam Boilers. 12mo., cloth . . 0 30

Prout (W.) Treatise on Chemistry, Meteorology, etc. 8vo. London . . 4 50

Quetelet (A.) Positions de Physique. 3 vols. 18mo. Brussels, 1834 . . 2 00

Rammelsberg (C. F.) Lehrbuch der Stochiometrie und der Allgemeinen theoretischen chemie. 8vo. Berlin, 1842 . . . . 1 75

——— Anfangsgrunde der quantitativen Mineralogisch, und Metallargisch, anaytischen Chemie durch Beispiele erlautert. 8vo. Berlin, 1845 . . . . . 1 75

——— Leisfaden fur die Qualitative Chemische Analyse, mit besonderer Rucksicht auf H. Rose, Handb. der analyt. Chemie. 8vo. Berlin, 1843 . . . . . 0 75

Raspail (F. V.) Nouveau Systeme de Chimie Organique, fonde sur de nouvelles methodes d'observations, precede d'un Traite complet sur l'art d'observer, de manipuler en grand et en petit, dans le laboratoire et sur le porte-objet du microscope. Deuxieme edition, entierement refondue, accompagnee d'un atlas in-4 de 20 planches de figures dessinees d'apres nature, gravees et coloriees avec le plus grand soin. 3 vols., 8vo., atlas 4to. Paris, 1838 . . . . 7 50

——— Nouveau Systeme de Physiologie vegetale et de Botanique, fonde sur les methodes d'observations developpes dans le nouveau systeme de chimie organique, accompagne de 60 planches contenant pres de 1,000 figures d'analyse dessinees d'apres nature et gravees avec le plus grand soin. 2 forts vol., 8vo., et atlas de 60 planches. Paris, 1837 . . . . 7 50

——— Le meme ouvrage, planches coloriees 12 50

Reech. Theorie Generale sur les Effets Dynamiques de la Chaleur. 4to., avec planche. 1854 . . . . 3 00

Regnault (M. H.) Cours Elementaire de Chimie, a l'usage des Facultes, des Etablissements d'Enseignement secondaire, des Ecoles Normales et des Ecoles Industrielles. 4 vols. 12mo. 4th edit. Paris, 1853-4 . . . . 5 00

——— Elements of Chemistry. Translated by Betton and Taber. 2 vols. 8vo. 700 woodcuts. Philadelphia, 1853 . . . . 7 50

——— Relations des Experiences entreprises pour determiner les principales lois et les donnees numeriques qui entrent dans le calcul des Machines a Vapeur. 4to. Paris, 1847. (Scarce.) 10 00

——— Cours Elementaire de Physique. 4 vols., 18mo., anglais, avec figures dans le texte. Sous presse . . . .

——— An Elementary Treatise on Crystallography. Illustrated with 108 Wood Engravings, printed on black ground. 8vo. London, 1848 . . . . . 0 75

——— Premiers Elements de Chimie. 1 vol., 18mo., avec figures dans le texte. Paris, 1850 . . . . 1 25

Reichenbach (Baron Charles.) Physico-Physiological Researches on the Dynamics of Magnetism, Electricity, Heat, Light, Crystallisation, and Chemism, in their Relations to Vital Force. The complete work, from the German second edition, with additions, a preface, and critical notes, by John Ashburner, M.D. 8vo. With woodcuts and one plate. London, 1850 . . . . 3 00

Reid (D. B.) Illustrations of the Theory and Practice of Ventilation, with remarks on Warming, Exclusive Lighting, and the Communication of Sound. 8vo. London, 1844 . 4 80

——— Rudiments of Chemistry, with illustrations of the Chemistry of Daily Life. 4th edit. 12mo. London, 1851 . . . . 0 75

Repertoire de Pharmacie. 6 vols. 8vo. 1846–1850 . . . . 7 50

Richardson (C. J.) Popular Treatise on the Warming and Ventilation of Buildings. 18 plates. 8vo., hl. cf. London, 1831 . . . . 2 00

Rintoul (A. N.) A Guide to Painting Photographic Portraits, Draperies, Background, etc., in Water Color. With colored diagrams. 12mo. 1855 . . . . 0 50

Roberts (W. L.) Scottish Ale Brewer and Maltster. 8vo. London . . . 5 00

Robertson (H.) A General View of the Natural History of the Atmosphere, &c. 2 vols., 8vo., cf. Edinburgh, 1808 . . . . 2 00

Rose (H.) Traite pratique d'analyse chimique, suivi de tables servant dans les analyses a calculer la quantite d'une substance d'apres celle qui a ete trouvee dans une autre substance; traduit de l'allemand sur la quatrieme edition par A. J. L. Jourdan. Nouvelle edition, avec des notes et additions, par M. Peligot, professeur de chimie au Conservatoire des arts et metiers. 2 vols., 8vo., fig. Paris, 1843 . . . .

——— Practical Treatise on Chemical Analysis, including Tables for calculations in Analysis. With notes and additions by A. Normandy. 2 vols., 8vo., cloth. London . 10 25

——— Analytical Manual of Chemistry, by Griffin. 8vo. London 4 75

——— Ausfuhrliches Handbuch der Analytischen Chemie. 2 vols., 8vo., hf. bound calf. Braunschweig, 1851 . . . . 8 00

Roseleur (A.) Manipulations Hydroplastiques. Guide pratique du doreur, de l'argenteur et du galvanoplastie (avec 90 figures en galvanoplastie intercalees dans le texte). 8vo. Paris, 1856 . . . . 3 75

Runge (F. F.) Chemistry of Dyeing. Part 1. 8vo. London 1 50

Ryland (A.) Treatise on Assay of Gold and Silver Wares. Post 8vo. London, 1852 . 1 75

Sabine (E.) Magnetical Observations at Hobarton. Vol. 2, royal 4to. London, 1852 . 12 00

Sacc (F.) Precis Elementaire de Chimie Agricole. 2e edit. 12mo. Paris, 1855 . 1 00

Safety Lamps for Miners, etc. Knapp's Chemical Technology. Vol. 1. 1856 9 00

Sanders (Dr. J. M.) Practical Manual on the Use of the Blowpipe . . Will be published in January, 1857.

Santini. Teorica degli objettivi acromatici. 4to 0 50

Scheerer (T.) An Introduction to the Use of the Blowpipe; together with a description of the Blowpipe, characters of the important minerals. Translated by H. L. Blanchard. 12mo. London, 1856 . . . . 1 00

Schoedler and Medlock. The Book of Nature; an elementary introduction to the Sciences of Physics, Astronomy, Chemistry, &c., &c. 8vo. London, 1851 . 3 50

Schroder (H.) Die Molecularvolume der Chemischen Verbindungen im festen und flussigen Zustande. 8vo. Mannheim, 1843 . 1 00

Scoffern. Chemistry of the Imponderable Agents; including the Principles of Light, Heat, Electricity, and Magnetism. 8vo. London, 1855 . 1 00

——— Manufacture of Sugar in the Colonies. 8vo. London . 3 25

——— Elementary Chemistry of the Imponderable Agents and of Inorganic Bodies. 8vo. London, 1855 . 1 50

——— Chemistry no Mystery. 12mo. London . 1 50

Scoresby (W.) Magnetical Investigations. 3 vols., 8vo. London, 1852 . 3 00

Sheir (John). Directions for Testing Cane-Juice. 12mo., cloth . 0 87

Smee (A.) Instinct and Reason; deduced from Electro-Biology. 8vo., cloth . 5 00

——— Elements of Electro-Metallurgy. Illustrated with woodcuts. 8vo., cloth . 1 50

Smith (R. B.) Italian Irrigation; being a Report of the Agricultural Canals of Piedmont and Lombardy; addressed to the Directors of the East India Company. 2 vols. 8vo., and plates, folio, cloth. Edinburgh, 1855 . 9 00

Smith (D.) Practical Dyer's Guide. 8vo. London . 19 00

——— Dyers' Instructor. 12mo., London . 6 50

Solly (E.) Introduction to Rural Chemistry. 8vo. London . 1 50

——— Syllabus of Lectures on Chemistry. 8vo. London . 1 50

Soubeiran. Traite de Pharmacie theorique et pratique. 3e edition. 2 forts vol. 8vo., avec 63 fig. imprimees dans le texte. Paris, 1847 . 4 00

——— Precis elementaire de Physique. 2e edit., augmentee. 1 vol., 8vo., avec 13 planches 4to. Paris, 1844 . 1 25

Sutton (T.) The Calotype Process: a Handbook of Photography on Paper. 8vo. London, 1855 . 75

Swedenborg. Principles of Chemistry. 8vo. London . 3 60

Tables generales des Comptes Rendus des seances de l'Academie des Sciences, publiees par MM. les secretaires perpetuels, conformement a une decision de l'Academie, en date du 13 juillet 1835. Tomes 1 a 31. 3 aout 1835 a 30 decembre 1850. 4to. Paris, 1854 . 6 00

Tardieu (A.) Voiries et cimetieres. 8vo. Paris, 1852 . 1 00

Tate (T.) The Little Philosopher; or, the Science of Familiar Things; in which the Principles of Nature and Experimental Philosophy are Systematically Developed from the Properties and Uses of Familiar Things. Vol. 1. 18mo. London, 1855 . 1 12

——— **(C.)** Theory and Experiments in Chemistry. 8vo. London . 6 50

Thenard. Traite de Chimie elementaire. 6e edit. 5 vols. Paris, 1834–6 . Very scarce.

Thieme (F. W.) Die Physik in ihre Beziehung zur Chemie, oder diejenizen lehren der Physik, &c. 8vo. Leipzig, 1840 . 75

Thomson (T.) Practical Dyer's Assistant. 12mo. London . 1 50

——— Chemistry of Organic Bodies—Vegetables. 1 large vol., 8vo., pp. 1092, boards. London, 1838 . 6 00

——— Heat and Electricity. 2d edition. 1 vol., 8vo. Illustrated with woodcuts London, 1839 . 4 00

——— Chemistry of Animal Bodies. 8vo., cloth . 4 00

——— History of Chemistry. 2 vols. 12mo. Scarce . 2 50

——— Treatise on Brewing and Distillation. 8vo. London . 1 90

——— Elements of Chemistry. 8vo. London . 3 25

——— First Principles of Chemistry. 2 vols., 8vo. London . 9 00

——— Outlines of Mineralogy, Geology, &c. 3 vols., 8vo. . 9 50

——— System of Inorganic Chemistry. 2 vols., 8vo. London . 12 50

——— System of Chemistry. 4 vols., 8vo. London . 18 00

Thomson (R. D.) Cyclopædia of Chemistry, Practical and Theoretical, including the Application of the Science to the Arts, Mineralogy, and Physiology. 8vo., with illustrations. London, 1854 . 3 75

Thornthwaite (W. H.) A Guide to Photography: Simple and Concise Directions for obtaining Views, Portraits, &c. 9th edit. 12mo. London, 1856 . 30

Tizard (W. L.) Theory and Practice of Brewing. 2nd edit. 8vo. London, 1846 . 7 50

——— Brewer's Journal. London, 1854 . 3 25

Tolhausen et Gardissal. Dictionnaire Technologique. Francais-Anglais-Allemand. 3 vols., 12mo. Paris 1855 . 5 00

Tomlinson (C.) Cyclopædia of Useful Arts, Mechanical and Chemical, Manufacturing, Mining and Engineering. 2 vols., 8vo., with splendid steel plates and woodcuts. London, 1854 . 12 00

Trosseau et Reveil. Traite de l'art de formuler, comprenant des notions de Pharmacie. 12mo. 1851. . . . . 1 25

Turner (E.) Elements of Chemistry, including the actual State and prevalent Doctrines of the Science. 8th edit. Edited by Baron Liebig and Dr. Gregory. 8vo. cloth . 9 00

Ure (A.) A Dictionary of Arts, Manufactures, and Mines, containing a clear Exposition of their Principles and Practice. 4th edit., corrected and greatly enlarged. 2 vols., 8vo., pp. 2,078, and 1,600 engravings on wood, cloth. London, 1853 . . . 5 50

——— Dictionary of Chemistry. 8vo. London 6 50

Van Mons. Sur les combinaisons faites par le Pyrophore. 4to. . . . 50

Violette et Archambault. Dictionnaire des Analyses chimiques ou Repertoire alphabetique des Analyses de tous corps naturels et artificiels depuis la fondation de la chimie, avec l'indication des noms des auteurs et des recueils ou elles ont ete inserees. 2 vols., 8vo., a 2 col. Paris, 1851 . . . . 4 00
Or half calf 5 00

Walker (W.) The Magnetism of Ships and the Mariner's Compass: being a Rudimentary Exposition of the Induced Magnetism of Iron in Sea-going Vessels. 12mo. London, 1853 . . . . 1 50

——— **(C. V.) et Fau.** Manipulations Electrotypiques, ou Traite de Galvanoplastie, contenant la Description des Procedes les plus Faciles pour Dorer, Argenter, Graver sur Cuivre et sur Acier, reproduire les Medailles et les Epreuves Daguerriennes, Metalliser les Statuettes de Platre, etc., au moyen du Galvanisme. 4me edition, 18mo. Paris, 1855 50

Watson (R.) Chemical Essays. 5 vols., 18mo. London, 1800 . . . 2 50

Webster (J.) Elements of Mechanical and Chemical Philosophy. 8vo. . . 3 00

Weekes (W. H.) A Memoir on the Universal Portable Eudiometer, an Apparatus designed for researches of Philosophical Chemistry. 4to., with plate. Sandwich, 1838 . 1 00

Weldon (W.) Elements and Laws of Chemistry. 8vo. London . . . 3 75

Wertheim. Theses presentees a la Faculte des sciences de Paris pour obtenir le grade de docteur des sciences physiques. Paris 1853 . . . . . .
Theses de physique, de chimie et de mineralogie.

Will et Liebig. Manuel Complet de Chimie Analytique, contenant des Notions sur les Manipulations Chimiques, les Elements d'Analyse Inorganique Qualitative et Quantitative, et des Principes de Chimie Organique. 2 vols. 18mo . . . 1 25

Williams (C. W.) Treatise on the Combustion of Coal. 4to. London . . 3 25

Wittstein. Practical Pharmaceutical Chemistry, translated by S. Darley. London, 1853 1 88

Wohler (F.) Handbook of Inorganic Analysis. Translated and edited by Hofmann. 12mo. London 2 00

Wolff (E. T.) Quellen-Litteratur der theoretisch-organischen Chemie, &c. 8vo. Halle, 1845 . . . . 1 00

Woodward (C.) A Familiar Introduction to the Study of Polarized Light. 2nd edit. 8vo. London, 1851 . . . . 1 00

H. BAILLIERE publiſhes a bi-monthly Liſt of all Works publiſhed in France and England on SCIENCE, which he will be happy to ſend gratis to any perſon forwarding his address, &c.

He alſo begs leave to call the attention of Librarians of Colleges, Profesſors, and the Scientific World in general, to his unſurpaſſed facilities for the procuring of Books, Inſtruments, &c., with economy and diſpatch, having houſes in London, Paris, and Madrid, engaged in the ſame branch of the buſiness. (Duty free for Public Inſtitutions.) His ſtock is always replete with the beſt and lateſt editions; from his great experience and knowledge of Scientific Works, and from his willingness and ability to give information about both old and new books, he is confident of being able to give entire ſatisfaction to all who favor him with their orders.

C. E. Bailliere, Agent.
H. E. Bailliere.

ALPHABETICAL INDEX.

www.ingramcontent.com/pod-product-compliance
Lightning Source LLC
LaVergne TN
LVHW010218110826
845151LV00004B/1126

* 9 7 8 1 4 2 5 5 2 7 0 8 2 *